A
CORNER
OF EVERY
FOREIGN
FIELD

TIM BROOKS

A CORNER OF EVERY FOREIGN FIELD

CRICKET'S JOURNEY
FROM ENGLISH GAME TO GLOBAL SPORT

First published by Pitch Publishing, 2020

Pitch Publishing
A2 Yeoman Gate
Yeoman Way
Worthing
Sussex
BN13 3QZ
www.pitchpublishing.co.uk
info@pitchpublishing.co.uk

A CIP catalogue record is available for this book
from the British Library.

ISBN 978 1 78531 639 5

Typesetting and origination by Pitch Publishing
Printed and bound by TJ International, Padstow, UK

Contents

For my darling daughters
Esme and Rose

Acknowledgements

I AM indebted in writing this book to the wealth of historical accounts of the game in England and across the world that have helped identify key moments, debates and players that have shaped the game as we know it. For the history of the modern sport, particularly away from the game's Test strongholds, I am thankful to Simone Gambino, Craig White, Tim Cutler, Darren Talbot and Bertus De Jong for their thoughts and perspectives. The amazing team at Emerging Cricket have all been very supportive and encouraging in pulling this book together.

I have also been fortunate to be able to interview many players from associate nations who have provided a unique insight into the opportunities and challenges in emerging cricket nations. I'd especially like to thank Freddie Klokker, Binod Das and Paras Khadka.

I'd also like to thank my good friends Ben and Nigel Keohane, both still reeling from Robin Smith's retirement even though it was nearly 20 years ago, for thoughts on content and structure. My wife Claire has been a constant source of inspiration and support, kindly not showing any outward signs of annoyance when evening key tapping has accompanied the nuanced drama that is *Masterchef.*

Chapter 1

Origins

WAS it John Le Mesurier who once likened watching cricket to a religious experience? In a very moving interview I can still recall I believe it was. Of course many others have shared the sentiment over the years and cricket has a surely unique appeal among sports to man's deepest, most spiritual needs. This explains why short smash and giggle forms of the game are so quickly labelled shallow and vacuous by traditionalists and devotees. It is a sport that doesn't so much attract followers as acolytes. If we run with the thesis that cricket is the most spiritual of sports, what then is its genesis, its creation myth? In the beginning there was willow. Well, being such a quintessentially English story it was probably oak but an opening paragraph is no place for pedantry I'm sure you'd agree.

In the absence of certainties it is safe to assume it all began, as everything does, in its simplest form. Bored boy whacks pebble with stick, enjoys it and tells his friend.

He enjoys it too and soon a group of boys are playing something recognisable as a game. Everything that was to come sprang from an innate, fateful moment of inspiration that led to that first, furtive thrill of velocity, strength and precision. If cricket was a play, and there are worse analogies, that primordial six was Lear on the Heath, stripped of everything but his instinct.

While many have tried to put a date on cricket's beginning, trying to identify and document that first moment is a futile, if no doubt entertainingly diverting, venture. History rarely offers definitives in social experience. Even if it could be isolated and labelled that moment wasn't cricket, yet was cricket distilled. What would eventually become cricket evolved from primitive bat and ball games recorded as early as the 13th century. The established story goes that cricket was one of a number of variants that sprung from a simple hockey-like game generally referred to as club-ball. It was most definitely a game rather than a sport and even 'game' implies more structure and form than it had. We are, as you'd imagine, largely in the realms of conjecture but what all accounts agree on was that this proto-cricket was played by boys, not adults, and was definitely not a team game until much later in its development.

Most academic interest in the origins of cricket has focused not so much on dating but on the word's philological roots. What is rather alarming, particularly as a proud Englishman who chose the title of this book, is that some have speculated that cricket may not have originated in England at all. Some say it is of Norse origin, perhaps coming over with the Normans, others that linguistically it must be French, possibly sharing the same base origin as another sport that has survived to the modern day, croquet. The prospect of the most English of games actually being an import from France (of all places!) has been the focus of a number of feature articles in recent years. Cricket may not be the easiest to fathom but it is ours, damn it. Surely it is ours!

The philological studies vary considerably and assertions seem to be made on very flimsy deduction. But it seems likely that *cricket* refers to the stick used to strike the small object. Initially this would have been a curved piece of wood, similar to a modern hockey stick, designed to stop and flick whatever was used as the ball. As fascinating as the philological arguments for a foreign origin are, the truth is that there is no corroborating evidence at all for the early game being played beyond England. Similar games were played no doubt, but without any distinctive enough to characterise as cricket.

※ ※ ※

Cricket was born in the weald, the vast forested area that once covered large swathes of Kent, Sussex and Surrey. From here it spread to the downland of Sussex and Hampshire. The first games were probably played by boys seeking amusement in the forest glades being cleared for timber or iron ore by their fathers, using tree stumps as the target and curved branches as the bat. They may have used pebbles or pieces of wood for a ball. It is likely that the aim of these early games was to prevent the ball hitting the stump, rather than to dispatch it as far as it would go. It is in the spread of this game from the weald to neighbouring downland regions that it acquired some of its distinct characteristics due to the different topography and landscape. In the absence of tree stumps they used what was at hand, a wicket being a simple sheep gate comprising two vertical sticks and a bail between them. This variant borne of necessity and pragmatism provided a distinct advantage over games in the weald, as the bail dropping was proof that the defences had been breached. A shepherd's staff would have made an ideal bat too.

It is impossible to chart how this simple medieval game evolved, how widespread it was or how many people played. By its nature it wouldn't have left any trace to archaeology and it didn't feature in any known written record until the mid-16th century. This could be because it was rare and confined to a limited area, but it could also be because it went largely unobserved and unremarked upon because it was played by boys, not men, and was informal and occasional. Pastimes and activities that are regularly cited in medieval literature and records are generally linked to the court or were gentlemanly pursuits. At this time sport meant chivalric, courtly pursuits like archery, hunting and jousting. The people who enjoyed them were worth writing about. The lives of peasants, labourers and simple artisans feature rarely if at all in an era where the means of writing and the patronage of publishing was largely the preserve of privileged classes. So perhaps we shouldn't be too surprised that cricket took a while to be recorded, or assume that it did not long predate its earliest attested reference.

Guildford hosts a few county games a season and its club has produced some England cricketers so it is perhaps fitting that the first recorded playing of cricket was in

Surrey's county town. In a legal document dated 1598 a game of cricket was referred to that must have taken place in the early 1550s. To offer a frame of reference it was the Tudor era, just as England was getting used to being a protestant nation, when the *Mary Rose* was being constructed from the ancient oaks of the weald. Although short, this first reference is telling. There is no indication from the context that cricket was a novel or unusual activity. It is recorded matter-of-factly, as if the reader would immediately understand the reference. This suggests that at least in the local area the game was reasonably well established. It is a fairly safe assumption therefore that it was played at least in a form recognisable as cricket in the 15th century. There is, sadly, no further detail to describe the game, its players or its context. But next time you are in Guildford watching a chanceless century by Ollie Pope, smile at the thought that your journey there was actually a pilgrimage to the cradle of the game.

We travel forward to 1611 before the next reference and the next major milestone for development of the game. You should add Chevening, near Sevenoaks, to the pilgrimage list, because this is where the first actual game of cricket was recorded. In Guildford 60 years before it had just been two boys playing with a bat and ball but the Chevening record shows that by the early 17th century cricket was being played by adults and was a team sport. Village cricket, that most English of institutions, that most cherished subject of the watercolourist, was being played over 400 years ago. Other references indicate that there were certainly occasional inter-parish matches within

Kent or Sussex prior to the civil war although there is no evidence of common organisation or a formalised league.

The progression from an impromptu game between boys to a team sport is a fundamental one and it happened far earlier in cricket than any other major modern sport. The emergence of teams gave cricket one of its most compelling attributes, that it is a team sport comprising a series of individual duels. A batsman facing a bowler, their skill pitted against each other, was a deeply personal episode within a team contest. That added dimension laid the foundations for a game to become a sport. Cricket had found its resonance and appeal as a team contest. The catalyst for cricket's early development was a social dimension and a desire to represent a place. This social context was critical to cricket's success as a sport, the way it developed and how and why it went global.

The harmony of church and square is part of cricket's pastoral charm and an image portrayed in many a birthday card. The parish as an archaic form of civic organisation was critical in the early spread of the game. In medieval times a popular parish social gathering were fetes organised to raise alms for the poor through the sale of local ales. These had a reputation for being rather too jolly and boisterous and puritan administrators replaced them with payment of poor rates. This removed a popular social occasion and villagers looked to alternatives, with cricket being a beneficiary.

Whether we'd recognise that first game in Chevening as cricket is an interesting question. The first descriptions and illustrations of games were still a century or more away. The fundamental elements of batting, bowling and fielding would have been present but in the details it would have been a very different spectacle. There were no common rules at this time so there would have been considerable variations as teams applied their own conventions to their games. The number of players was not fixed and methods of dismissal may also have varied. A modern observer witnessing one of these early games would be struck immediately by one fundamental difference: the ball was rolled along the ground. The batsman would protect the wicket and if possible strike the ball through the field to score a run. It would have been played on a village green or common land so the ball may have deviated on uneven ground. This would have required considerable concentration on behalf of the batsmen to navigate the demons of the pitch. Other than assistance from the pitch it was tough for the bowlers, as there was no leg before and a deadly accurate ball rolling between the two stumps and failing to dislodge the bail would be a reprieve for the batsman. The batsman would score notches rather than runs, marked on a wooden precursor to the scorecard. To get a notch a batsman would have to run to the other end and return. It is likely that early totals were very modest, perhaps around 30 per team.

The players at Chevening would have been working men, who we must assume learnt the game as children. We don't know the occupations of the players in that first match but judging by the composition of later teams it is reasonable to infer that they would have included blacksmiths, horse grooms, bakers and other staple tradesmen of the agrarian economy. Cricket began as a rural, working class sport. Class would become one of cricket's defining characteristics, with the sport at the fulcrum of English society's obsession with status. But that was to come. In the reigns of the early Stuarts it was a simple, unaffected local game. It had yet to add the layers of cultural, political and moral context that was to see it heralded as the very embodiment of Englishness.

Almost without exception the earliest references to the game are found in a legal context and the picture painted one of suspicion and condescension. Cricket was clearly not approved of, had a subversive reputation and was certainly not a suitable pastime for a gentleman. This was partly due to how dangerous it was. The legal cases focus on damage to property, injury and even death. We know all too well that in spite of modern protections a hard ball can be fatal, and in the absence of balls pragmatic alternatives may have been even harder. But the main reason the earliest games were so dangerous was that you could strike the ball as often as you liked. A batsman could scoop the ball into the air near a fielder and then run over to strike it again. Unsurprisingly this led to many injuries and some untimely demises. This helped give cricket a reputation as a rough, brutish, dangerous game that encouraged violence. The elements that make the game exciting such as power, strength and velocity could also make it thuggish, if not played in the right spirit. The concept of the spirit of cricket very likely predated any organised form of the game.

This roguish reputation became further entrenched under the puritan rule of Oliver Cromwell, who ironically is the first person ever known to have played cricket in London. Cricket did not feature on a list of permitted activities and those caught playing cricket on the Sabbath were fined for unruly, unsaintly behaviour. Although the puritans attempted to force cricket out of existence this persecution was to be prove pivotal in its subsequent rise in profile and popularity. While seeking succour from conformist Cromwellian London the aristocracy of southern England left court life for the pastoral charm of their country estates. Missing courtly intrigue and desperate for diversions, they watched their estate workers playing cricket and a thought occurred to them that transformed the game. It was a thought borne of boredom, wealth and one-upmanship: betting.

By the latter half of the 17th century betting was rife amongst the upper classes. Social capital and notoriety was won by placing eye-watering bets and getting one over a rival. Traditionally this urge was sated at the horse races or at bloodsports such as cock fighting but as betting mania grew the aesthetes sought other things to bet on. For the earls and dukes in Kent and Sussex the answer could be seen from their vaulted leaded windows. Picture the scene. William Sackville, of Knole House, Sevenoaks, erstwhile hunting estate of Henry VIII, is bored to distraction in his exile from hedonistic London. He strolls around his deer park and sees estate workers cheering, running and striking a ball. He pauses to watch, taking in the scene. He then rushes back to the house and sends a hurried, excited message to his friend the Duke of Richmond, at Goodwood, near Chichester. Sackville visits and they watch a game. 'You think your men are better than mine?' he asks. 'I'll wager they are,' his host replies with relish. A game is scheduled. A local youth joins the staff as an under-gardener. He doesn't know a petunia from a potato. But you try defending against his pace and accuracy. And so country house cricket was born.

As the wagers grew so did the pressure to field the best team. Physical prowess became a key attribute of employability in the area. The players in local parish teams became a talent pool. Cricket had piqued the interest of those in society circles. Not for its own merits but as an excuse for a bet. The game itself was just a means to an end. It was only the result and the stake that mattered. Those first country house games set a theme that runs deep through cricket's history: class. The amateur patron and the professional player.

Charles Lennox was born in London at the height of the summer of 1672. His mother was Louise de Keroualle, a Breton noblewoman and mistress of King Charles II, the boy's father. Of royal blood but not in the royal line, the boy was raised in West Sussex and as a toddler was made the Duke of Richmond, just one of a range of titles bestowed on him by the king. Charles grew up in Goodwood House, near Chichester, Sussex, in an area widely regarded as a cradle of the game. Without the threat of kingship to burden him the boy grew to a life of indulgence and idleness, along which journey he became an early patron of the game. He made Goodwood one of the early centres for great games and through his wish for a strong local side on which to wager helped raise standards and spread the game in the area.

He split his time between Goodwood and the courtly society of restoration London. Charles and his circle celebrated his birthright with gusto, revelling in the excesses and moral profligacy so despised by the puritans who had killed his father. Following his lead, London wanted sport in the broadest sense of the word. Richmond and his fellow cricketing nobles brought their pastoral pastime with them, and being men of influence who could afford gossip-stirringly huge wagers they made cricket a society sport. As Richmond entered his twenties he got bolder and the wagers grew ever larger. It was the beginning of the era of the great games. At the age of 27 Charles helped organise the first cricket match ever to be covered in a newspaper.

It was the first week of July 1697. The ducal rivalry had seen local teams bolstered by the best players in the wider area, drafted in at expense to help win the wager. This had created the first cricket professionals, drawn from parish sides to represent the local dignitary. In its turn this process led to the formation of the first county representative team, with Richmond's Sussex men facing those over the border in Kent. County rivalry and local pride, along with the thrill of the money at stake, created interest and drew the crowds. This was to be the biggest cricketing occasion yet seen. The stake was 50 guineas.

Four years after this match he bore a son, like him a Charles. The son shared his father's affection for the game and his passion and commitment made him the most active and significant of the game's early patrons. He played cricket as a boy, one of the first generations of his class to play the game as well as bet on it. At the age of 21 he became MP for Chichester but on the death of his father a year later he resigned to assume his ducal duties. It was then that cricket became an almost all-consuming passion. He scheduled regular fixtures in the 1720s, captaining what was a de facto Sussex XI. Regular opponents were Sir William Gage, baronet, of Firle Place, Sussex, and Alan Brodrick, 2nd viscount Hamilton, of Godalming, Surrey.

The most famous of these proto county fixtures was played in Peper Harow, near Godalming, Surrey, in July 1727. It has been remembered as one of the most significant matches of cricket's early history as it was the first played to a written set of rules. There were rules governing games before this but they were subject to variation from game to game and location to location. These noblemen wanted to agree the rules to ensure they didn't lose a wager and dent their pride on a technicality or inconsistency. There was also a wish to standardise the game. This was one of the critical steps in the medieval game becoming a modern sport. The importance of these games, the concentration of talent and the fact they were played to consistent, agreed rules has seen them classed as first class matches, significant fixtures of superior standard.

Richmond's star player was his groom, Thomas Waymark, sometimes regarded as the first cricket professional and the game's first dynamic all-rounder. He was born in Mitcham, Surrey, in 1705, a town notable for having the first ever cricket club. He was ostensibly employed as a groom but was undoubtedly retained for his cricket ability over his skill with horses. He began his career in the 1720s but his most celebrated years came in the 1730s and 1740s. Principally playing for the duke, but also loaned as a 'given man' to other sides, he was considered a class apart in ability and agility. His career spanned a formative stage of the sport's development and he played in most of the notable matches of the era. In the 1740s he left Sussex and his patron and moved to Berkshire, where he played for that county and London. He played in the match with the earliest surviving scorecard, a 1744 game between London and Slindon.

The duke may have lost his star player but his love of cricket only intensified. He established a team at Slindon, a small, picturesque village in the South Downs close to Goodwood, who were arguably the best cricket team in the world in the 1740s. Other than proximity the reason for the duke's interest and patronage was that the village had produced one of the best young players of his generation, a certain Richard Newland. His career helps take the story on from Waymark. The standout talent of a trio of cricketing brothers, he was the leading batsman of the 1740s and the leading light in a village team that regularly beat county sides. His stardom was such that his presence would see bets on his personal performance, with one bet that he'd score 40 runs himself, an incredible score at the time when batting was so difficult.

At this stage there were still two variants of the game. The eleven-a-side format we recognise but also a personal duel, known as single wicket. This pitted the most talented players against each other, the ultimate distillation of an all-round performance. The top single wicket players became celebrities and their contests drew large crowds. It was said to be a remarkable feat of endurance as much as a display of skill, players having to field off their bowling.

By the mid-1740s Newland's fame was such he assembled his own XI rather than play for the village side. With cricket beginning to blossom under the early Georgians, though still largely restricted to London and the southern counties, representative teams became more popular and brought the best players together from their various parishes. The patrons' teams, like Slindon, provided the nucleus for county sides. The next logical step was of course an 'all England' XI. With considerable pride at stake, not to mention social capital, leading teams of the time wanted to prove they were the best. From the 1730s there are references to teams such as the London cricket club taking on the rest of England, by which was meant the leading players from all other clubs. Newland was a regular in such teams, thereby spreading his fame far beyond Slindon. Cricket was gaining in popularity and the 'great matches' attracted considerable public interest. A 1744 fixture between Kent and All England was so popular the organisers charged 6d entrance fee and publicans ensured the punters were lubricated and well nourished. Eerily forecasting the food forecourts of T20 venues, local traders vied for lucrative stalls at the game. Cricket could not only draw a crowd by now but could generate income too.

By the middle of the 18th century there were signs of a power shift from the southern shires to London. Through influential and charismatic patrons and players cricket joined the roster of activities adopted by the club scene, a society institution that was at the epicentre of Georgian London. Betting remained absolutely central to its allure but the upper classes were now enjoying taking to the field themselves, albeit many were a little too stout and uncoordinated to make much of an impression on scorecards. This trend saw grounds like Richmond and the artillery ground in Finsbury become famous venues of the game. Just as London was beginning to claim hegemony the focus switched back to the shires with the formation of the most talented group of cricketers yet to play the game, in the small east Hampshire village of Hambledon. In 1750 the Duke of Richmond had died and a year later Newland retired to farm his land in Slindon. Without these two titans of local cricket Sussex lost ground to Kent, which became the dominant county force in the late Georgian era. But Newland's contribution to the game was not finished, as while tilling the land in his retirement he taught his nephew, Richard Nyren, the game.

Nyren moved west from Slindon to Hampshire around 1760 and was influential in the founding of the Hambledon club. The club played at the windswept Broadhalfpenny Down ground, which by the 1770s became the most famous ground in the world. This small, out of the way hamlet drew the best players in the country and the cream of society, a more remote cricketing variant of the Epsom races. Nyren's bowling was described as 'provokingly deceitful'. Though a village team, Hambledon players were professionals, earning match fees equivalent to a decent week's wages by those wanting to wager on the best team in the country. As such Nyren, his fellow opening bowler Thomas Brett and Billy Beldham, regarded as the best batsman of the early era, could dedicate their time to training. In Nyren's case he balanced this with running the Bat and Ball pub by the ground. This professionalism saw the sport develop the technique and nuance it is such admired for, moving beyond sheer strength and athleticism. Beldham and team-mate Tom Seuter were the first batsmen to come forward to the ball, often leaving the crease to drive. Their skills influenced visiting players desperate to bear comparison with the best of their age. To combat their dominance bowlers began using deceptive flight and variations. Nyren described Beldham's technique as 'the beau ideal of grace, animation, and concentrated energy'. Cricket was starting to distinguish itself as a sport of rare skill, embodying romantic ideals of grace and beauty.

Given the logistical challenge presented by Hambledon's remoteness its fame and good fortune couldn't last forever and inevitably cricket was drawn back into Georgian London's orbit. If London was where the money was it seemed logical that London should host the big games. While Richmond Green had long been a venue for big matches and cricket would have been a familiar sight on the capital's green spaces, the city lacked a ground and cricket lacked a home worthy of its society status.

Among the plethora of gentlemen's clubs in Georgian London was the Star and Garter of Pall Mall. This counted aristocrats and royals in its membership and had a particular fondness for cricket, alongside horse racing and other pursuits of the season. The cricketers of the society formed the White Conduit club in 1782, named after the White Conduit Fields in Islington, then lying just beyond the city's early suburban sprawl. The gentlemen employed professionals to coach them and add quality to their ranks. Their list of members read like a chapter of *Debrett's* and it was two aristocrats, the 4th Duke of Richmond and the 9th Earl of Winchelsea, who took a decision that would have a profound impact on the development of the sport. Wanting more privacy for their games away from the hoi polloi of Islington fields, they financed another of their members, William Lord, to find the club its own venue.

Lord identified several sites at the northern edge of the city and the club moved to the district of Marylebone. His first ground was on the site of Dorset Square. Once acquired the Whites Conduit Club moved to a permanent home and remodelled themselves the Marylebone Cricket Club (MCC). With such influential members this became the de facto home of the London Cricket Club and took over from the artillery ground as the principal cricket centre in the capital. But from its inception the MCC were far, far more ambitious than merely being the most prestigious club in London.

These men of influence volunteered themselves as the rule-makers and arbiters of their sport. Quite why or how they felt they had this all-encompassing mandate isn't clear, beyond the fact that the club contained many of the leading patrons of the game and they came from a class bred to govern. In 1788, a year after they were founded, they assumed ownership of the laws of the game. Previously, leading clubs had met in what could be seen as a loose federation to organise and manage the game. MCC members would have played a key role in this process. But now they seized control. It was one of the most significant moments in our story so far. From its simple, sylvan, working class roots cricket had become a tool of the establishment. It was overseen by a governing class who would mould the game through the prism of their world view. It was child's play no more.

What was the game like in 1788, the year *The Times* was founded, parliament was given a report on the madness of King George III, the year before the French Revolution? Its rules had been largely defined 44 years earlier, at the Star and Garter club of course. The earlier, lethal practice of hitting the ball twice and obstructing the field had been wisely outlawed. Overs consisted of four balls, there were coin tosses and no-balls. Deliveries could now be pitched rather than rolled and as a consequence the curved hockey-style staves were now early versions of the more familiar straight bats. In the 1770s certain key revisions were made, some to combat innovations that were just not cricket. For instance, when in 1771 a Chertsey batsman used a bat as wide as the wicket, it was decided a maximum width should be defined. At the same time the lbw rule was introduced. However, the addition of a third stump was not yet required, giving bowlers of the era the considerable chagrin of seeing a batsman's smug, relieved face when the ball went between his two stumps. The game was still confined to a few southern counties, though well established at some of the leading public schools. As a leading society draw it attracted large crowds and large wagers. It had also made a few furtive appearances in the world at large, but more on that shortly.

The MCC took the game very seriously and its members sought to use their influence to get rid of its rowdier elements and its undesirable variability. It was a gentlemanly pursuit and they wanted it to reflect gentlemanly virtues and ideals. To what extent this was a deliberate strategy or just reflected the beliefs of the class of its members isn't clear. In time the club would not only make the rules, but award status and administer the game beyond British shores. Was this by design, some kind of coup d'etat by the privileged of the provincial? I think that is too dramatic. It was just a natural evolution of governance by a class who considered themselves morally and intellectually better placed to govern than anyone else. You could call it arrogance or you could call it duty and service, depending on your perspective. But all would agree that with the MCC at the helm cricket's journey was destined to take a certain path.

Chapter 2

Cricketing celebrities and exporting to the empire

IN the aftermath of the Napoleonic Wars the first cricketing superstar made his first forays into the game. It was a time when the sport was gripped by the round-arm controversy, a new style introduced by some to unsettle the under-arm status quo. Round-arm wasn't explicitly outlawed but was considered ungentlemanly and umpires were leant on by the MCC to no-ball the perpetrators. Eventually, and begrudgingly it was accepted and made cricket a far more dynamic sport. Imagine Malinga coming on to replace someone bowling underarm! This was the context for the emergence of Fuller Pilch. He rose to prominence in his native Norfolk in the 1820s before moving to Kent to earn a considerable salary from the game. He took batmanship to another level and earned the sobriquet 'the unparalleled'. In Kent he earned a living as a professional and was a mainstay of the county team. He revolutionised batting, playing a range of strokes in front of the wicket that had seldom been seen before. In an era when batting was notoriously difficult due to terrible pitches (and the addition of a third stump) and no protection at all Pilch scored ten first class centuries in his career, a feat put into perspective by the fact that a score over ten was relatively rare at the time.

Pilch was a star and as such was courted for many money-making innovations of the day, some of which had a considerable impact on the spread of cricket within England and its consolidation as a major sport, spanning class divides. By the 1840s, when Pilch was in his prime, the interest in betting had dimmed, and crowds were attracted by the action rather than the wagers. The introduction of the railways was a huge factor in social mobility and played a pivotal role in cricket spreading beyond its traditional heartlands in the south. Naturally cricket had spread north, taken by those who had played it at school and teachers and clergy taking roles up country and taking their love of the game with them. It was relatively strong in Essex and in Pilch's native Norfolk, and there were clubs in cities like Sheffield, Nottingham and Manchester. But these were isolated outposts.

One man saw a commercial opportunity, enabled by the railway and showcasing the country's leading players. William Clarke was a Nottinghamshire player with an eye on a profit and in 1846 he created the 'All-England Eleven'. This brought together the best players in England on a constant tour to cricket clubs willing to pay large fees to test themselves against the best in the land. This served as a catalyst for development and spread the game north, as although the host teams were generally thrashed they picked up proper techniques. As the years went on the team recruited the early Victorian stars such as Alfred Mynn, the 21-stone 'Lion of Kent', George Parr and John Wisden, he of the yellow *Almanack*. They were paid well, though Clarke took the largest share and became very wealthy. Though by all accounts an unscrupulous businessman, Clarke nevertheless left a dual legacy to the game, progression from a southern game to an English sport and the nucleus of a national team.

Though the game had grown in profile and scale in the careers of Pilch and Clarke it didn't yet have the visibility or level of societal interest to win the hearts of the nation and enter the national consciousness. Clarke's entrepreneurialism had added to a crisis of confidence for the amateurs, whose grip on the game was slowly loosening. Although the gentlemen of the MCC had assumed moral leadership, in practice the power was with the professionals. They were simply more athletic, talented and watchable. For in an England modernising at breakneck pace on the coat-tails of the Industrial Revolution, success mattered. It was gaining greater social capital than the old feudal notions of deference.

The burgeoning middle classes had money and ambition. Society was no longer a binary divide between the gentry and the rest. With the professionals key to drawing the crowds and an increasingly complex web of contracts and commercial rivalries the MCC found it difficult to exert any control on or even coherence to first class cricket. The proto county sides often refused to play if the opposition included players associated with certain commercial ventures that threatened their own. The MCC did have the venue, at least. In the course of the 19th century Lord's had lost its pond and grazing sheep, added a tavern and stands and consolidated its pre-eminence as the focal point of the game.

The amateurs' saviour came in an unlikely form, the son of a Bristol doctor. William Gilbert Grace was born in 1848 in a village just outside Bristol. His father loved the game and cleared an orchard on his land so his sons could practise. He then formed a local village side that was to lay the foundations for a Gloucestershire county team. W.G. played for the side as early as nine and was one of the leading players by his early teens. His talent was such that he was courted by both sides, the amateurs and the professionals. His elder brother, one of the leading cricketers of the age in his own right, went with the money and joined Clarke's band of men. But though he was far from blue-blooded, W.G. made his first class debut for the Gentlemen versus the Players in 1865. It was a significant coup for the MCC, for Grace was to became one of the best and most influential cricketers of all time. And, crucially, he was their man. He was a professional of course, but as a doctor. As a cricketer he was never a salary man, though he didn't let that stop him amassing a fortune.

As W.G. was breaking into the top echelons of the game cricket was entering a bridging phase, retaining many of its arcane, pastoral traits but beginning to adopt some reforms integral to the modern form of the game. One of these was overarm bowling, long rallied against by the MCC but despite their protestations, and encouragement of umpires to no-ball its proponents, finally, begrudgingly, it was accepted into the rules. This made batting far more challenging, technical and dangerous. There were so many injuries that pads were introduced, presented by *Punch* magazine as one of the symbols of modernity along with the steam train. It was particularly galling for the MCC as gentlemen were invariably batsmen and were targeted with relish by a new breed of firebrand professional.

In addition to the overarm revolution Grace also saw the birth of formalised county cricket while still a young player, being a proud champion of Gloucestershire cricket himself. County sides in this era played whoever they wanted to and there was no structure or governance. Northern counties had grown in strength and some could more than hold their own against the sport's traditional strongholds of Surrey and Sussex. Their competitiveness was given added edge by the north flexing its newfound economic muscles and the working classes determined to get one over the privileged gentry of the south. Is there a hint of this still in Surrey versus Lancashire fixtures? The leading team of the 1860s and 1870s was Nottinghamshire, a long, long way from the influence of Lord's. There was inevitable tension between the counties, especially the professional-laden ones of the north, and the MCC. The MCC, who remarkably took it upon themselves to also write the rules for the new sport of lawn tennis, only to be trumped by the All England Club, wanted absolute control of top-level cricket. Some counties preferred a more democratic form of governance, sometimes referred to as a cricket parliament.

Those long hours in the orchard with his brothers had forged a formidable technique and by his third year of first class cricket Grace was clearly the most talented player in the land. In 1868 he scored 224 not out for All-England versus Surrey. It was his maiden century and propelled him to stardom. By 1871 he was a colossus. Seventeen first class centuries were made that year, with W.G. accounting for ten of them. His statistics were simply astonishing, averaging 78 that season, almost twice as much as the next man. He was also the first to score 2,000 runs in a season. It is sometimes forgotten that he was also a very successful bowler. As his career developed so his statistics got more and more ridiculous. In 1876 he scored 839 runs in three innings in the space of six days, including two triple centuries, the first ever made in first class cricket.

While his statistics illustrate his freakish talent they don't quite explain the extent of his considerable fame. He is one of the most recognisable of all Victorians and it is said he was the greatest personality of the day. When Grace played, the gate fee doubled. His iconic beard and huge physical presence gave him an almost otherworldly, superhuman aura, reflected in the way he played. His social status and ambiguity of class may also have helped him achieve hero status, in a culture that had a complex, conflicted relationship with status, social betterment, Christian values and sense of English superiority. He was at once one of the elite, but champion of the people. As Birley put it in his seminal *Social History of English Cricket* 'while he rescued the establishment, he was not part of it'.

Grace wasn't the first national sporting hero – a few boxers had preceded him in that accolade – but W.G. took it to another level. His fame quickly transcended cricket, that still only appealed to certain levels of society. He managed his life and his profile carefully and was astute at making his 'expenses' as an amateur stretch far beyond his needs. With Grace in their camp the MCC managed to resist the modernisation and democratisation that swept progress through much of Victorian society. They retained control through the critical decades when cricket was consolidating as a modern sport, the domestic structure we now know was taking shape and the game was poised to go international. The MCC comprised an elite imbued with imperialist zeal and a belief that English values, embodied in cricket, would civilise the world.

The *Wisden Almanack*, that book-bound bundle of yellow bliss, was launched in 1864. The first edition was something of a hotch-potch, ranging beyond cricket for pieces on the history of China and advice on collectable coins. What did the cricket scene it covered consist of? There was not yet a formalised county game or internationals. But there was a plethora of first class fixtures played by all number of teams, most of which at some point in the season were lured to Lord's and the MCC. The old universities were amongst the best teams in the country and Eton versus Harrow the society match of the season. The now packed marketplace for representative XIs was ever expanding, spreading cricket's tentacles further into distant shires. *Wisden's* publication of scorecards, particularly those from the first, furtive foreign tours, was to give impetus to an exciting new frontier to the game. The British Empire.

Grace was, of course, destined to play a vital role. His fame seemed to expand in unison with his waistline and resisting the urge to retire to commit himself full-time to general practice at 30, he played at the top level until his 50s. Though affable he wasn't always the easiest character and his determination to win at all costs often saw him clash with amateurs, for whom playing cricket in the right spirit mattered more than anything. More than performance, more than winning. Even to this day most cricket fans will be aware of the possibly apocryphal quote attributed to the great doctor when bowled for a duck. He said, so legend has remembered, pointing to the crowd 'they've come to see me bat, not you umpire', while replacing the bails. Many of his contemporaries noted his pedantry with the rules when his team could benefit, and the great Lord Harris once reflected, blithely, that Grace 'relied rather too much on the umpire for leg before'. The establishment took him under their wing but he never fully accepted their conventions. Back when gentlemen not only eschewed the pull shot but considered it immoral, Grace and his elder brother delighted crowds with the stroke. In the Victorian age Grace was cricket, but his behaviour 'wasn't cricket'.

Below first class cricket the sport had successfully infiltrated the institutions that produced England's empire builders. It had been played in some public schools since the 1640s and by the mid-19th century was viewed alongside rowing as embodying the ideal blend of virility and Christian values. It taught patience and fortitude, values the imperialists thought distinguished the English from what they deemed hot-headed races beyond their shores. Birley sums up the virtue of cricket seen through the eyes of public schools and the military as 'discipline and reliance on one another'. It was this characteristic that would see cricket being played in all corners of Earth.

※ ※ ※

Cricket was always destined to cross continents and spread across the world because of the people who played it. As England, and then Britain, started to forge an empire so its traders, administrators and military officers set sail to conquer, build and sustain it. The first written reference to cricket being played beyond Britain was by officers in Aleppo, Syria, in 1676. It is likely it was played earlier than this by some of the first English colonists in the new world. As cricketers, young men would naturally want to indulge in their hobbies wherever fortune took them or wherever they were posted. You can well imagine that for some their passion for the game may even intensify as a means of battling homesickness and retaining a vital link to their heritage. For those who were responsible for men, whether that be a military unit or a ship's crew, cricket could serve to boost morale, foster unity and reduce the risk of ill-discipline.

The Duke of Wellington, heroic vanquisher of Napoleon and future prime minister, made an order that all new barracks should incorporate a cricket ground. It was a formalisation of a long-held tenet of the British army that cricket was not only a recreational activity to be encouraged to keep the men fit and out of mischief, but an integral part of building the requisite discipline and skills of soldiery. In military outposts as diverse as Calcutta, Corfu and Kingston cricket was played. The level of cricketing infrastructure depended on the nature of the location. For instance, in places fully incorporated into the empire and directly ruled by Britain cricket would be taught in schools, played in clubs, and was part of the cultural and official fabric of British life in the colony. Take for instance Jamaica or, on a much smaller scale, Gibraltar. In other cases where Britain had a limited or fleeting foothold, such as in Corfu, facilities may only have stretched to a ground and an enthusiastic coach. Where facilities were sufficiently developed, representative teams often played neighbouring colonies, visiting sides and even undertook tours. Over decades and even centuries this model could see a distinct cricket culture develop with a strong enough foundation to progress beyond the military and civic need it served, and if allowed, spread beyond the confines of British control to the country at large and local populations.

These mercantile and military catalysts for growth would see cricket go wherever the English gained footfall. As the empire grew so the game's reach extended. That such a quintessentially English sport, typically played by the very class who built and administered the empire, was taken to its far flung outposts is hardly revelatory. It is as natural as hoisting the union flag on an English ship. What is fascinating is the extent to which cricket took root and why. To understand that you first have to accept what may initially appear to be counterintuitive: that while the English are rightly proud of the summer sport and took it across the globe, the motivation has largely been to play it themselves rather than see it be played. There are exceptions of course, but invariably cricket's Anglican missionaries have viewed it as an English sport played across the world. Cricket's history has rarely been far removed from broader colonial and post-colonial narratives.

In 1868, just as W.G. was consolidating his position as the most celebrated cricketer in England, a 13-year-old boy was making his debut in the Eton v Harrow match at Lord's. Though his 23 didn't set the world alight this slender youth was destined to shape both English cricket and the international game. The honourable George Canning Harris was born a cricket fanatic and a staunch imperialist. His father, the 3rd Baron Harris, had been governor of Trinidad, where George was born, and Madras and on his return to England in 1859 had become president of Kent Cricket Club. While W.G.'s amateur status could be described as expedient, there was no doubting the pedigree of George Harris. In many ways he was a throwback to the aristocratic patrons of the last century and had little truck with modern, more socially fluid ideas.

On leaving Eton in 1870 he immediately made his first class debut for Kent. While experience wasn't on his side his station in life was and he was drafted on to the committee of the county club before he'd gone up to Oxford. He played for the university, then one of the best teams in the country, and played for Kent in the high summer after term had ended. In only his second year at Oxford he was made the captain of Kent, a role he retained for the next 18 years.

The county cricket system that Harris began his career in was still informal and haphazard. By this time the press became interested in declaring a county champion, but the criteria they used varied and there were no fixture lists or agreed governance. It was a device to provoke discussion after the fact rather than a clear goal counties aimed for during the season itself. An important step forward came in 1873 when the annual meeting of the club secretaries agreed player qualification rules. A player could not play for more than one county in a season and could choose between a county they were resident in or a county where their family were from and where they had occasional residence. This stopped counties being invitational teams and allowed for a more considered evaluation of which counties were strongest.

An interest in international cricket predated the consolidation of domestic structures and was a child of the commercial All-England era. It was natural that once Clarke, and latterly his many imitators, had established the All-England XI they would be enticed by a larger, international market. At the same time there was an appetite amongst cricketers in the empire to show their mettle against the best of the mother country.

In the early 1850s a group of influential figures in North American clubs came up with the notion of hosting an All-England XI. It took a few years to get the finance in place to support the tour but eventually, in 1859, a team was selected comprising George Clarke's All-England XI and the breakaway United All-England XI, formed seven years before under the stewardship of John Wisden. It was captained by George Parr, captain of Nottinghamshire, sometime player for the MCC and known as 'the lion of the north'. The squad included a sprinkling of players from the strongest counties of the era: Surrey, Sussex, Cambridgeshire and Notts. The squad included Surrey star Billy Caffyn and John Lillywhite, whose family founded the famous sports outfitters.

Although it contained many of the leading players of the time it was neither a best English XI or subject to any formalised, representative selection process. Rather it was an extension of the commercial arrangements for the All-England XIs and a question of availability and remuneration. The MCC were not involved. They played against XXIIs so there were no first class matches but the team played in Quebec, New Jersey, Pennsylvania, Ontario and New York, and even found time for some sightseeing at Niagara Falls. They played to large crowds at the initial games but then the weather turned cold, forcing the players to wear coats for the final fixtures.

Two years later an England squad toured Australia. Again it was a commercial venture, a contingency enterprise when the promotor's plan to lure Charles Dickens for a book tour fell through. The first game against Victoria drew 45,000 spectators over the three days, ensuring a profit for the tour with a further 11 fixtures to come. Unsurprisingly given the interest and profits generated there was a further Australia tour, this time under Parr, in 1863, with a New Zealand leg added at the end.

These tours were commercial and professional, two concepts considered deeply distasteful by the MCC. Although the Marylebone men had assumed ownership of the rules and saw themselves as the moral guardians of cricket they didn't seek to encourage spread of the game. There were no rival amateur tours, for instance, even though they must have been aware of the success of the tours and the burgeoning interest in the colonies. The emergence of Lord Harris as an influential amateur and administrator was to change perspectives to the outside world: he ushered in a less insular attitude though very much driven by an imperialist, paternalistic vision.

The 1870s saw more counties form and innovations such as the heavy roller introduced. This helped eradicate the scourge of 'dead shooters' careening into the base of the stumps from a good length, while also removing pebbles from the pitches, that had tragically been responsible for several deaths as balls reared up dangerously. The early batsmen breathed a sigh of relief. Imagine facing Jeff Thomson on Brighton beach!

In 1873 W.G. led a touring side to Australia that included his brother Fred and players from Surrey, Sussex, Nottinghamshire, Yorkshire and Middlesex. In a departure from previous tours the party included five amateurs, albeit those on the more 'amenable to payment' end of the amateur spectrum.

In early 1877 two tours were planned for Australia, both by members of the 1873 party. Fred Grace, younger brother of W.G. and fated to die tragically young at the age of 29, had planned to tour with a mixed squad of professionals and amateurs. In parallel John Lillywhite planned to tour with professionals. Grace's venture foundered, leaving the way clear for Lillywhite. It was considered in Australia a much weaker squad than previous tours and didn't feature star amateurs such as W.G. Nevertheless, the match against a combined Victoria and New South Wales team at the MCG on 15 March was later designated the first Test match, the term itself being coined some time later. Alfred Shaw bowled the first ball in Tests and Charles Bannerman scored the first run. Australia came out as victors to the delight of a reported 12,000-strong crowd. The popularity and profitability of the match saw another game scheduled and this time England won comfortably. The Australian press gave the matches top billing though it made very little impression back in England. Just another tour, and not even with the strongest side. Nevertheless, Test cricket had begun.

When the Australians came to England in 1878 the MCC belatedly took an interest, though with a team including W.G. they lost to the tourists by nine wickets. Though not a Test match it helped prove that Australia were worthy Test match opponents. Having their appetite whetted and we can only assume belatedly eager to control foreign games as they did domestically the next Australian tour was not led by a professional, but by the ultimate establishment amateur, Lord Harris. He took a team of amateurs, though added a few professional bowlers to provide the hard yards. Once again the side was relatively weak and Harris's men had to contend with the Australian hero Fred 'The Demon' Spofforth, who claimed the first Test hat-trick. Harris lost and there followed some ugly rioting scenes, covered with relish in the English press.

By 1880 the England v Australia series was a guaranteed annual tour but the distasteful memory of the riot meant they struggled to secure fixtures. But Harris arranged a Test match at the Oval in which W.G. struck 152, securing a win witnessed by a crowd of 20,000. The 1881 tour reverted to a professional affair, led by Shaw and Shrewsbury. It was beset by match-fixing allegations and related skirmishes and the local press accused the English of staying up into the small hours drinking and fraternising rather too closely with the betting tent. England lost a four-match series 2-0. The needle that has been a bubbling undercurrent of England and Australia contests to the modern day was there in the earliest Tests.

Thus the scene was set for an event that would make England versus Australia Tests the stuff of sporting mythology. It was 1882 and England, chasing a mere 85, were well placed to win at the Oval. Even with an uncovered pitch a sub-hundred target should have been a formality. It may have been were it not for the most devastating bowler of his day, who had proved the scourge of England on previous tours. The 'Demon' Spofforth saw England collapse from a secure 51/2 to be bowled out seven runs short of the target. Contemporary reports bristle with tension as England sought to eke out the remaining runs and defy the irrepressible Demon. It was so harrowing to watch for one anxious spectator that he chewed through his umbrella handle. It was a desperately disappointing result and the media presented it as a national embarrassment. England had lost on home soil to an upstart colony. *The Sporting Times* sensed the mood of the nation and ran a mock obituary for English cricket. Its body was to be cremated and its ashes taken to Australia. Imperial pride had been wounded, Australian nationhood asserted and an enduring rivalry assured. The Ashes was cemented at the fulcrum of national interest and cultural resonance.

At the beginning of the Test era it was the convention that the host county would select the team in home tours and the promoters for away tours. This led to an inevitable variation in squads, although a natural deference to the titled meant Lord Harris was in strong demand. The integrity and structure of the England team we take for granted in the modern era just wasn't present, as seen when two rival representative teams, an amateur and a professional, toured Australia in 1887.

Back home the county secretaries formally adopted a means of agreeing a champion county and thus the first official championship was played in 1890. This comprised Nottinghamshire, Surrey, Sussex, Kent, Middlesex, Gloucestershire, Middlesex and Lancashire. Somerset, Essex, Warwickshire, Derbyshire and Hampshire had joined by 1895.

In the inaugural year of the County Championship a young man far, far away from home started his studies at Cambridge University. The slender young man was destined to become one of the most celebrated batsmen ever to play the game, with a style, elegance and touch rarely seen before or since. Born in Sadodar, India, Ranjitsinhji was born into the ruling family of the Nawanagar state and learnt cricket from an English games master in an English-style private school. He was bewitched by the quality of the first game he saw in England, Surrey versus the touring Australians in 1888, and playing cricket at a high level became his dream.

His batting was callow at first and he struggled against top quality bowling, tending to back away and expose his stumps. But he persevered and began to convince some of his talent. Despite more promising form he found it hard to get a game for his college, possibly stemming from a degree of racial prejudice. He finally made his first class debut for the university in 1893 and soon became a fans' favourite, as a dynamic player with an audacious new shot, the leg glance. His notoriety, and the royal associations he had somewhat over-egged, saw him turn out for the Gentlemen against the Players. In 1895 he began his career at Sussex and by the following season the clamour was building for him to play for England.

Lord Harris had all but finished his first class career by 1889, the last few years of which he had served as Under Secretary of State for India and then War in the House of Lords. From 1890 to 1895 he was the governor of Bombay. His conservative, imperialist views certainly suffused his approach to colonial government, and, on his return from India and having been made president of the MCC, it seemed to influence his decision to block the elevation of the prolific Ranji to the England team. He did not favour having a mix of racial backgrounds in the national XI. His was the traditionalist, southern view, but ever eager to throw a cat into establishment pigeons the Lancashire committee had no such qualms when including Ranji in the squad for the Old Trafford Test. As well as the relish of ruffling the MCC's feathers Lancashire knew Ranji's presence would boost admission numbers considerably, for his elegance but also the faint whiff of scandal.

Ranji was sublime in what must count as one of the most memorable Test debuts of all time. He made a supremely elegant 154, caressing the ball as none had done before with exquisite timing and touch. His innovative leg glance drew gasps from the crowd. *Wisden* and the press at large swooned over the Indian prince and his feats helped cricket become further entrenched in the hearts of the nation. He ended the century as the first man to pass 3,000 runs in a season.

From almost dying out during the Napoleonic Wars, cricket had prospered in the 19th century, gradually introducing the reforms and acquiring the attributes that are familiar today. Through entrepreneurship and capitalising on the opportunities of the modern age, it had steamed throughout England, establishing itself as a popular sport. In a microcosm, cricket's development mirrored broader societal trends in the Victorian age: conservatism versus modernism, privilege versus meritocracy, status through birthright or status through achievement. Through this lens it had grappled with round-arm, over-arm and betting scandals. And what this all distilled down to was a simple question: was cricket a sport for the many or a sport for the few? In the next century this would play out through an altogether broader political sphere as cricket went global.

Chapter 3

Development of cricket in the empire

W HILE cricket took some time to find a form and structure at first class level it was quicker to settle into a natural place in the formative institutions of English life. Although the development of first class cricket in England was by nature haphazard and episodic, the vision was clearer and passage of the sport smoother at lower levels. The parish and village game grew organically as interest spread, in turn feeding a growing number of clubs that in many cases formed the origin of county sides. In parallel, and from an early stage in many cases, cricket was eagerly adopted by public schools. Cricket is known to have been played in some schools by the mid-17th century and many influential figures recorded playing in their school years. One such early cricketing scholar was Horace Walpole, son of Britain's first prime minister, who played at Eton in the 1720s.

By the early 19th century as well as Westminster, Harrow, Eton, Charterhouse, Rugby and Winchester cricket is known to have taken root in many grammar schools, broadening its exposure in the social spectrum. Matches between establishment schools attracted a lot of prestige and attention and the Eton v Harrow game transferred to Lord's in 1805 and was arguably the most anticipated game of the season. In the first half of the 19th century Lord's ran a public schools' week.

So why was cricket so eagerly adopted by schools? Well part of it of course stems from its popularity with boys, especially as it was a historic pastime south of the Thames. But it must have been favoured by masters too in order to be adopted as an important representative sport for the school. It was the public schools after all who invented the sport's obsession with striped blazers. As its empire expanded and English society began to adopt Christian morality in a rebuke to the hedonism of the early Georgian age the leading schools sought ways of shaping the moral education of their boys and preparing them for roles in public service and empire.

Rowing was very popular with Christian headmasters building fortitude, determination and absolute discipline. But you needed a river. Cricket was more flexible, had a team ethic and was moulded to their purpose. Its increasingly complex rules provided structure and order, which in turn promoted discipline and respect. It also blended individual fortitude and team cohesion. These were all attributes young men of breeding would need as they assumed positions of leadership and responsibility. Cricket also provided the obvious health benefits of strength, fitness and hand to eye coordination as well as providing stimulus for the agile mind (especially for a captain planning the strategy of the game and his men). Given they were all born to lead there must have been consternation at their being only one captain!

Most of the boys would have gone up to Oxford or Cambridge and if particularly talented would have followed a well-worn path from first class university cricket, to MCC representation and the counties. It was a path Michael Atherton still followed in the late 1980s. For many it wasn't the talent for the game that shaped their futures but enjoyment, warm nostalgia and the values it instilled. As the boys left school so they took cricket with them. This undoubtedly helped cricket spread and consolidate in England but also took the game abroad. Naturally these born leaders took positions of authority and leadership and remembering their schooldays, would have been predisposed to play the game and encourage it among the men they led. This route from schools out across the empire and beyond played a significant role in the spread of the game. It is easy to imagine old school friends meeting out in the empire (Kingston, Jamaica, perhaps) renewing acquaintance and setting up a match between their plantations.

England's earliest colony, Roanoke, was founded in what is now North Carolina in 1584 in the reign of Elizabeth I, but a lack of supplies meant it was short-lived. Her successor, James I, had better luck founding Jamestown, near present day Williamsburg, Virginia, in 1607. It isn't known whether any of the settlers knew of cricket, and given the leaders were from Huntingdonshire and Lincolnshire and the game was restricted to the Wealden counties at this time you'd have to assume they didn't. But it isn't beyond the realms of possibility. By the Civil War Bermuda, Cape Cod, the Bahamas and Antigua had been added to the colonial map. With more settlers in the region the chances of cricket having been played increase though the historical record stubbornly refuses to oblige with references.

For the earliest reference to cricket being played outside Britain we have to cross the world in the year 1697 to Aleppo, a city that has never to this day seen cricket established to any degree. Henry Teonge, of Worcestershire, was a naval chaplain who kept a diary of a voyage that progressed through Malta, Cyprus and Turkey before arriving in Syria. On 6 May the party rode out of the city to a river basin where they hunted ducks before playing cricket. No locals were involved and no legacy of the game remained. It was simply a group of Englishmen seeking recreation playing a game they knew. They just happened to be a long, long way from home.

Establishing dates is of course a little academic as it can be reasonably assumed that if English merchants, military men or settlers went anywhere in any number that cricket may have been played, especially after it began to grow in profile in England from the beginning of the 17th century. But humour me. The next earliest definitive reference dates from 1736 in Lisbon where the crews of two naval ships played each other. Later, British port purveyors would establish clubs in Lisbon and Oporto.

The third reference is altogether more significant. William Stephens had learnt the game at Winchester school, progressed to Cambridge University and then moved to Georgia to run a plantation in the 1730s. He recorded that cricket was played in the town square by a mixture of settlers and slaves in 1737. The context for the reference doesn't suggest this was unusual and the fact slaves were playing indicates they must have had some prior introduction to the game and therefore points to even earlier roots in the new world. In 1751 a game was played in New York to 'London rules', a reference to the famous rules of association agreed by the London club in 1744. That cricket was being played is natural enough given the empire had been extant and growing in the new world for over a century. But it is interesting to reflect that it was being played in the colonies before it had consistently spread to all corners of Britain.

By 1800 the number of references and their geographic locations had expanded. The game was being played in Canada and India and almost certainly in South Africa, Gibraltar and Barbados. The most common model for the spread of the game was commanders setting up matches in British garrisons, then often arranging fixtures with neighbouring British outposts in the region. By 1850 this trend saw cricket played in Bermuda, Burma, Corfu, Egypt, Hong Kong, Singapore, New Zealand, Sri Lanka and Mauritius. It wasn't just growth through Britain's increasingly widespread military presence, British traders and emigrants had introduced the game to Chile and Argentina. With this growing and increasingly widespread list you could make a case that cricket was a global sport by the time of the Great Exhibition, that infamous display of Britain's role at the centre of the world. But such references to cricket are far from evidence it was a global sport. How much was it played? By whom? And to what extent was it absorbed into local cultures?

Let's return to North America. In Canada a game was played in Montreal in 1785 and through the establishment of teams in garrison towns and an encouraging level of local interest it became relatively well known by the 1830s. As is so often the case much of its growing profile was due to the passion and commitment of a single individual, George Barber. As publisher of the *Toronto Herald* and a teacher at Upper Canada College he was very well connected. He founded the Toronto cricket club in 1827 and introduced cricket to the college. The fixture between these two institutions began in 1836 and continues to this day.

In the USA the St George's Club of Manhattan was established in 1838. As the name suggests it was an English club. The majority of its players were British born and Americans were not allowed to play. This exclusive approach was resented by Americans who had been playing the game for over a century. It gave the impression it was an English game, with no one else welcome. Despite these constraints to its influence the St George's Club was a strong centre of the game in the Americas. The interest north and south of the Hudson was sufficient for regular games between St George's and Toronto to be staged by 1840 and this led to what would prove to be a historic fixture at the St George's Club, Manhattan, in late September 1844. It pitted Canada against the United States and was the first ever international, not only in cricket but in any modern sport. The core of the US team were from St George's but also included players from other main centres such as Philadelphia, Washington DC and Boston. A reported 20,000 watched Canada emerge victorious in a low-scoring, two innings match played over two days. The match started a long-running rivalry for the Auty Cup, named after Chicago resident Karl Andre Auty, which was played for every year since until 2017.

With clubs growing, interest building and annual internationals giving a patriotic hook to drive further development, cricket was gaining a foothold in the region. In Canada not only was the game consolidating in the Toronto area but was spreading to the west with the nucleus of what would become clubs forming in Victoria and Winnipeg. The level of ambition and confidence of this cricketing outpost is shown by the invite to an All-England XI to tour, originally planned in 1856 but finally achieved in 1859. As we've seen this was the first international tour by a representative English team. It was masterminded by William Pickering, a cricketer freshly emigrated from England and captain of the Canadian team. Games were played in Quebec, Ontario, Philadelphia, New Jersey and New York. Media and public interest were considerable and it was undoubtedly something of a coup. It was also a financial gamble that paid off handsomely.

It was a pivotal moment in the global game. International cricket was established and Canada and the USA were fast-growing regions of the sport beyond England, with the latter not even in the empire. The eagerness to arrange the 1859 tour despite a huge commercial risk on securing the services of the All Star XI demonstrates that they looked to England for influence and heroes. Nevertheless, partly as a result of the tour cricket could be said to be the most popular and established sport in both countries. There were grand plans for further international tours. In Canada the first prime minister, Sir John MacDonald, declared cricket the national sport.

Just as cricket was on the brink of taking root in the region civil war broke out. It was to be baseball, a young American sport adapted from the traditional English rounders-like game bass-ball, rather than cricket that the troops played during the war helping to establish it as the all-American game. Baseball is thought to have come over with British settlers in Canada in the middle of the 18th century and moved south of the border from there. In the 1850s its popularity in New York increased significantly, becoming something of a craze.

Though less established than cricket at this point it had a home-grown appeal over the stuffy English image the St George's Club had helped lumber cricket with. It was easier to organise and play than cricket too, not requiring a prepared pitch or as much specialist equipment. This helped it become the game of choice for relaxation amid the Civil War.

Cricket had lost its moment as a national sport. Although club cricket continued in the 1860s and further English sides toured it had begun to fall well behind baseball in participation and its place in the national consciousness. With the exception of Philadelphia, of which more shortly, it became restricted to certain circles and select clubs, unable to break through as a mainstream sport as had seemed possible in 1859. In Canada the signs looked more promising with formal clubs being founded in the west, the prime minister's ringing endorsement and even a visit by the great W.G. as part of an English touring team in 1872.

※ ※ ※

A mere 12 years after the first written reference to cricket Elizabeth I sought to extend England's influence, wealth and power beyond its shores and created the East India Company. The company was formed after a successful petition to the queen by merchants keen to challenge Spanish and Portuguese hegemony of trade in the East. Appetites were whetted in 1592 when Francis Drake captured a Portuguese ship laden with gold, jewels and spice. The capture also brought into English possession the ship's log book with details of trade routes, ports and treasure in India, China and beyond. Armed with the log book and a royal charter, inferring a monopoly on trade east of the Cape of Good Hope, they made speculative early expeditions in the opening years of the 17th century setting up trading stations in Java and the Spice Islands. They soon turned their attentions to India and with the help of James I royal diplomacy signed a trade treaty with the Moghul emperor Jahangir. With growing confidence and local patronage they set about taking over Portuguese possessions and claiming strategic bases of their own in Surat (1619), Madras (1639), Bombay (1668) and Calcutta (1690). Their operations in these bases were later subsumed into fortified garrisons.

Given the growing English presence in India in the late 17th century it is likely that some cricket was played, although the earliest reference was not until 1721, when English sailors played near the city of Cambay, in modern day Gujarat. The first city to see regular matches played was Calcutta. Initially there were irregular matches between the army and East India Company in the second half of the 18th century. Cricket in the city was consolidated in 1792 with the foundation of the Calcutta Cricket Club, on whose site the famous Eden Gardens ground now stands. It was unequivocally an English club with no attempt to spread the game to the local population. This reflects a pattern seen elsewhere in the empire where the English saw cricket as their game, just being played in exotic climes.

However, in another Indian city, Bombay, local interest in the game was stirred. The Parsi community were the descendants of refugees from Persia in the Middle Ages and as wealthy traders were keen to establish strong links with the English, and what better way than to adopt the English game. As early as the late 18th century a Parsi team played an Old Etonian XI and there was clearly sufficient interest in the game by 1848 to establish their own club, which they called the Orient. It stood adjacent to the major English sporting club of the city, the Bombay Gymkhana. With no equipment available locally they had to make do with whatever they could borrow or contrive but unlike so many sporting clubs born in adversity, that wither and disband once key individuals leave the fray, the Orient club flourished and in 1877 defeated their English neighbours.

Elsewhere, cricket clubs were founded in Madras and Karachi by 1850 and games between cities were established in the 1860s. By this time interest had also spread to the Hindu communities and Hindus in Bombay established the Union club in 1866. This made for an interesting cricket culture in the city, with cricketing and cultural rivalries interweaved amongst English, Parsi and Hindus. Feeling left out, the Muslim community established the Mohammedan Cricket Club, later known as the Muslim Gymkhana. The popularity of the game by this time can be seen in the publication in Hindi and Urdu of a coaching manual. Cricket was entrenching itself in Indian culture.

For one of these communities ambition took Indian cricket international. Buoyed by their success over the English in 1877, the Parsis arranged a tour of England and Australia but the funding fell through and it wasn't until 1886 that a tour was pulled off. It was extensive, featuring no fewer than 28 matches, but the inexperience of the tourists told and they only won a solitary game. But clearly they didn't find defeat too chastening as they returned two years later, this time faring a lot better and winning eight games. The star in their midst was, like the great W.G., a tall, strapping doctor. Mehlasa Parvi took 170 wickets on the tour at an average of 12! He certainly didn't lack for pace, causing an uprooted stump to cartwheel nine yards in a match in Norwich.

Parvi's talent and improved competitiveness of the team in general generated interest in tours in the other direction. In 1889 an all amateur side including Lord Hawke visited India. For the most part their opponents were fellow Englishmen but when they faced the Parsi team Dr Parvi took nine wickets in a heavy defeat for the tourists. At this critical juncture in the development of Indian cricket we renew acquaintance with two old friends, Lord Harris and the master leg-glancer Ranjitsinhji.

Lord Harris had become governor of Bombay and by all accounts prioritised organising cricket over administering the city. His zeal and commitment, albeit seen through a very conservative, imperialist vision, undoubtedly helped further embed cricket into the culture of the city. He was also influential in encouraging further teams to tour, with Lord Hawke captaining a touring side in 1892. Ranjitsinjhi's heroics in England had inspired fellow princes back home to form teams in their states. In this way cricket spread from Calcutta and Bombay to cover vast swathes of the country. The domestic game was initially structured on religious grounds, with regular 'presidency matches' played between the Parsis and Europeans from 1895, later joined by Muslims and a combined Jewish and Christian team in the 20th century.

※ ※ ※

Just as cricket was starting to spread following the restoration in England the Dutch, bitter rivals in trade and imperial ambitions, discovered the 'southern continent' on the far side of the globe. Despite taking great pains to map Terre Australis, the Dutch East India Company thought the cost outweighed the benefit in the case for colonisation of what maps called New Holland. A century later just as Britain's grip on its American colony was slipping, James Cook, captain of the *Endeavour*, landed at Botany Bay, liked what he saw and, confident that the east coast of Australia had never been claimed by the Dutch, claimed it for Britain. Later in the 1770s the French and Swedish also devised plans to colonise parts of Australia, though as a cursory knowledge of history will attest these plans came to naught.

In the 1780s a combination of new-found industrial wealth and confidence, a prison capacity crisis and wounded pride from the loss of America saw the British government found a colony at Botany Bay noting opportunities for plantations of sugar, cotton and tobacco and a strategically cited base for Pacific trade. Norfolk Island, off the coast of Australia, was also an attractive acquisition to offset the loss of timber supplies in America. The first fleet that arrived in the colony of New South Wales carried a thousand people, over three-quarters of whom were convicts. Sydney Cove, down the coast from Botany Bay, was chosen as the site of settlement due to its safe harbour and source of fresh water. It would be speculation to suggest that some of those first settlers may have played cricket but those of a romantic disposition would consider it plausible. A newspaper feature in 1804 indicates that cricket must have been firmly established in the colony by 1800 and the first recorded match was in Sydney in December 1803.

By the mid-1820s Hyde Park was hosting matches between established clubs in the city and the game also became established in Van Diemen's Land, later renamed Tasmania. In 1832 the *Sydney Gazette* asserted that cricket was the 'prevailing amusement of the colony'. The presence of the British military and an eagerness to accentuate the Britishness of the colonies help explain its popularity.

In 1838 a match was played on the site of the Royal Mint in Melbourne and the Melbourne Cricket Club was founded. One of its founders, Alfred Mundy, was a military man of aristocratic birth, his family seat being

Shipley Hall in Derbyshire, who resigned his commission as lieutenant in the year of the club's founding. Another was Frederick Powlett, of Shropshire, who was later treasurer of Victoria. His cricketing pedigree was clear, being descended from the Reverend Charles Powlett, founder of the famous Hambledon Cricket Club and on the committee that drew up the original rules in 1844. Given the status of its founders it is not surprising that the MCC soon became the most prestigious club in the country. Cricket also spread to South Australia and Western Australia at this time.

With cricket expanding in its various Australian colonies the MCC of the Port Talbot district sent an invitation for a representative game against the best of Van Diemen's Land. The following year Victoria won its battle for separation from New South Wales and the inter-colony cricket match was an integral part of the Victorian celebrations. It was played in Launceston and is now considered the inaugural first class match in Australia. It was an intriguing contest, with Victorians bowling overarm and the Tasmanians underarm. The captain of Tasmania, John Marshall, was a mere 58 years old and remains the oldest cricketer to have played at first class level in Australia. The game attracted a crowd of 2,500 and was covered extensively by the press. Despite the logistical challenges of inter-colonial matches in such a vast country the appetite was certainly whetted. The following year the Melbourne club hosted on the banks of the river Yarra, winning by 61 runs. The Victorian gold rush then diverted attention from the decider, which wasn't staged until 1854. By then the Australian MCC had moved from the flood-prone riverside ground to a site in Richmond Park, today one of the most famous and loved grounds in the world, the MCG.

Victoria played New South Wales in 1855 for a wager of £500 at the MCG, drawing a crowd of 5,000. Annual inter-colonial matches between Tasmania, NSW and Victoria continued with South Australia joining in 1877, hosting matches at the Adelaide Oval. Western Australian teams started competing in the 1890s.

With inter-colonial matches not long established but growing affection for the game in the country recent English emigrant owners of the Cafe de Paris at Melbourne's Theatre Royal sought to organise a tour by a representative English side. With sufficient financial inducement the plan came off, the touring side led by Surrey cricketer Heathfield Harman Stephenson, who was awarded a hat for taking three wickets in consecutive balls, thereby coining a cricketing term. His other claim to fame was umpiring in the first Test match hosted in England, at the Oval in 1880. The quality of play was variable but commercially it was a great success, drawing considerable public interest. Unsurprisingly, further tours followed.

As cricket was growing in the cities it was also being introduced in the outback. English pastoralists in rural Victoria taught the game to Aboriginals working in their cattle stations. A key figure in this movement was Thomas Wentworth Wills, born in NSW but educated at Rugby and Cambridge. While in England he played first class cricket for Kent and the MCC. On his return to Australia he captained a strong Victorian side and found time to devise Aussie Rules football, a winter sport intended to keep cricketers fit and active. In 1861 he suffered a tragedy when, following an epic eight-month trek into the Queensland outback, his father and 17 others of his group were killed in an Aboriginal raid. Despite this he founded and coached an Aboriginal cricket team that toured Australia in 1867. Many of this side were included in a touring party put together by Charles Lawrence.

English-born Lawrence, in his youth a professional cricketer in Scotland and captain of an All-Ireland XI, was a Surrey player when selected for the 1861 tour to Australia. He opted to stay and became the first professional cricket coach in Australia for the Albert Club, Sydney, home of the legendary Fred Spofforth. He also represented NSW as a player. In 1868 he became coach of the Aboriginal XI.

Unaarimmim was the captain of the side. Born in a cattle station near Harrow, Victoria, he became one of the best players in Victoria and was once described as the 'W.G. of Aboriginal cricketers'. He was a champion of indigenous rights at a time when Aboriginals were often treated as second class citizens. The Aboriginal touring party's arrival in London in May 1868 caused quite a stir, with the conservative press being less than charitable. The *Telegraph* appeared surprised when meeting the team to find them 'clothed and in their right minds'. It may not have been their cricketing prowess that drew a crowd of 20,000 to their first fixture at the Oval. In 47 matches played over six months the team won a creditable 17, with their captain winning particular admiration. As part of the show they often demonstrated boomerang throwing after the close of play. A young W.G. Grace narrowly beat the squad in a distance challenge, throwing 118 yards. On their return two of the team played colony-level cricket. A rule made in 1869 required permission from the governor for any Aboriginal to leave Victoria. This made being a cricket professional impossible.

With the spread of cricket and the concentration of talent in the inter-colonial matches the standard of Australian cricket got stronger and stronger and produced players of the calibre of Charles Bannerman. Bannerman had been born in Woolwich, England, and emigrated to Australia as an infant. He joined the Warwick club in Sydney, where he was coached by former Surrey and All-England star Billy Caffyn. He became a professional at 20 and played for New South Wales.

There had been further tours by English sides in his early years as a professional and these helped bring the best players in the country together. In March 1877 Bannerman found himself selected for the Australian side in a match that was later recognised as the first Test match. He opened the batting at the MCG and therefore, though this wasn't apparent at the time, faced the first ever ball and scored the first ever run in Test cricket. He then went on to score a few more. Dropped while still in single figures, he finished the first day undefeated on 126 and added a further 39 the next morning before being forced to retire hurt after fast bowler George Ulyett broke his finger. He was the first Test centurion and 165 remains the highest score for an Australian Test debutant. It is testimony to his skill and performance that day that none of his team-mates made more than 20 in either innings.

On the Australian tour to England in 1878 he also made a century, though this wasn't classified as a Test match. These feats won him plenty of admiration and celebrity in a country that already saw sporting success as part of its identity. But he struggled to cope with the spotlight and his Test career was cut short after only three games. He played on as a first class cricketer until 1888 but was plagued by gambling debts and personal problems. His famous 165 was the highest score of his first class career. He later umpired in 12 Test matches.

Charles's brother Alick, younger by eight years and born in Australia, enjoyed a longer international career, scoring over a thousand runs in 28 matches. He was a short, slight man with a barnacle-like defensive technique that earned him the nickname 'barn door'. *Wisden* mused that he was 'the most famous of all stone wall batsmen'. Ditties were composed of his remarkable patience and he took his cricket very seriously indeed, once reprimanding a colleague for singing comic songs in the slips.

The hero of early Australian cricket was undoubtedly Fred Spofforth. His potency was central to the fame Australian cricket was acquiring which was immortalised in the creation of the Ashes. For the English it was hard to stomach that they, the inventors and rule makers of the game, should lose to a colony that had only been playing top class cricket for a mere 30 years. For Australia it was a display of national pride and strength. Spofforth, who invented the hostile tactic of staring opposition batsmen down until they wilted under the gaze, an art form Merv Hughes was to perfect a century later, embodied the athletic, strong, ultra-competitive ethos that was woven into the fabric of Australian culture. He was the first to take a Test match hat-trick and the first to take 50 Test wickets. In 18 Tests he took 94 wickets.

With the Ashes rivalry firmly established inter-colonial cricket was further formalised in 1891 after Henry Holroyd, Earl of Sheffield, touring with the English Test side, donated £150 for a trophy for the best colony side in the country, and henceforth the premier cricket tournament in Australia has borne his name, the Sheffield Shield. Queensland, where cricket had been played since the 1850s, was finally awarded first class status, but didn't join the Sheffield Shield until 1926. Western Australia joined in 1947 and Tasmania in 1977.

※ ※ ※

The Dutch founded Cape colony as a victualling station around the area of what is now Cape Town in 1652. Their control gradually spread into the hinterland as they discovered bountiful farmland and mineral wealth. The British took advantage of conflicts between the Dutch and French in the late 18th century to seize the colony in 1795 to prevent French acquisition. It was held on behalf of the Dutch until 1803, within which time cricket was played on African soil. Amongst the crew was Charles Anguish, one of the founding members of the MCC and a first class cricketer in England before his departure. During the Napoleonic Wars Britain seized it again but with longer-term colonial ambitions and they formally took administrative control when it was ceded to Britain in the Treaty of Amiens.

The first recorded fixture in South Africa was in 1808, a military affair with the garrison XI facing the artillery corps. It was probably played in the area of Green Point, now a vibrant, liberal district of the city. The fact it was billed as a grand match in the press indicates cricket was present and organised from the very outset of colonisation. It remained a military-centred, settler game for some time. In 1843 the first cricket club, one of the oldest sporting clubs still in existence in the world, was formed in Port Elizabeth. Their St George's Park playing field was later to host the country's first Test match. By late 1844 there was a club established in Cape Town and following the seizure of Pietermaritzburg from the Boers in 1843 cricket was also introduced to Natal. The military remained the sport's main champion and conduit for growth with cricket played in Bloemfontein and Durban in the 1850s. The sport was consolidated in the civilian population in Cape Town through its introduction to schools and those leaving schools and moving into more rural areas helped the game to spread. A club was founded in the Transvaal, at Potchefstroom, in 1863.

Along with fixtures between this increasingly extensive network of clubs in 1862 a mother country versus colonial-born fixture was staged, quickly establishing itself as the main event in the cricketing calendar. In 1876 there was an attempt to formalise the inter-club matches, in a similar way to inter-colony fixtures in Australia, through a Port Elizabeth initiative to present a champion bat trophy. Initially this competition featured the hosts, Cape Town, Grahamstown and King William's Town. Although not an annual tournament, the champion bat was played regularly.

In 1888 a ground at the foot of Table Mountain originally owned by a brewer, fitting given the prodigious consumption of lager at the site in modern times, was leased for cricket purposes, levelled, drained and turned into the famous Newlands ground. The same year the Wanderers ground was created at the mining camp in Johannesburg.

The novelist H. Rider Haggard lived in the country in the 1870s and was of the belief that the army's passion for cricket was a hindrance to their efficiency, noting, wryly perhaps, that they sometimes prioritised moving cricket gear over vital military supplies. It was an army man, Major Wharton, who organised the first tour of an English side in 1888. It was captained by Sir Charles Aubrey Smith, a bowler for Sussex, who would later become a Hollywood star, featuring in films such as *The Prisoner of Zenda*, *The Four Feathers* and *Rebecca*. He would later found the Hollywood Cricket Club and played alongside fellow Brits abroad David Niven and Laurence Olivier. But let's not get ahead of ourselves.

The English XI was not as strong as the truly representative sides playing Australia at the time, but nevertheless contained some talented players in Surrey's diminutive Bobby Abel, Lancashire spinner Johnny Briggs and the breaker of Bannerman's finger, George Ulyett. Beyond this core the team was supplemented by some without first class experience. Nevertheless, two fixtures against combined South Africa XIs in early 1889 were subsequently designated as Tests. This decision was controversial, as first class cricket was not played before that date in South Africa and standards were not yet as strong as in Australia.

The tourists played fixtures against provincial and club sides, mostly playing on matting due to the variability of playing surfaces. Although South Africa lost both Tests a few players made an impression. Bernard Tancred, born in Cape Town and a member of the Grahamstown club, top scored for the hosts, making 87 runs in the series. At Newlands he became the first Test cricketer to carry his bat, making an undefeated 26 as his team collapsed for 47. The following season he became the first player to make a first class century in South African domestic cricket. He would later spy for the British in the Boer War. The South African captain in the Second Test, William Milton, also played rugby for England and later in his career governed Southern Rhodesia. But as a whole the squad didn't go on to have long first class careers. It was an inexperienced squad of occasional cricketers who by fate became Test pioneers in their country.

The legacy of the tour was that the sponsor, Scottish shipping magnate Donald Currie, was impressed by the cricket he saw and donated a cup to the winners of the domestic competition. The Currie Cup, as it has been ever since, was awarded first class status from 1890. The first winners were Kimberley, latterly known as Griqualand West. In 1894 the South African Cricket Association was formed. By 1902 standards had increased and they proved competitive against a full-strength Australian touring side, albeit losing both Tests.

Before the First World War South Africa were known for their battery of googly bowlers. The delivery, pioneered by Bernard Bosanquet, had been learnt from its creator by Reginald Schwartz, a London-born son of a Polish trader. As a young man he played rugby for England before representing Middlesex at cricket and emigrating to South Africa. When he returned to England in 1904 as a South African international he bowled his 'Bosies' to great effect. He also passed on the skill to Bert Vogler, who for a few years in 1907/08 was considered one of the best bowlers in the world. With Aubrey Faulkner and Gordon White, who also had the googly in their armoury, Bosanquet had left quite a legacy in the colony, much to the chagrin of the English batsmen who faced them.

※ ※ ※

Seeking to muscle in on Spanish trade in the new world, English adventurers established footholds in the West Indies, initially at St Kitts, Nevis and Barbados in the 1620s, only a decade or so on from the founding of Jamestown. From these bases further settlements were made in the following decade such as Antigua, Jamaica and the Virgin Islands. The British West Indies was then expanded through the spoils of the Seven Years' War in the mid-18th century. With such widespread settlement it is likely that some cricketers emigrated and may have played on their plantations as early as 1700. However, a lack of written references suggests if it was played at all it was occasional and ad hoc. The impetus for development of the game instead came from the military, who established cricket in its network of garrisons. Clubs sprung from these garrison sides.

An image on a belt buckle showing a slave being bowled suggests cricket was being played on plantations before Britain's abolition of the sale of slaves in 1807. It is one of the most intriguing of cricket's historic artefacts, discovered in the mud of the River Tweed in 1979. It depicts a mixed raced man manacled by the neck batting with slave huts and a cane-crushing windmill in the background. The presence of a cane mill means it probably predates the devastating hurricane in Barbados in 1780, while the depiction of three stumps dates it after 1777 when the third stump was typically added. It probably belonged to the Hotham family, who had estates on the Tweed and in Barbados.

At the same time as the buckle was made a plantation owner in Jamaica recorded a game of cricket on his estate. Several authorities of the West Indian game, including former Jamaican Prime Minister Michael Manley in his comprehensive *History of West Indian Cricket*, have suggested that enslaved boys on plantations were required to bowl at the sons of their masters, probably in clearings in the sugar cane. This makes the depiction of the man batting potentially significant, with the great West Indian cricket authority C.L.R. James associating this with a scene of defiance and self-expression, despite the context of servitude.

By the mid-18th century the islands would have been an increasingly complex social mix of colonists, military, slaves and free men. While at this time the military would have kept cricket within their white, English elite, the situation beyond the garrisons may have been more nuanced. With a miserable life of servitude, drudgery and back-breaking work in the fields it is possible to imagine that an ability to demonstrate athletic prowess and skill was a welcome diversion, and along with music and stories perhaps one of a limited number of forms of self-expression. From the perspective of the colonial masters on the other hand cricket is likely to have been seen as a way of instilling discipline and what in an imperialist's world view may have been described as 'civilised virtues' among their workers.

By the turn of the 19th century several clubs were active, with the first known press cutting referring to a meeting of the St Anne's club in Barbados in 1806. By the middle of the 19th century there was an established club in Trinidad, colleges in Jamaica were playing the game and cricket was established in British Guyana. Most clubs were English and white only but some allowed black players to join. This exclusive approach saw local players form their own clubs, such as the Barbados Cricket Committee and the Melbourne Cricket Club of Jamaica, that would go on to produce such luminaries of the game as Michael 'Whispering Death' Holding and Courtney Walsh.

As cricket was consolidating and gradually becoming more culturally and racially diverse in the region it started to look outwards too, with tours in the last quarter of the 19th century to Canada and the USA.

In 1894 an English touring team under the captaincy of Middlesex batsman Robert Lucas arrived in the islands after completing their American itinerary. It was a squad of mixed ability, including future Test player Hugh Bromley-Davenport but many not of first class calibre. They played in seven different islands, including the first ever first class fixture in Jamaica.

In 1896 that perennial empire cricket tourist Lord Hawke led a further tour. This time it featured a stronger squad, with future England captains Pelham 'Plum' Warner and Henry Leveson-Gower among them. At the same time another English team under Arthur Priestley, featuring some Test players such as Andy Stoddart, were also touring. This tour contained a particularly important fixture against an all-West Indies team, featuring players from Trinidad, Guyana and Barbados. This team was captained by Aucher Warner, brother of Plum, Attorney General of Trinidad and Tobago who had played against Lucas's team in 1894. He played for Trinidad against his more famous brother who toured with Lord Hawke.

Aucher led a racially mixed team featuring some of the earliest titans of West Indian cricket. These included fast bowlers Clifford Goodman and Archie Cumberbatch. Cumberbatch, who took 45 wickets in five matches on the tour, was a high-class bowler who had to move islands several times to survive as a professional cricketer. His steepling bounce off a good length will conjure a clear image for anyone who has watched West Indian teams over the years.

As in Australia and South Africa the next important development came in the establishment of inter-colonial matches. In February 1865 a team from Guyana played a Barbados team in Bridgetown. Although the teams practised within the garrison walls a pitch had to be prepared in the savannah for the game. This was an unconventional surface to say the least, with long grass in the outfield and sharp pieces of exposed coral in the pitch requiring several changes of ball. Given this it is surprising this game is considered to be the first first class game in the region. A return fixture was arranged in Guyana for later in the year, with the players treated to a riverboat trip and festivities after the match. Tragically, two of the team died during the river trip when a boat capsized in the Koestabroek Falls. This social element of the game was important in building friendships and bonds between the outposts, fostering a regional sense of identity to counter the seclusion of garrison life.

In the latter half of the century with inter-colonial rivalries intensifying and acquiring embryonic elements of national contests, and with a greater, albeit still limited, degree of racial mixing, some leading black players were included in the squads. The prevailing prejudices of the day often saw them subject to discrimination, such as being forced to dine separately.

After the clutch of tours in the final years of the century Lord Hawke arranged for an all-West Indies team to tour England in 1900. Unfortunately, availability issues for some of the leading domestic players meant it was not a full-strength squad. The tour had a dramatic start for one of the leading players, Lebrun Constantine, who was left on the dock when the squad left saying he couldn't afford to travel. A public fund was started on the spot and the player was sped off on a fast motor launch to catch the transatlantic crossing. This shows the pride in this representative side.

The touring side was captained by Aucher Warner, featured players from six colonies and was a mixture of white and black cricketers. There were two black professionals and three black amateurs in the squad of 14. The degree of control applied by the mother country can be seen in the fact that the captain of the touring side had to be approved by the MCC, who had a West Indies Cricket Committee.

Given the quality of the South African games later awarded Test status it is interesting that the games were not granted first class status, despite the fact that the tourists were all first class cricketers in the West Indies. This is partly explained by the poor start they made to the tour, struggling to adjust to conditions and facing strong county sides. Sadly, public interest waned after a few heavy defeats even though the tourists went on to win matches against Leicestershire, Hampshire and Surrey.

Despite a knack of losing the toss, bad running and scrappy wicketkeeping, several players made a favourable impression. Having joined the party on his dash from the dock, Constantine repaid the public's faith by making the first century by a West Indian abroad. While his talent was eclipsed by that of his son, the rarely gifted Learie Constantine, he was nevertheless pivotal in winning respect both for West Indian cricket and players of colour. St Vincent batsman Charles Ollivierre topped the averages and made the highest score of the tour, a sparking 159 against Leicestershire, considered one of the best innings of the English season. One report thought his style of play reminiscent of Ranjitsinhji. Praise indeed. A year after the tour he moved to Derbyshire and became the first black cricketer in the County Championship and was the first West Indian cricketer to be well known outside the islands. Of the bowlers, Bajan Tommie Burton took 78 wickets and 'Float' Woods 72 wickets. Woods was ferociously quick, perhaps on his day the equal of Surrey and England's Tom Richardson, widely considered the quickest in the world. He took 107 wickets in only 17 first class games and inspired future generations to bowl quickly and rough the white men up a bit.

The tour was an interesting insight into societal views on race. In 1900 only West Indies and India had top class cricketers of colour. As with the Aboriginal touring team 42 years before and the emergence of Ranjitsinhji, colour certainly provoked intrigue and interest, and in the hands of some in the press this spilled over to outright racism and mockery. But there are no reports of any significant abuse and many of the black tourists recorded that they enjoyed the tour and were welcomed. Although that generation of West Indians would not play Test cricket, they began to make a compelling case with their English county scalps.

Aucher Warner was instrumental in formalising the inter-colonial matches into a regular competition. This began in 1893 but was made an amateur-only competition, leaving the growing number of talented black professionals without access to top class cricket. This exclusive approach undoubtedly constrained the ability of the islands to field the strongest sides in representative fixtures.

The MCC arranged a tour in 1910 under the captaincy of Arthur Somerset, a modest first class cricketer and minor aristocrat, featuring three Test cricketers including John Hearne. The fact the squad was relatively weak suggested the MCC didn't yet see the West Indies as Test calibre opposition. This appeared to be vindicated when the tourists won the two matches against the all-West Indies team. However, in a follow-up tour in 1913 the West Indian team won by an innings against a similar strength squad, with Harry Ince, a stylish batsman with a technique compared to Frank Woolley, making 167.

When the Great War began the West Indies were a talented side but had not done enough in high profile representative games to make a case for greater recognition. Whether the general standard in the West Indies was significantly inferior to South Africa, awarded Test status before they'd even played first class games domestically, is debatable. Whether race and imperial mindsets played a role is equally difficult to divine. What is clear is that several non-white players from both the West Indies and India had risen to prominence and gained reputation and respect outside the countries of their birth. It was no longer just a white man's game, though it was still for the white man to shape, govern and confer or withdraw opportunity.

Chapter 4

High hopes in distant fields

THERE are a few examples where cricket took root and developed to a good standard without either a colonial or military influence. One such is Argentina. During the Napoleonic Wars Britain tried to wrestle control of the River Plate delta from the Spanish but failed. British prisoners are thought to have played the first cricket in the country in 1806. Despite thwarted military attempts the region saw considerable immigration from England, as merchants and bankers settled in the country. By the 1830s Argentina had the highest proportion of English anywhere outside the Commonwealth. There was certainly enough critical mass for cricket to become established.

James Brittain, founder of the first bank in the country, arranged games at his property in Buenos Aires and in time this developed into a club. *The British Packet*, a newspaper serving the English community, ran a report of a match in 1831 featuring the Buenos Aires Cricket

Club, the oldest surviving sports club in the country. In the 1860s the club played against Montevideo and in the same decade a club was founded in the city of Sante Fe by workers of an English company building the Rosario to Córdoba railway. By the 1870s English expats had founded clubs in Córdoba, Flores, Rosario and Quilmes. To this point the clubs were exclusively for English players but it was slowly spreading to Argentines through a few select schools.

By 1900 a national league was established, providing more regular games to complement the annual North versus South fixture and international games against Uruguay, Brazil and Chile.

Lord Hawke, always keen on a cricketing tour to distant climes, took an MCC side to Argentina in 1912. The quality of local opposition was considered high enough for the games to warrant first class status. The hosts won one of the three representative matches. At this time Argentina were regular tourists themselves, visiting Philadelphia and the West Indies and by their presence helping nurture the small expat cricketing communities in other South American countries.

Much nearer to home the Netherlands was the country in continental Europe where cricket became most established. As with Argentina, trade and mercantile connections provided the initial spur but it was to be the deep admiration of influential Dutchmen for the English game that was to see it popularised amongst the country's privileged leisured class.

As in England cricket proved an attractive activity to principled principals of private schools, seeking physical activity that provided intellectual challenge and embodied a set of gentlemanly principles such as fair play. These attributes saw cricket introduced to the Noorthey boarding school in Voorschoten, near The Hague, by 1845. It was one of the most elite institutions in the country, being entrusted with instructing young royals. Peter de Raadt, who founded the school, was not a lone eccentric in adopting the game though. The network of gymnasium schools, the highest level of public education designed to groom future leaders in society and ready them for university, also adopted the game. This was particularly the case where schools employed teachers from England.

As students from these elite schools graduated, some wanting to continue to play the game formed clubs. The first was in 1875 in the Eastern town of Deventer, that stages international games to this day. The inspiration for the foundation can be seen in the name of this first club, *Utile Dulci*, meaning 'work and pleasure'. This high-minded, idealised, classically inspired name shows that the game was viewed as much more than a fun and athletic pastime for friends. Playing cricket was a social and class marker in the country, with the elite seeking identification with the English game and the values it represented. It was viewed as more sophisticated and cultured than provincial, local games.

Within a decade clubs were established in The Hague and Haarlem. The latter was established by an English teacher so full of zeal for the tutoring of an idealised generation to shape the modern world he named his club 'progress'. The progressives played their cricket on a rough strip among wind-scattered sand dunes by the North Sea.

Players from this club formed the Rood en Wit (red and white) club. By the 1880s Haarlem had become a centre, another riff on a theme being a club named 'unity', and there were several clubs in Amsterdam. Players were drawn from The Hague, Haarlem, Noorthey and Deventer to face a touring team from Uxbridge Cricket Club in 1881.

In Deventer the players certainly adopted the Corinthian spirit of fair play, considering strokes played behind the wicket ungentlemanly and terming it 'Spanish hitting', a reference to the villain of Dutch history, the Habsburg overlord the Duke of Alba. The Uxbridge tour caused some consternation amongst the gentlemen cricketers, exposing the poor quality of play and facilities and inconsistency of rules and playing conditions. The English side provided the exemplar to which they aspired. In order to take collective, concerted action they formed the Nederlandsche Cricket Bond (NCB) in 1883. To put that date into perspective, the Netherlands had a national governing body of the sport before the Test match nations of Australia and South Africa. The second oldest board in the world was not in the empire, but a short hop over the North Sea.

Despite being founded to improve conditions the NCB diverted most of its energy to arranging lavish cricketing festivals. Think the equivalent of Henley Regatta but with bats rather than oars. The exclusivity of the game was assured by the clubs whose boards vetted nominees for membership. It was social standing that mattered rather than ability. This insular, guarded approach along with the free time required to play longer-format games ensured cricket was limited to a narrow social elite.

In 1899 the board employed an English coach who introduced overarm bowling and worked on technique. Although a local league was established by the 1890s the clubs took more interest in consolidating links with England, the NCB sending the gentlemen of Holland on a tour of England in 1891. Desperate to be acknowledged and respected, the NCB's preoccupation was courting favour with and organising games against the MCC. They pursued that aim with considerably more fervour than consolidating and spreading the game in their own country. Like Argentina they did serve a role as the most established cricket community in their region with games against Belgium and Germany helping cricket get a foothold, albeit on a very small scale, in those countries.

Late in his career W.G. founded the London County team, a metropolitan side based in Crystal Palace and given first class status largely due to the fame and influence of its founder. In 1903 the club played Leicestershire, nothing remarkable in that of course, but what does catch the eye on the scorecard is that a Dutchman, Carst Posthuma, took ten wickets. He was one of the earliest foreign-based players to play first class fixtures for a domestic team in England, and he wasn't from the empire! He owed this opportunity in the twilight of his career – he was 35 at the time – to being spotted on the MCC's tour of the Netherlands the year before.

Known as 'the grand old man of Dutch cricket', Posthuma was born in 1868 and joined the Rood en Wit club as a young man. He quickly established himself as the best player in the country, as a left-arm seamer and hard-hitting batsman. He scored the first century in the country in 1894. In 1900 he became the first to take 100 wickets in a Dutch season. In the five games he played for London County he took 23 wickets at an average of 15. Given he was past his peak at the time, this suggests he was of sufficient calibre to have been a successful county cricketer. When PJ Bakker joined Hampshire in the mid-1980s, becoming good chums with Gower by all accounts, much was made of him being the first Dutchman in English cricket. Not so; Posthuma had led the way many, many years before. Remarkably, he continued to play for the Dutch national team until he was 60. His influence and legacy was seen off the pitch too, with a passionate advocacy of improved pitches and facilities.

Further north cricket had also gained a foothold in Denmark, where echoing the Argentine example the game had been introduced to the country by English railway engineers in the middle of the 19th century. Cricket was enthusiastically adopted by a small group of aristocrats who had learnt the game during their schooling in England. In an example of how the commitment of a single individual can make a profound impact, one of those men, Mr Hoskjaer, published an article in 1866 extolling the virtues of the game and instructed (it was a firmer request than merely asking it seems) them to distribute it to all grammar and secondary schools and teacher training colleges. He had clearly been won over by his schoolmasters' championing of the game!

As in England Denmark had a simpler, pre-existing bat and ball game they termed langbold. Probably similar to rounders it required similar physical abilities as cricket, such as hand to eye coordination, and this helped players transfer their skills to cricket.

Hoskjaer was influential in developing a playing manual for langbold and cricket. It was quite a read as the following attests:

'one dares to suppose that just as cricket is beneficial in developing physical powers and suppleness so it is in developing the mental capacities, and that not least through this game requiring the making of quick decisions and an energetic execution of these, so does this strengthen that energy of decision which is the Englishman's chief advantage over other nationalities'.

This last point makes it clear that cricket was seen as an English game, not a universal game to be played anywhere, and that in playing it you could develop English virtues. This very clear identification of cricket as English was the basis of its appeal to some, but it can only be assumed was less attractive to others. The introduction of cricket in some schools, notably the Soro academy, helped spread the game through the country as its cricket-playing students left and settled elsewhere. By 1890 there were clubs in Odense, Aalborg and even on the Danish islands of Falster and Bornholm. Though less widespread than in the Netherlands, the cricket community was sufficiently cohesive to attract touring teams from Britain in the closing years of the 19th century.

Although the Civil War was a critical factor in the rise of baseball as the national sport and the decline in popularity of cricket in Philadelphia, the game continued to develop. Unlike in New York where clubs were typically anglicised and not welcoming of local players, in

Philadelphia it was more inclusive. The Haverford College team, founded in 1833, had been the first American team and although this was short-lived other clubs were formed on the same basis. By 1856 there were four clubs in the city and healthy competition. The time commitments of the game limited the involvement of working men and therefore the cricket scene was dominated by gentlemen of independent means.

In 1872 our two friends W.G. and Lord Harris were part of a touring party that played a game at the Germantown club, one of the main clubs in the city. As was often the case when sides were not evenly matched it pitted the 22 of Pennsylvania against 12 of England. W.G. took 21 wickets. In October of the following year John Barton King was born in the city, into a middle-class family in the linen trade. When he was five Philadelphia played their first first class game, against an Australian touring squad stopping over on their way back from England. As with most boys in the USA Bart King would have been introduced to baseball from an early age. But thankfully for cricket something or someone saw him join the Tioga Cricket Club as a 15-year old in 1888. Initially he was a batsman but his strong physique saw him tried as a bowler and he never looked back. As a 16-year-old he took 37 wickets for 99 runs in the 1889 season.

Four years later King was in the Gentlemen of Philadelphia side that faced the touring Australians, in the inaugural first class fixture in the country. The Australians were jaded from the Atlantic crossing and the Belmont ground had short boundaries that they were not used to. Nevertheless, the result shocked the cricketing world. The Philadelphians amassed 525 and then bowled out the tourists for 199 and, following on, 268. King took a five-for and scored 34 as a number 11. Jack Blackham the Australian captain was impressed, saying he thought the standard of the players equal to those in England. Praise indeed.

By this time the cricket community had been influential in securing King a move from the family linen trade to insurance, not necessarily due to his aptitude with premiums but to ensure he had sufficient time to play cricket. King had moved to one of the major clubs, Belmont, and cemented his reputation as the leading bowler. In 1897 King toured with the Philadelphians to England where they were to face all the counties, the main universities and the MCC. Not all the counties played a full-strength side but when they came to play Sussex it was their strongest XI. King simply blew them away, taking 7-13 as the south coast county were bundled out for 46. He took 13 wickets in all in a famous eight wicket victory.

The key to King's success was a delivery he called 'the angler' which came in to the batsman through the air. He is considered to be the inventor of what we call swing bowling. His American roots may well have played a key role, adapting the baseball pitchers' swerve into cricket. Despite this eye-catching victory the rest of the tour was a little muted for the tourists and a victory over Warwickshire aside, they may not have had the expected impact. But for King personally it was a triumph, taking 72 wickets at 24. The counties were very interested indeed and vied with each other to offer this amateur sufficient financial inducement to stay and turn out for them. One county even attempted to secure a match, excuse the pun, with a rich widow with £7,000 a year. By the turn of the century Philadelphia was attracting annual tours from English representative teams led by leading comets of the day such as Plum Warner and Bernard Bosanquet, inventor of the googly.

In 1903 he returned to England again and had become even more deadly in the intervening years. Against Lancashire he ran through the top order, taking 5-7 in his opening three-over spell. In all he took 9-62 helping Philadelphia win by nine wickets. Against Surrey he starred with the bat, scoring 98 and 113 not out along with six wickets to secure yet another famous victory. Back home he was breaking domestic records consistently, making 315 in a match in 1905 only to surpass his own record with 344 not out in 1906. This remains the highest ever score made in the Americas.

His last tour of England came in 1908. By then 35, King was instrumental in Philadelphia claiming another four county scalps and he ended the tour topping the first class averages for the English season with a miraculously miserly 11.08. This stood as the best bowling average for an English season until 1958.

With Philadelphia firmly established as one of the leading teams in the world and King a colossus of the sport, cricket in the USA was dealt a crushing, far-reaching blow. In a decision that had nothing to do with calibre and everything to do with politics they were excluded from the Imperial Cricket Council formed in 1909. Their temerity in winning independence from the British Empire meant they didn't meet the critical eligibility criteria. As with the

Civil War this was to be a pivotal point in the development of cricket in the Americas. Although King, now 39, was able to claim 9-78 in a victory over the touring Australians in 1912 the US had been frozen out of the new world order, structured as it was on imperial lines.

It is difficult to predict the impact first class and Test status would have had in the US but the interest and impetus it would have provided would have surely kept cricket in Philadelphia strong and perhaps laid the foundation for regrowth in other regions. But it was not to be. King retired in 1916. In all he made nigh on 20,000 runs at an average of 36.47 and took 2,088 wickets at an eye-opening 10.47. His success in England and against touring sides ensured he won worldwide fame with the England captain, the veritable Plum Warner saying he was the equal of the greatest bowlers of all time. His greatest weapon was late, booming inswing. Even the greatest players of the age found this unplayable. The ICC's decision denied King and his team-mates a legacy. If politics had not intervened he may have been the first in a long line of US cricketing heroes winning fame on the global stage. The US may have been at the heart of the global cricket community to this day.

Chapter 5

Missed opportunities and the irresistible rise of football

THE eve of the 20th century is an interesting point to reflect on how cricket had developed, whether it had fully evolved from a game to a sport and how it was faring against new sports such as football and baseball. These competitors were new kids on the block compared to cricket but as the 20th century approached they had the wind in their sails and were competing with cricket for participation and profile.

The distinction between sports and games is not a simple one. Sports are considered a relatively modern phenomenon, with a certain degree of structure and organisation, whereas games are as old as civilisation itself. There are no definitive criteria to judge when the latter becomes the former. Seeing sport as a form of entertainment is a helpful way of viewing its origins and development. In medieval England entertainments ranged from courtly pursuits such as hunting and chivalric tournaments, to popular entertainment such as troubadours, cockfighting and bear-baiting. Games included cerebral affairs such as chess and backgammon and more physical pursuits such as archery, hammer throwing and wrestling. These would often be an integral part of feast days and festivities held in towns and parishes to mark religious occasions and milestones in pastoral seasons, such as harvest festivals. These were occasions when often-dispersed rural populations would meet, make and reaffirm bonds of kinship and oil the wheels of commerce and society. Three known English medieval games developed over the centuries to become modern sports. We've seen how stool-ball and its numerous provincial variants provided the foundations for cricket. Another stick and ball game, shinty, was to become formalised in hockey. The third, mob football, was perhaps the most intriguing and significant.

Forms of ball games involving hands and feet were known in ancient times in China, Japan and Greece, all varying in objective and structure. The nearest of the ancient games to what would later be played in medieval English villages was the Roman Harpastum, a frenetic game, involving many players where teams sought to smuggle a small ball over their rival's line through sleight of hand and exchange between players. It is not known whether this was brought to Britain by the Romans and influenced anglicised forms of early football, though certain elements of the games were certainly similar. Annual shrovetide celebrations brought many people together and the weight of numbers and excitement of the festivities made a mass participation game possible.

This was the setting of mob football, still played to this day in Ashbourne, Leicestershire, where village teams of indeterminate number use all means possible to transfer a pig's bladder to the rival village's marker. Sometimes a variation on this was to kick the ball into the parish church of your rival. The result was a tumult of seething limbs lasting for many hours with a violent ebb and flow through marketplaces and thoroughfares. The ball could be moved by carrying, kicking or throwing and the only rule appeared to be avoiding maim and murder if possible. This anarchic spectacle was clearly extremely dangerous and in 1835 it was banned from being played on a public highway. This forced more moderate and controlled forms of the game to evolve.

Henry VIII was known to order boots specifically for football but in the main it was a pursuit of the common man. By the late 16th century there were accounts of the game being tamed somewhat, with referees and if not written rules then certainly set formations of players. It was adopted by some public schools as a means of encouraging physical prowess and toughening up callow young boys. However, the form the games took varied significantly from school to school. In some, such as Rugby, running with the ball was prevalent while for others footwork and passing were more prominent. This variation was clearly an obstacle to inter-school matches. By 1843 the rules at Eton allowed controlling the ball with hands but not carrying the ball or running with it. In Rugby a set of rules agreed in 1845 became the basis for what was to become a different sport: rugby football. In 1848 Cambridge University attempted to set out the rules for the dribbling variant of the game and this formed the basis of what came to be known as association football, or soccer. In October 1863 12 schools and clubs favouring the dribbling style met in London and formed the Football Association. The FA agreed a code of laws taking elements of the Sheffield and Cambridge rules, though Blackheath quit after 'hacking' was outlawed. This helped facilitate the founding of the Rugby Football Union, initially comprising of 21 clubs.

Until the 1860s cricket as the first codified modern sport had been unopposed as the English game. It had developed rules quicker, formed clubs earlier and attracted public and press interest long before other sports took root. It therefore had an advantage of established pedigree and profile over these newly founded rivals for popularity. But the middle decades of the 19th century were characterised by the onset of modernity, with not only industrial revolution but far reaching changes to social mobility, class distinctions and individual and regional identity.

Was cricket well positioned to flourish in this new age of modernity? In some ways it was. It had an established following, an extensive network of clubs and grounds, county cricket was beginning to emerge to consolidate regional rivalries popular with the public and it had celebrities like the doctor from Gloucester. The emergence of alternative organised sports certainly didn't come at a time when cricket was on the wane. It was continuing to spread across the country thanks to the railways and the commercial endeavour of the All-England XIs. But, and there is always a but, cricket was run by gentlemen of a certain class and with a world view that found the onset of modernity and its challenge to the established order of society difficult. This was seen in the great amateur versus professional power struggle. Was this governing class, this rural elite amenable to spreading the game through a modern, urban industrial society? Could someone from the present day seeing the dominance of football over all other sports look back to this critical period and foresee a shift in the sporting landscape?

By 1870 football had seen touchlines and goalkeepers added and all forms of handling prohibited for on-field players. The following year the FA created a cup competition featuring all of its teams. All the clubs were amateur and mainly drawn from the London area. In March 1872 the first FA Cup Final was played, at the Oval cricket ground. Later that year 4,000 spectators watched the first football international, with England and Scotland contesting a 0-0 draw. Initially the clubs sourced most of their players from the football-playing public schools. The first FA Cup winners, the Wanderers, were mainly from Harrow, a school where they would also have played cricket. In its infancy, therefore, the player base for football was similar to cricket and it would have been very natural to play one in winter and one in summer.

In the first half of the 19th century there was still a very clear dichotomy between the rich and leisured class and the poor. The rich had the luxury of playing three-day matches unencumbered by the travails of work. In contrast, working men worked draconian hours and had precious little time for participating in or watching sport, beyond the traditional festive holidays. The leading players could become professionals but these represented a very small percentage of society as a whole. Changes to labour laws, increased social mobility and the growing wealth of the middle class in the 1850s changed this traditional dynamic. One of the aspects of cricket gentlemen liked was that it was played over several days, but they alone had the luxury of enjoying this. Football was played over a much shorter duration and therefore was more accessible to players and spectators alike. It was fast and dynamic too, compared to the snail-like scoring rates of 19th century cricket. Cricket was being challenged for both flexibility and entertainment.

Even though the County Championship was formed, Test match cricket began and cricket was propelled to broader fame through W.G., the period 1870–1900 was one of missed opportunity for cricket. The influencers and power brokers in the game sought to insulate cricket from modernity rather than shape cricket as a game that embraces all and looks to the future. The MCC had always tended to resist reform, as seen in their fight against round-arm and then overarm bowling. They were suspicious of progress for in it they saw a threat to a game they had tailored to their own image. When county organisations saw the success of the FA Cup and suggested emulating its growing popularity in a shorter, more accessible form of the game they were rebuffed. This was part of the amateurs resisting the encroachment of professional influence.

Shorter games at the top level may have opened up the game to a broader spectrum of society who could have found time to play the game themselves. The fact that the format was heavily weighted in favour of the leisured classes ensured the exclusivity many craved, but in spite of the growing number and profile of professionals this contributed to an 'us and them' culture. There is a sense too that within this tension between amateur and professional there was a north and south dimension. Northern cricketers tended to be pragmatic, those from the south more dogmatic in attempting to freeze the game in time, in a time, naturally, when society saw them as born leaders and moral guardians. The MCC could be pragmatic too, such as in courting W.G. as a leading amateur and one of the establishment, but only when they felt cornered and forced to act, not in their approach to the game as a whole.

The result of this was that many clubs founded to play cricket quickly adopted football and the new sport, being more inclusive and suited to those with little time off work, slowly came to dominate. A great example of this is AC Milan, the famous club of Van Basten and Maldini, that was founded for cricket but made its name in football. In the critical formative years when football was not yet established its English founders kept interested local players out, considering cricket a solely English preserve. This pattern is repeated in numerous examples across the world. The cricket clubs of Argentina became sporting clubs, gradually phasing cricket out as they adopted tennis and golf. In New York the main club was English only, in Lisbon the port merchants failed to invite locals watching from the sidelines to play. In valuing exclusivity over popularity the cricketers of this period were giving football free passage to become the world's dominant sport. Cricket conferred social status and therefore they didn't want any Tom, Dick or Gianluca playing. Cricket's challenges echo through the ages. Street 20 and cage cricket are the latest attempts to make a rural sport urban and The Hundred a further truncated format to appeal to the time-poor.

Chapter 6

Governance: that novel idea

B Y 1900 the three Test nations of England, Australia and South Africa were playing regular fixtures and stars such as Grace, Ranji, Spofforth and Trumper were icons of the sport. In addition the travelling triumvirate of Warner, Harris and Hawke were taking sides across the world, with several national sides arguably as strong as those with Test status. But those three sides shared the vital characteristics of being in the empire and white.

In 1907, only a few years after the bloody Boer conflict, South African diamond tycoon, politician and cricketer Abe Bailey set out a proposition to the MCC to create an imperial cricket board. He knew his principled, imperialist audience well and made what must have seemed a convincing pitch:

'Inter-rivalry within the Empire cannot fail to draw together in closer, friendly interest all those many thousands of our kinsmen who regard cricket as our national sport, while secondly it would probably give a direct stimulus to amateurism.'

Two years later this vision saw the formation of the Imperial Cricket Conference, comprising England, Australia and South Africa. Its remit was simply to organise Tests between its members. England as colonial master assumed natural paternalistic authority, with the MCC president and secretary filling those roles for the ICC. Its level of ambition was alarmingly low. There was no commitment to grow the game, spread its reach or broaden its appeal. Just three teams were involved when cricket was being played across the world. The MCC itself had toured India, West Indies, New Zealand and the USA and had witnessed the quality and potential in those countries. The Netherlands and Denmark had national boards. All were omitted. It was a select club of white, imperial teams. Cricketers of the calibre of Bart King and Charles Ollivierre were left out in the cold.

It was an amazingly short-sighted decision and shows that cementing imperial ties was far more important than securing the international future of the game. After all it was an English game, that just happened to be played by Englishmen across the world. The ICC's insular approach is emphasised in comparison with FIFA.

A review of the MCC minute book from 1907 to the outbreak of the Great War gives an impression of the issues and priorities of the club in this period. Given their founding objective to be custodians of the laws it is fitting that much time was exercised considering various revisions. This included in relation to scoring runs off no-balls, deciding when a team could declare and the need for umpire supervision of pitch rolling. There was society business, like asking George V to be a patron, and some sartorial decisions like the design of the cap for England players. The committee considered reports of its tours and reprimanded poor behaviour of its representatives, such as excessive rowdiness on board ship. There was also their role as a venue owner, such as a decision to ensure the club against the risk of detonations organised by the Suffragettes. Sub-committees were established to deal with a range of issues, from expenses to improvements to the game. On the latter issue they considered a proposal to train more English bowlers in the art of the googly, presumably to counter the Bosie bowling of the South Africans. It was in amongst this business that in 1907 the MCC first considered Abe Bailey for an Imperial Cricket Contest. This was approved to be held in 1909 but when Australia rejected the invitation the imperial contest turned into an Imperial Council, designed only to facilitate the contest. Following formation of the ICC the next order of business was to discuss a report of a banquet held for the Australian team. The Council agreed to a Triangular tournament to be hosted in England in 1912, with the hope of repeating the format every four years.

The year 1912 proved to be one of the wettest of the 20th century, causing havoc with the pitches and the play. This inauspicious weather combined with a weakened Australia team saw rain-interrupted, uncompetitive matches and the tournament was viewed very much as a damp squib by supporters. England won four out of their six matches, with South Africa losing five. The latter's googly bowlers found damp English wickets less receptive to their wiles than the matting pitches of home. The weather aside, the tournament showed that nine Tests in a summer was perhaps a case of supply exceeding demand and the English public had limited interest in fixtures not involving their own team. The experiment was not repeated, though critically the ICC was not disbanded.

The reasons for Australia sending a weakened team are worth further scrutiny. As with the MCC in England, Australian cricket administration had navigated the tensions between amateurs and professionals. The original Australasian Cricket Council, bringing together the state administrations of New South Wales, Victoria and South Australia, was founded in 1892 but without sufficient funding it foundered and was disbanded in 1898. As with early tours by England, representative sides' international tours were managed by individual promoters. The tours were often very profitable for promoters and players and an attempt was made by the state authorities to channel some of this profit to support cash-strapped clubs. In 1905 some of the states came together to assume control of tours from the players.

The Australian Board of Control for International Cricket was founded by New South Wales and Victoria, with Queensland, South Australia and Tasmania joining by 1907. The players did not have representation and felt their opportunity for influence and profit had been stamped out. This resentment had steadily simmered and came to a head in advance of the Triangular tournament, where six of the leading players led a boycott, after their demand to select the team management of the tour and take a portion of the profits was rebuffed. In March 1912

Australian captain, Clem Hill, a selector of the team, came to bloodied blows with fellow selector Peter McAlister over team selections and choice of manager. Hill resigned and in solidarity five other leading players, including star batsman Victor Trumper, refused to tour England for the Triangular tournament. In their absence the team performed badly and by all accounts behaved badly, with the manager George Crouch saying that the behaviour was so lamentable that the party were 'socially ostracised' by the British public. However, this did not lead to a shift in the balance of power. The players were subservient to the board from then on.

Despite football being a baby in the cradle in comparison with cricket it established an international body in May 1904, five years before the foundation of the ICC. The idea for a body arose from the increasing number of international matches being organised and the benefit of greater coordination. Initially it was anticipated that given their creation of the game England's Football Association would take the lead. However, the FA and other home nations rejected the idea. Despite this the national associations of France, Belgium, Denmark, Sweden, Switzerland, Spain and the Netherlands became founding members of FIFA. Germany notified their intention to join by telegram on the day of foundation.

The central focus was to schedule international tournaments. FIFA's first charter wasn't particularly ambitious, merely seeking to standardise rules and organise fixtures. Like the ICC there were no explicit commitments to promoting growth of the game. However, it had more members and wasn't constrained by any imperial vision. In practice the nascent organisation struggled without the influence of the FA and after considerable diplomatic efforts the FA were persuaded to join in 1905. It soon expanded beyond Europe and by the Great War South Africa, Chile, Argentina, USA and Canada had joined. Cricket was well established in Canada, USA, Argentina, Holland and Denmark but the ICC did not welcome them into their membership. Without a political subtext football naturally took a more inclusive approach to growth and had a much broader base from which to grow the global game.

In England football had gained popularity through the creation of the FA Cup and then the Football League in 1888. Its flexibility and association with towns helped gain a strong following. Like cricket it also navigated some amateur versus professional tensions. In the FA Cup the East London team Upton Park complained that their opponents Preston were playing professionals. It was true, many had been recruited from the cream of professional Scottish players. Amid the furore Preston threatened to form a breakaway British Football Association with like-minded clubs such as Aston Villa. But the FA arbitrated and allowed professionals as long as there was a strong local link to the club they played for. Compared to other entertainments of the age watching a Football League match was expensive, at 6d. It has been suggested this price point was arrived at deliberately, to exclude poorer, rowdier elements of the crowd.

Football was attracting lower middle- and skilled working-class followers. In those days the rules allowed for muscular entertainment such as goalkeepers being bundled over the line by forwards. Affordable, accessible transport was an issue for some fans but as railway networks improved so crowds increased. By 1900 crowds for major matches were hitting 100,000. Football had come a long way in 50 years, from public school variants to six-figure crowds.

While cricket's origins were as a rural game football was an urban phenomenon. Cricket clubs like Sheffield had provided the nucleus for county sides but football was the child of a more modern age. Cricket's county structure didn't limit where cricket was played or who by but it perhaps impacted its marketability as a sport. With towns associated with particular trades and invested with a considerable amount of civic pride there was the basis for a nationwide following. Cricket on the other hand was more complex, with first class counties and minor counties. Many fans had to travel a considerable distance to their nearest major ground. With limited leisure time, the choice for those who could afford it was often a short visit to watch the entirety of a game or a long visit to watch part of a longer sporting contest. The celebrity of W.G. and Ranji helped counteract this disadvantage to an extent. Cricket was in the midst of a Golden Age but football was beginning to grip the nation.

Although the Triangular tournament was a failure, an insight into some of the world's leading players who participated in it (and one who should have done but didn't) helps paint a picture of cricket in the twilight years of its so-called Golden Age.

The victorious England captain was the much heralded polymath and all-round sportsman C.B. Fry. Seemingly capable of turning his hand to and excelling at everything, he was once described as 'probably the most gifted Englishman of any age' by John Arlott. He was born in Croydon to a middle-class family and won a scholarship to Repton School where he excelled in classics, languages and sport. He captained the school at cricket and football and in the latter was talented enough to play in the FA Cup while still at school. He then progressed to Oxford by another scholarship and won blues at football, cricket and athletics. His sporting prowess won him early fame but he ran up large debts that he desperately tried to pay off through a range of extra-curricular activities including private tutoring and nude modelling. But the stress caused a nervous breakdown and this saw him incapacitated for exams and scraping a fourth-class degree.

He was rescued from his debts by cricket and went on to enjoy a long and successful career with Sussex and Hampshire. At Sussex he established a formidable pairing with Ranji, a friendship that would later see Fry assist Ranji at the League of Nations, where the Prince was representing India. He had made his Test debut back in 1896 and had been recalled as captain for the 1912 Triangular, at the age of 40, in what proved to be his last Tests (although in 1921, at the age of 49, he was asked to return once more as captain but a finger injury prevented it). He was the elder statesman of the team and in some ways a throwback to an earlier, 19th-century era. Neville Cardus said of him in his obituary that he 'belonged – and it was his glory – to an age not obsessed with specialism. He was one of the last of the English tradition of the amateur, the connoisseur, and, in the most delightful sense of the word, a dilettante.'

Even though he wasn't a specialist he was a batsman of rare talent, once making six consecutive first class hundreds and finishing his career averaging over 50 and scoring 94 centuries. His fame spread far beyond cricket and today he is perhaps more widely known for purportedly being offered the throne of Albania and his party trick of jumping backwards on to a mantelpiece. In an extraordinary life he had three failed attempts to become an MP, held the world long jump record, was a noted publisher and launched an adventure magazine for boys. His like would never be seen again: an emblem of the Edwardian age. Other sporting all-rounders in the 1912 series were Reggie Spooner who played rugby for England and Johnny Douglas, who won a boxing Olympic gold in 1908.

Another old hand making his swansong in Tests was our old friend Plum Warner, a fellow amateur and firmly part of the MCC establishment. Spending more time at sea than many in a naval career, he had toured the world. The same age as Warner but from a markedly different background was Sydney Barnes. The son of a Staffordshire metal worker, Barnes was a product of league cricket rather than public schools and universities. The All-England XIs had brought cricket to provincial towns and the legacy of their visits was often a network of local sides. At 15 Barnes played for Smethwick Cricket Club, a member of the Birmingham and District League, the oldest club league in the world. Reversing the general trend, its inspiration was a football club formed in the area. At 21 and having attracted the attention of county sides he opted instead to join Rishton in the Lancashire League as the pay was much better, particularly with win bonuses.

He played a handful of games for Warwickshire when they joined the County Championship in 1895 as a fast bowler, without great success. Annoyed by what he saw as favourable treatment to amateurs he focused on league cricket, slowing his pace and experimenting with spin bowling variations. By this time he was lucratively balancing league cricket with a steady job as a clerk in a Staffordshire colliery. In an unprecedented move Barnes was selected from the Lancashire League to join Archie MacLaren's England touring side to Australia in 1901. The colliery clerk made his Test debut in December at the SCG and took a five-for. He demonstrated his calibre by taking 19 wickets in two Tests, but fell out with MacLaren. It was a clash of cultures, Barnes expecting due reward for services rendered and MacLaren expecting public school pluck and spirit from his charges. Barnes played for Lancashire for the next two seasons but was annoyed that they paid £3 a week when he could make £8 playing for his league club on a Saturday. He asked the county to match the salary but they refused, so he went back to the leagues for good.

He came back to Test cricket in 1907. In the Australia tour that preceded the 1912 Triangular he proved a revelation. Stung by his use as a change bowler in the first Test, he proved a point when returning to open, taking four wickets for one run and went on to take 39 wickets in the series. In the three matches against South Africa in 1912 he took 34 wickets. In the following tour to South Africa he took 49 wickets in just four Tests. In all, Barnes took 189 wickets at just 16.43 with a strike rate of 41. These are the most devastating statistics ever for a Test bowler. After the war Barnes played for Bradford League side Saltaire. His presence drew huge crowds and knowing his worth his match fee went up to £18, supplemented by crowd collections. In his mid-fifties he played first class cricket for Wales, taking 12 wickets against the touring West Indies. Remarkable. His mastery of swing allied to the ability to spin the ball both ways and his knack of dissecting a batsman's weaknesses made him virtually unplayable on his day. Barnes was resolutely anti-establishment and revealed the depth of cricket below county level.

The English opener in the Triangular series was Jack Hobbs, a true legend of the game and in many ways the first modern cricketer. Born in Cambridge in 1882 one of 12 children of a slater, Hobbs's childhood was marked by poverty. His father, a local club cricketer, took a job as umpire and net bowler at Fenners, the university ground. He then took a better paid position as groundsman at Jesus College, with young Jack getting his first cricket representing the choral team. While still at school he entered domestic service to help the family make ends meet. He practised hard at his game in his spare time but didn't show any particular aptitude or win any admirers. Unlike his captain in 1912, he wasn't a natural.

In 1901 at the age of 19 his form improved and he was selected for a Cambridge side to face a team of professionals led by Surrey and England opener Tom Hayward, himself Cambridge-born. This proved to himself that he could face professionals. After following his father by taking a groundsman and net bowler role at Bedford School, the alma mater of another England opener, Alastair Cook, he returned to Cambridgeshire as a club professional, scoring a century on debut. Then tragedy struck and his father died of pneumonia, leaving the family at risk of destitution. The community rallied round and Hayward returned with a team to raise money in a memorial game. Hobbs took his father's job as groundsman at Jesus. Through Hayward he got a trial at Surrey in 1903 and was taken on to the ground staff on a very modest income. He had to serve two years' residential qualification to represent the county. During this he returned to play for Cambridgeshire and averaged 58 for the minor county. The following year upon qualification Surrey gambled on him as an opener to partner Hayward, the great Bobby Abel having recently retired.

He made 88 runs on debut, impressing opposition captain W.G. Grace and after stroking 155 in his second game was awarded his county cap by Surrey captain, the 6th Earl of Roseberry. Two influential people to impress so early in a fledgling career. He developed his technique further and became a consistent run scorer and forged a formidable partnership with Hayward. By 1907 he was a contender for an England cap, or to be more accurate an MCC touring cap, and due to some withdrawals from professionals unhappy with the financial remuneration he was selected for the winter tour to Australia. He suffered horribly from seasickness and missed the beginning of the tour but was selected for a Test debut on New Year's Day 1908, at the age of 25. He made three half-centuries in the series and impressed. By the 1908 season he was considered one of three best professionals in the game, along with Hayward and Lancashire's Johnny Tyldesley.

The making of him was his success against South Africa's googly bowlers who had proved a handful on their matting wickets. Hobbs averaged 67 on the tour and was widely praised by the press. Precision had come into his game and he was regarded as an excellent judge of length. In this way he became something of a model for modern batsmanship, going either fully forward or fully back and playing each ball on its merits. In 1911 he was in sensational form on the Australia tour making 662 runs at an average of 83, the highest series aggregate in Test cricket history. He was the leading run scorer in the Triangular tournament. After a late start to his first class career Hobbs was regarded as the best batsman of his generation by the First World War.

When first class cricket resumed in 1919, Hobbs was given a £400 contract. In the mid-1920s, by which time Hobbs was in his 40s, he formed a very successful partnership with Herbert Sutcliffe. In 1925 he scored 3,000 runs, hit a record 16 centuries and surpassed W.G.'s record of 126 first class centuries. He became a significant public figure, feted by film studios and parliamentary parties. This recognition and standing saw him break what had previously been considered a glass ceiling for professionals, first joining the selection committee and then captaining England as injury cover. He continued to play in Tests until 1930, at the age of 47 retiring as the leading run scorer in Tests. He played on for Surrey until 1935 at the age of 52. He had surpassed W.G.'s career runs and had hit a scarcely credible 197 first class hundreds. Beyond the sheer awe of his statistics he played a role in proving professionals could be supremely gifted batsmen. He became the first professional cricketer to be knighted. He has been named in several best XIs in the history of the game.

Hobbs's opening partner in the Triangular was Wilfred Rhodes, who is famous for the sheer longevity of his career, playing his first Test in 1899 and his last in 1930! The son of a Yorkshire farmer and second XI club cricket captain, he was born in 1877 in Kirkheaton. Inspired by his father he took up cricket seriously after leaving school at 16, getting fired as a railway worker for leaving early to play for his local team. After elevation to the first XI of his village side he became a professional for a Scottish club in Galashiels. He changed from a medium-pacer to a spin bowler and tried his hand at county cricket. After some trial matches he made his debut for Yorkshire in 1898. Unlike Hobbs his success was immediate and he took 145 wickets at 14 in his debut season and was recognised as the best spinner in the country. He made his international debut in W.G.'s last, in 1899. He was another modern player who began his career rubbing shoulders with an earlier generation.

Between 1900 and 1902 he took an incredible 725 wickets. Always capable with the bat, by 1904 Rhodes was not only the premier spinner but also a genuine all-rounder. As the years went by he pressed his case with the bat, becoming a very respected opener who developed an excellent understanding with Hobbs. A dour, competitive man who focused on results in favour of flamboyancy, he was the ultimate jobbing cricketer, reliably performing the role needed of him by Yorkshire or England. He was a pragmatist, working on metronomic accuracy to compensate when the sharp spin of his youth deserted him, changing his technique to make greater use of his pads when his batting became less fluent.

As his batting improved his bowling became less devastating, although he regularly achieved the double of 1,000 runs and 100 wickets. After the war he dropped down the order and worked hard to regain his form with the ball. In the 1920s he earned good money in the off-season teaching Indian princes the game. When he finally retired in 1930 he did so as a record breaker, playing over 1,100 first class games, taking 4,187 wickets and in facing the West Indies at the age of 52, the oldest ever player in Tests. He was the first player to score 2,000 runs and take 100 wickets in Tests. He was made a life member of the MCC late in life.

Another great in England's 1912 side was Frank Woolley, like Rhodes a spinning all-rounder. Born in Tonbridge, where his father ran a cycle shop, as a young boy he took a keen interest in cricket and spent much of his time at the town cricket club. This was used by the county as an out ground and they made it the home of their youth development programme when Woolley was in his teens. He joined the ground staff and developed quickly as both a batsman and left-arm spin and medium-pace bowler. He had broken into the Kent team by 1905, still only 19 years of age. He became established in the team quickly and went on to become one of the county's most long-standing and revered stars, playing until 1938 at the age of 51. A tall man, he was an elegant and graceful batsman who scored very quickly, known particularly for natural timing. As a bowler he had a natural, fluid technique. He made his England debut against Australia in 1909. He went on to become an all-time great, scoring over 50,000 first class runs.

The England team showed the depth of talent in the game and the strength of the cricket tradition at the public schools, universities, clubs and leagues. Barnes's background couldn't have contrasted more than that of Pelham Warner. The amateur tradition saw its zenith in C.B. Fry but Hobbs and Rhodes proved that England could not do without professionals and their performances and long service helped gain recognition.

The Australian captain, in the absence of Clem Hill, was Syd Gregory. At 42 he was older than his English counterpart by three years and was the most capped Test cricketer in the world, with over 50 caps. He came from a cricketing dynasty with his father Ned playing in the first Test series in 1877 and his uncle Dave being Australia's first Test captain. Like Hobbs, his father was a groundsman, curator of the Sydney Cricket Ground. He made his debut for New South Wales at 19 and the following year was selected for the England tour. His finest hour was scoring Australia's first Test double century in a remarkable defeat, England having followed on, in 1895. He was a steady if not spectacular batsman, averaging 24 in 58 Tests with four centuries. Away from the game he worked for the postal service, as a tobacconist and later for the water board.

The great champion of Australian cricket, picking up the mantle from the Demon Spofforth, was Victor Trumper, absent in 1912 as part of the player revolt. Born in Sydney in 1877, his talent as a teenager saw him play state cricket at just 17. After modest returns he made a breakthrough in 1898 averaging 63 and he was rewarded with a last-minute selection for the Ashes touring squad in 1899. It is fair to say the 21-year-old made quite an impression, scoring a century against England at Lord's and a triple century against Sussex. After the Lord's hundred he was visited in the changing room by W.G. who presented him with a bat saying 'from the present champion to the future one'. Initially he failed to live up to this early promise but on the 1902 tour of England he dominated a very wet, tricky summer averaging close to 50 when many others failed.

Batting came very naturally to him and he didn't attempt to model his technique on others or adopt an orthodox approach. He just played. C.B. Fry said of him:

'He had no style, and yet he was all style. He had no fixed canonical method of play, he defied all orthodox rules, yet every stroke he played satisfied the ultimate criterion of style – the minimum of effort, the maximum of effect.'

Those who saw him play urged posterity not to judge him on his statistics, though these were impressive enough, but rather on his audacious natural ability best shown on tricky wickets where he often flourished when others could barely lay bat on ball. Tragically Trumper died young in 1915, at a mere 37, of Bright's disease. Despite playing less than a quarter of the games of Rhodes his stature was recognised, being named one of the six cricketers of the *Wisden* century (1863–1963), along with Grace, Hobbs, Barnes and Tom Richardson. He was the only non-English player of the Golden Age-era included. The only other non-English included was a certain Don Bradman. Trumper was the subject of one of the most famous cricket photographs of all, with muscular physique dancing down the wicket with bat held high above his head. It has entered the cricketing consciousness as a symbol of power and confidence, not just of Trumper but of the Australian nature and an epoch of the game. If we believe Geoff Boycott batting was virtually impossible in the era of uncovered pitches, Trumper bounding down the wicket makes a mockery of that. Trumper was honoured with a stand named in his honour at the SCG and a public park in the city. The bat he received from Grace is proudly displayed in Australia's national museum, testimony to how important cricket was in forging a national identity and expressing the spirit of a young nation.

We've already met some of the South African squad through their legion of Bosie bowlers, who made life very difficult indeed for England touring sides. In the 1912 tour one of their key players was Aubrey Faulkner. Born into a wealthy family in Port Elizabeth in 1881, he went to the prestigious Wynberg High School in Cape Town, the second oldest school in the country, where he learnt the game.

Despite the affluence of his family he endured an unhappy childhood with his father a violent alcoholic. He escaped to join the army, fighting in the Boer War. Following the war he played for Transvaal and having been taught how to bowl googlies he made his South Africa debut in 1906, taking a six-for and helping his country secure their maiden Test victory. He went on to become an influential all-rounder, scoring the first double century for South Africa. In 1912 he had moved to England to pursue a county career. However, he was lured into Nottinghamshire club cricket by the retail magnate Julien Cahn. He made himself available for the Triangular tournament but had a modest series. In 25 Tests he scored 1,754 runs at 40 and took 82 wickets at 26.

He had a successful war being promoted to major but struggled when peace resumed, his cricket restricted by bouts of malaria. He gave up first class cricket although he was coerced into a Test return in 1924 at the age of 42 after the team couldn't buy a run. It was 12 years since his last game. His powers had long since declined and he scraped 25 runs. The following year he became the first to found a cricket school, helping the development of a handful of future England Test players and went on to write a coaching manual. He suffered from bipolar disorder and bouts of depression, gassing himself in the bat drying room of his school in 1948.

By the First World War cricket had been firmly established in New Zealand, with a first class tournament, the Plunket Shield, played from 1906. Cricket was first recorded by Charles Darwin in the 1830s with club cricket established by the middle of the century. The first English touring side visited in 1864 and from then a New Zealand leg was generally added to an Australian tour. Canterbury began annual first class fixtures with Otago in 1865 with many players in Australian state sides taking part. By 1873 Wellington, Nelson and Auckland had become first class sides.

One of the country's early stars was William Barton, who, after learning cricket at Cranleigh School emigrated to New Zealand in 1877 at the age of 19, where he became a bank manager. His cricketing prowess was shown when he made a battling 45 against a touring Australian side featuring the Demon in 1880. His club form in Auckland was prolific and without a representative team of their own he was considered for selection by Australia for their tour of England in 1886. A representative side begun playing in 1894 and the New Zealand cricket council was formed that year. By the war New Zealand were playing regular first class internationals against England, Australia and Fiji but they were not invited to join the ICC.

On the outbreak of war in 1914 several county captains left their sides to enlist and Jack Hobbs had to move his benefit match from the Oval after the ground was requisitioned by the army. Although county cricket continued for a time, audiences dropped and W.G. published a letter saying he thought games should cease so that the country could squarely focus on the war effort. Cricket continued in various forms around the world, with a cricket match staged at Gallipoli in 1915 to disguise a hasty retreat. *Punch* cartoons used cricket caricature to emphasise German underhandedness, with balls being caught with nets and umpires being struck with bats. Cricket took its share of the fallen, with Test cricketers such as England's Colin Blythe, South Africa's Reggie Schwartz and Australian quick Tibby Cotter lost. Warwickshire bowler Percy Jeeves, used by P.G. Wodehouse as a model for his fictional manservant, also fell.

With Britain's love of doleful self-reflection, several books have been published that point to 1913 as the perfect year that saw the country at its finest. Of course, the emotional heft in such sentiment comes from the awful juxtaposition with the Great War that began the following year. For cricket the war marked the end, so established wisdom goes, of its Golden Age. The dehumanising aspect of trench warfare and dystopian images of brave souls limping through a treeless wasteland with mustard gas plumes and roaring tanks made for a bleak prospect.

Chapter 7

The inter-war years

AT the end of the war the shock and disgust at what had transpired contributed to a feeling that the world would never be the same again, that a rift had been created with a more innocent past. This public mood led cricket to face something of an existential crisis; after all, it was part of the old world that people feared may be lost. There were profound social changes too that concerned the cricket establishment. The leisured classes, from which the amateur spirit had sprung and who saw themselves as the guardians of cricket's soul, had been squeezed by death duties, rising taxes and the realisation that gainful employment wasn't a monopoly held by the working and middle classes.

This unease manifested itself in several ways. Many in the county game concerned by the trend for diminishing numbers at the gates, a high number of draws and a need to match football for excitement put forward ideas for reforms for the 1919 season. This included shortening boundaries, having penalties for batting out maiden overs and shortening matches to two days. Some ideas, like banning left-handers, were very radical indeed. There was a feeling that cricket needed to move with the times to retain its status as the national game. Predictably this provoked an impassioned defence of the traditional game by the likes of Harris, Hawke, Plum Warner and *Wisden* editor Sydney Pardon for whom a regular theme of his editor's notes was that the game should not be tampered with.

As it was cricket received a boost from those desperate to enjoy the English pleasures they had fought so hard for and gate receipts increased in the first few seasons after the war. But the gentleman governors of the game begrudged the dearth of quality amateurs, which made it increasingly difficult to resist a power shift to professionals. They also resented the increasingly popular maxim that winning was everything. Two-day matches proved unpopular and the Championship reverted to three days in 1920. After Warner's Middlesex won the Championship in 1921 it was not won again by a southern county until after the Second World War. This power shift to the north saw the MCC's moral guardianship of the game slip a bit further. Yorkshire and Lancashire became the powerhouses of the game and the former had almost tripled their pre-war spectator numbers by 1921 to close to 300,000 in a season. The supporters came to see their side win, which they invariably did.

This shift saw many amateurs feel bruised and it sparked a flurry of articles wistfully looking back to a halcyon age where the game was less commercial, less utilitarian and more charming. There was also a growing disconnect with the cricket-watching public, with the establishment balking at the wish for entertainment and feeling that the crowd were ignorant and cheered at the wrong things. Sport as a business was anathema to the amateur ideal, as was the heresy that cricket should adapt to remain popular in the modern age.

Birley summarised the first few years after the war as: 'Neo-feudal assumptions of the MCC, the dream world of county cricket, built in the image of a leisured class that no longer existed in sufficient numbers to pay for its pleasures, could not survive without taking on board alien values that it hated and tried to destroy.'

League cricket in the north was very popular in this period, with many clubs having enough financial might to bring in well-known players. It also provided a pool of talent for local counties and therefore in due course for the England team. But the MCC didn't like it as the cricket wasn't played in the right spirit. It was ultra-competitive and mercenary in their eyes. League games lasted four and a half hours and were played to a finish. This provided a format closer to a 90-minute game of football. There was certainly considerable space for a format between four hours and three days.

As was ever the case the MCC sought to preserve traditional values and quash reforms. But they were really struggling to justify the convention that an amateur should be England captain due to a lack of viable candidates. As we've seen they made a desperate attempt to recall C.B. Fry at the age of 50. The captain dictated the flow of the game and instilled its spirit. Could professionals be trusted with that responsibility? Despite a triumphant return for county cricket after the war England got thrashed in Australia. Was there also the potential for a power shift in the global game?

While in England the war had led to a nervy return for cricket and a resumption, if not intensification, of the old amateur and professional tensions, peace saw a renewed assertion of strength and confidence in the empire. Australia were very eager to resume the battle for the Ashes and doled out a humiliating whitewash to England when they toured in 1920. *Wisden* and the MCC thought the tour should have been delayed a year. Elsewhere, other cricketing centres in the empire had a point to prove.

The West Indies had played first class cricket for many decades and hosted regular international tours, but had not made a sufficient impression before the war to be included in the ICC. There were no stated eligibility criteria for attaining Test status and with a clear political agenda at play too the critical factor in joining the club was impressing the MCC. This meant being competitive against them on the field and following their lead in the spirit of the game. In practice this meant acceptance of the West Indies into the magic circle of the game rested on the shoulders of their leading players.

The opportunity to impress came in a tour of England in 1923. It was managed by Henry Mallet, an English cricket administrator who had turned out for the MCC back in 1901 and was president of the Minor Counties Cricket Association. He took an interest in West Indian cricket and managed their 1906 tour to England, when we can only assume they didn't impress sufficiently to be in consideration for inclusion in the Imperial Cricket

Council. George Challenor was 17 on that tour and 17 years later he was the most accomplished batsman in the Caribbean. With an uncle who had played in the early inter-colonial matches he was of cricketing stock, at the peak of his powers and familiar with English conditions. He was one of the revelations of the English season, scoring over 1,500 runs, averaging over 50 and making six first class centuries. He was a major factor in wins over five first class counties. In recognition the MCC made him a member and in so doing his team got a foot in the door of recognition by the establishment.

Another who made a big impression also had a link to the 1906 tour. Learie Constantine was the son of Lebrun, who we are already acquainted with. Born in Trinidad in 1901, he had little choice but to play cricket with his father overseeing his development. Captain of his school team, he was playing inter-colonial matches by 20 while also training as a legal clerk. He was an unconventional player in many ways, capable of extreme pace with the ball and destructive hitting with the bat but not consistently. A proto Andre Russell if you will. He was a superbly athletic fielder and this and a feeling of latent talent yet to be fully realised won him plaudits. One of whom, captain of West Indies Harold Austin, was a good man to impress. Despite modest returns he was perhaps fortuitously selected for the England tour.

He didn't set the tour alight but in patches he did enough to get influential people talking. He made a quickfire, unorthodox 77 against Oxford University and bowled some very slippery spells that made leading players like Jack Hobbs take note. Pelham Warner, himself born in the West Indies, thought him the best fielder in the world. On his return to Trinidad he had determined to become a professional cricketer. At the time there was a racial split in both society and the game in the Caribbean. It was difficult for black men to climb above the first few rungs of a professional career and in cricket there tended to be black local clubs with a point to prove against more established, colonial-style white-dominated clubs. His club, Shannon, certainly had a culture of promoting the black cause in an unjust society and this influenced Constantine's views.

The successful 1923 tour had done enough to prove that the standard of West Indies cricket had improved since the war and in 1926 they were one of the new sides voted into the ICC. Constantine peppered MCC captain Freddie Calthorpe with bouncers on their West Indian tour that year, having to be persuaded that injuring an establishment figure may not be wise. In 1927 the West Indies established an international board to coordinate domestic cricket and international tours.

Constantine was selected for the West Indies' first Test tour, to England in 1928. Constantine didn't intend to return, becoming disenchanted with the constraints he faced to advancement back home. He simply had to impress and he played in a way that drove his destiny. Against Middlesex he savaged the attack in making 86 in less than an hour to rescue his side in the first innings. He bowled express pace to take 7-57 and then scored 103 in an hour to win the game. It won him instant fame and, critically, a lucrative professional contract from Nelson in the Lancashire League.

West Indies lost their first three Tests by an innings and this inevitably led to some questioning the decision to award them Test status. In fairness the England team of 1928 was incredibly strong. In January 1930 on home soil they had national pride at stake. Opener Clifford Roach scored the first Test century by a West Indian and in the second innings a 21-year-old called George Headley scored 176 and helped earn the side a draw. They won the third Test with Roach making a double century, Headley stroking a century in each innings and Constantine taking nine wickets. It was nowhere near as strong a side as they had faced in 1928 but it was nevertheless a breakthrough. What is more, three black players had proved the match-winners.

Constantine balanced his professional career in England with international tours for the West Indies. He was annoyed that white cricketers of often modest ability were made captain when they had little in common with the players. They were beaten heavily in their first tour of Australia. Constantine played in Tests until 1939 and his record doesn't speak of greatness in itself, rather it was how he played that ensured his enduring fame. He was dashing, cavalier and entertaining with both bat and ball. The sheer confidence and at times arrogance he displayed on the field showed the Caribbean that black players could dominate a white man's game.

He was a celebrity in Nelson but faced some racist abuse and determined to use his profile to challenge the prejudice. He joined the League of Coloured Peoples as a campaigner and published a book, sometimes cited as an important landmark in an expression of West Indian nationalism. He took a key position at the ministry of labour championing black workers' rights, successfully sued a London hotel for racial discrimination in a landmark case and took up legal studies to be called to the Bar. He also wrote a clutch of books on both cricket and race relations. On cricket he proposed some radical ideas, including a one-day World Cup. When he moved back to Trinidad in his fifties he became a politician championing black rights and he was influential in Trinidad gaining independence in 1962. His life and career was an example of just how closely politics and cricket could align. On the field he gave pride to a dominion that needed heroes and self-confidence, off it he helped challenge racial prejudice and saw that dominion become a nation.

His team-mate Headley, who had taken to Test cricket like a duck to water, abandoned his plan to become a dentist to join Constantine as a Lancashire League professional after the England tour of 1933. His pay of £500 was considerably more than his fruit-picking job back in Jamaica. His contract released him for Test cricket and in 1935 he excelled once more, hitting a then West Indian Test record of 270 and averaging an absurd 97 to help the West Indies secure their first Test series victory.

Cricket had also consolidated in New Zealand after the war, though funding to sponsor tours was a limiting factor in greater exposure. The MCC toured in 1922/23 under Archie MacLaren, playing several fixtures against the New Zealand national team. A new generation of players, including opening batsman Charles Dempster, had increased competiveness against touring sides. This clearly showed sufficient progress in quality and competitiveness since before the war to warrant their inclusion in the ICC in 1926.

Although India took a prominent role in the imperial war effort cricket continued through the conflict. Indian cricket remained a complex mix of colonial British influence and organisation, a growing number of princely sides in the areas beyond direct colonial rule, clubs aligned on religious grounds and smaller local teams. While cricket was embedding itself throughout India and Indian culture its structures were not conducive to concentration of talent. Cricket's general popularity was boosted by the fact that football did not become established in Asia as it had in Europe and South America.

A group of young players from differing backgrounds had emerged since the war and were making a case for greater recognition of Indian cricket. One of the leading players was C.K. Nayudu. Born in 1895 in Andhra Pradesh, the son of a wealthy landowner, solicitor and politician, his father had been educated at Cambridge University where he had played cricket. C.K. showed early promise in school cricket and made his first class debut in 1916 for the Hindus against the English.

In 1925 the MCC arranged a tour to India with the intention of helping cement imperial ties and kinship between English imperialists and the mother country. However, the funding for the tour came from the cricket-loving Indian prince, Bhupinder Singh of Patiala, who had captained the first all-India tour of England in 1911, who wanted them to play Indian sides. MCC captain Arthur Gilligan was also keen that the tour could help develop Indian cricket more broadly. Against the Hindus at the Bombay Gymkhana Nayudu played one of the most important innings ever by an Indian, striking 153 in less than two hours with 11 sixes. It was this innings that led Gilligan to make the case to the MCC to grant India

Test status. Gilligan's personal intervention undoubtedly accelerated India's recognition as a Test nation at a time when many in England would have been uncomfortable with breaking the hegemony of white nations. It may have helped too that the chairman of the ICC in 1926 was Lord Harris, erstwhile governor of Bombay.

Gilligan encouraged Indians to create a national board of control to organise domestic cricket and select representative teams. In addition to religious, imperial and regional complexities in the Indian game there was also the question of class, or in an Indian context caste. A breakthrough had come in the career of Palwankar Baloo, a Dalit, the lowest 'untouchable' caste, whose sheer ability overcame social stigma and prejudice. A slow left-arm spinner, he took 179 wickets in 33 games and was a star on the 1911 tour.

The creation of the Board of Control in November 1927 brought all the different elements of Indian cricket together. Naturally it had an establishment base in its leadership, with Bhupendra Singh and Cambridge-educated Anthony de Mello taking key roles – 60% of those original BCCI members were English. But, significantly, it was not constituted on an English basis. English players were not allowed to qualify through residency. It was unequivocally an Indian team. As in England where an amateur was felt to be needed as a captain India felt they needed a prince, not necessarily because of tactical nous but as a representative of the country at social functions.

Perhaps the best qualified would have been Ranji's nephew, Duleepsinhji, who like his uncle was a cricketer of rare talent. But Ranji had persuaded him to further his career in England as the standard of cricket was superior. The next obvious choice was Patiala, not as talented but certainly very committed. However, his promiscuity (he is supposed to have sired 88 children) did not go down well with the British viceroy, Lord Willingdon. He turned to another prince, the Maharajah of Vizianagram, as a candidate. Politics played its hand and both princes withdrew, leaving the slightly ridiculous situation of having the Maharajah of Porbandar, who had no calibre as a player whatsoever, as captain for India's first Test tour of England. In practice he had the good sense to let Nayudu lead on the field.

The Board of Control recognised that cricket in the country needed more structure and a national first class competition, the Ranji Trophy, was founded in 1934. In a slightly farcical situation both the princes of Patiala and Vizianagram wanted to be seen as patrons and both presented a trophy to the winning team. It featured 15 teams representing either British administrative units or princely states.

※ ※ ※

By the early 1930s there was a consolidation of cricket in the main centres of empire and five Test nations, albeit not of equal status or playing an organised programme of regular fixtures. There was progress elsewhere too, such as in Sri Lanka (then Ceylon). Cricket had been established by the British military in the 1830s and spread through English-managed coffee and tea plantations. It took root through the major westernised schools. As in India clubs were formed along religious and racial lines. Clubs received tours from Calcutta and visited Singapore, Hong Kong and Malaysia in the late 19th century. The country was well situated to serve as a stop-over tour for visits to India by Australia and England.

In 1922 the Ceylon Cricket Association was formed to improve standards. Following this several first class tours were organised that included matches against a national representative XI. By the 1930s the standard of local players had surpassed those of English colonialists. The standard continued to improve as they received regular tours and by the late thirties they were considered the best non-Test side. In other colonial bases, such as Hong Kong, Singapore, Burma and Malaysia, cricket had largely been restricted to the English and did not develop to the same extent.

In the Americas cricket since the war had retained something of its pre-war promise, especially in Argentina, but it was contracting as English commercial interests reduced. Although tours continued to be organised the player bases were contracting to just the main centres, like Buenos Aires, and to a limited number of private schools. Other sports such as tennis, rugby and golf were becoming more prominent within country clubs. In 1927 Argentina were strong enough to defeat an MCC touring side captained by, yes you guessed it, Plum Warner. Though they didn't boast a player of the calibre of Bart King, in Dennet Ayling and Herbert Dorning they had two very capable bowlers who both claimed five wicket hauls against the MCC.

In 1932 a Best of South America XI toured England and played seven matches, considered first class. Of the

15-strong squad ten were Argentine, with three from Brazil and two from Chile. They were all of British origin and many had been to English public schools but they were testament to the quality, albeit in relatively modest numbers, of local club cricket. They gained a memorable victory over Julien Cahn's XI and gained a creditable draw against the MCC at Lord's. This concentration of regional talent ensured a relatively competitive tour but the experiment was not repeated. With the decline of cricket in Philadelphia tours to North America all but ceased, with cricket largely retreating to English enclaves. In Canada there was a sign of the sport reviving a little with wins over the MCC in 1936 and 1937.

In 1930 FIFA staged the first football World Cup, in Uruguay. This followed successful international football tournaments at the Olympics, that had grown from exhibition matches to a competitive tournament by 1908. By 1912 it had expanded to 14 teams, all European, and by 1920 included a non-European team, Egypt. The 1924 tournament had 22 entries and included teams from South America and North America. In contrast cricket in the Olympics withered on the vine. Originally planned to feature in 1896, the event was cancelled due to a lack of teams registering. In 1900 cricket did feature but it was a curious affair. The British team were in fact just a club, the Devon and Somerset Wanderers, and their only opposition was France, who were a team of English expats. It is a curiosity of sport that France has a silver medal for cricket. Belgium and the Netherlands had considered entering but withdrew when their bid to co-host the event failed. There were plans for cricket to be included in 1904, hosted by St Louis, USA, but not enough teams entered. It hasn't been seen at the Olympics since.

Although successful, growing and attracting significant public interest, FIFA had an issue with Olympic inclusion because football was an increasingly professional sport and this didn't sit well with the Olympic amateur ideal. It is this that saw them break away to form the football World Cup in 1930. This was hosted by Uruguay and featured seven South American teams, four from Europe and two from North America. Many European teams had declined to attend due to the distance and length of the trip. It was a very high-profile event, hosted in the 90,000-capacity Estadio Centenario stadium built for the tournament and marking the centenary of the country's formation. The attendance for the tournament was close to 600,000, with over 30,000 per match. The hosts beat Argentina in the final with the hubbub around the match causing havoc in Montevideo harbour with all number of vessels arriving carrying passionate Argentine fans. The visiting fans are said to have chanted 'victory or die' as they entered the stadium, giving an indication of the tribal nature of football that has never really been seen in cricket.

For the 1934 tournament, hosted by Italy, 32 teams entered the qualification process. It was European-focused, with 22 of the 32 teams, but also included teams from South America and Africa. A European and South American rivalry had been established that remains a feature of international football to this day. Football was the second most popular sport in the USA in the twenties with a successful professional league attracting many leading players from Europe. But squabbles between rival governing bodies and the impact of the Great Depression saw it reduced to an amateur, marginal sport. Like cricket it had failed to resist the all-consuming national passion of baseball.

Notable absentees from the first World Cup were the home nations of Britain. The FA had ongoing tensions with FIFA and informed the global representative body that the premier international tournament was the one played between the nations of the British Isles.

Rugby union had been introduced to the empire by the 1870s with clubs formed in Australia, New Zealand and South Africa. In New Zealand it spread quickly throughout the country while in South Africa is was spread from the Cape Colony into the interior by Boer farmers. There were clubs in Canada too but its growth was limited by the popularity of Canadian football, a similar game to American football and sometimes grouped together under the title gridiron. Gaelic football in Ireland and Aussie Rules in Australia were other variants alongside rugby league that developed from the same root game. In South America rugby was introduced by British settlers and was played in cricket clubs.

After disagreements over laws in early home nation internationals the International Rugby Football Board was founded by Wales, Ireland and Scotland in 1886, but England refused to join as they didn't accept equal status. There ensued a stand-off for several years when fixtures didn't take place before England joined in 1890. The board faced an early challenge over amateurism and professionalism, that perennial theme of sport. Northern clubs wanted to pay compensation costs to players for loss of earnings but the board took a principled stance on protecting amateurism and this led to a north/south divide, with the northern clubs forming the rugby league. Rugby league was adopted in tandem with rugby union in New Zealand and an 'all gold' team, a pun emphasising the mercenary nature of the professional rugby code, was created and toured both Australia and Great Britain. This helped establish the game in Australia and from then there were regular international tours featuring Great Britain, Australia and New Zealand. In rugby union the IRFB remained a home nations body until after the Second World War.

The proliferation of team sports by 1930, as well as individual sports such as tennis and golf, meant cricket had to find its place in a broader sporting context. It no longer had the clear run it enjoyed before 1850. At heart it remained an establishment game, thanks largely to the MCC and other national boards who modelled themselves on it, although league cricket in England and localised cricket in the West Indies and India showed it could be an everyman sport too. It was always an empire game, unlike football, and although the MCC toured various outposts they did so more for the enjoyment than a commitment to develop cricket in the sport's hinterland. Rugby was played on a similar basis, although was a more restricted game at this stage. Football was dominant in Europe and South America, while baseball pushed other sports to the margins in North America. Critically for its later development, cricket was the only sport to gain widespread popularity in Asia.

Chapter 8

Bodyline and its aftermath

ALTHOUGH there were new Test nations, the fulcrum of the international game remained the Ashes. The MCC would only select their strongest XIs for Australia and the public on both sides of the world were emotionally invested in the contest, as seen in the level of interest and the size of crowds. In the first series after the war Australia had gained the ascendancy but England had a rising star who would become one of the game's greatest ever players. Australia then produced a statistical freak. The battle between Walter Hammond and Don Bradman defined the inter-war years.

Walter Hammond was born in a castle in 1903. But he was no cricketing aristocrat. His father was a corporal in the artillery squadron at Dover based in the fortress. As a boy his family moved with army postings and some of his first cricket was played in Malta. In the Great War his father served on the western front and was promoted to major but died in the last throes of conflict. His mother

sent him to board at Cirencester Grammar School where
he excelled at football and cricket. An innings of 365 in
a school match won him local acclaim. He had intended
to train at agricultural college to become a farmer but his
headmaster arranged a trial at Gloucestershire and he won
a contract in 1920 at the tender age of 17. He was talented
but raw and with barely a score to his name Gloucester
sent him to coach at Clifton College, where he honed his
technique. Needing money in the off-season, he played
football professionally for Bristol Rovers but, fearing
injury, was a little hesitant in the tackle. Despite his coach
feeling he could reach international standard he decided
he had to focus solely on cricket.

Between 1923 and 1925 his statistics remained modest
but some eye-catching centuries saw the great and good
groom him for future England honours. He dropped down
the order from opener and made 250 against Lancashire
in 1925. His fast-medium bowling also developed, putting
him into the batting all-rounder category. The MCC
selected him for a pre-Test West Indies tour in 1925/26
and he averaged 49, including a score of 238 against the
full West Indian side. He clearly enjoyed a bit of pace on
the ball. He fell very ill at the end of the tour, possibly from
either a mosquito bite or through a sexually transmitted
disease, and he was admitted to a nursing home on his
return. He missed the 1926 season as a result.

He made up for lost time in 1927 by becoming only
the second cricketer, after W.G. (who else?) to score a
thousand runs in May and ended the season with a shade
under 3,000 runs at 69. This won him a *Wisden* cricketer
of the year accolade and a place in the Test squad. On his

Test debut against South Africa that winter he scored a half century and claimed a five-for. Perhaps still recovering strength after his illness and with the toil of a season behind him he didn't quite deliver on his promise, though many all-rounders would envy averaging 40 with the bat and 27 with the ball. He made three double centuries in 1928 and was all set for his first Ashes tour. His debut century was 251, the second highest score ever in an Ashes Test. In the next game he scored another double century and in the following game a hundred in each innings. In a 4-1 series victory he had scored 900 runs, a record for a Test match series, at an average of 113. After this he was considered the best player in the world.

Born five years after his English counterpart, Don Bradman was born in rural New South Wales in the village of Cootamundra, originally a gold rush settlement but by the early 20th century a gentle, agricultural community. He was raised in the nearby town of Bowral, strategically located on the railway line from Sydney to Melbourne. Of English forebears, his hometown had an anglicised feel with the planting of deciduous trees. He later put down his success to countless hours as a boy using a stump to strike a golf ball reverberating off a water tank in his garden. He became a prolific schoolboy cricketer at his local public school, hitting centuries as a 12-year-old.

His uncle was captain of the local team and young Bradman became scorer, filling in as a player when they were short. His father took him to the SCG for the 1920 Ashes Test and he made it his ambition to play at the ground. His genius may have been denied the game if he had persevered with an early teenage switch to tennis but by 17 he was dedicated to cricket and scored a triple century for Bowral in the local league. Those kind of scores get you noticed and with Australia's Ashes dominance in the early twenties reversed by England's victory in 1925/26 the selectors sought to freshen up an aging team. He entered a trial organised by the NSW cricket authority, did well and made an 80-mile Saturday commute to Sydney grade club St George's. By 18 he was playing for the NSW second XI. He made his first class debut at 19 and stroked a century on debut.

He started the 1928/29 season working in real estate and playing for his state team, but moved to Sydney and joined a sports retailer. He scored a century in each innings in the first Sheffield Shield game of the season and then a century against the touring England team secured him a place in the Ashes squad. His rise had been effortless but making his Test debut in only his tenth first class match, he had perhaps his first taste of failure. He only made 1 and 18 and Australia were bustled out for 66, losing by a mind-boggling 675 runs. He was dropped but served as substitute fielder when England thrashed Australia again. He had a long, long look at the best player in the world as Hammond amassed 251 in a mammoth 605 deliveries. Recalled for Melbourne, he became the youngest ever player to score a Test century but although Australia performed better another double century by Hammond saw England win again.

Bradman scored another century as Australia finally got a consolation win in the final Test. Although his team were in the doldrums Bradman had been a breakthrough success. He finished the domestic season by hitting 340, the highest ever score at the ground. In advance of the next Ashes tour he made a then first class world record 452, at more than a run a minute.

The build-up to the 1930 Ashes pitched Hammond against Bradman, both young men, both record breakers. Bradman's game was characterised by quick footwork, almost unerring judgement and fast scoring. There was some speculation about how his technique would fare on livelier pitches in England. Hammond was a sublime off-side player with a powerful drive and what has been described as a majesty to his game. He could be unsettled by extreme pace and wasn't quite as fluent against a leg side line but it was considered near impossible to stop him scoring. He was moody in temperament, possibly in part down to the effects of mercury from his treatment five years before, and wasn't considered a team man. He tended to arrogance and following his record-breaking series in Australia would have been wary of the challenge of the boy from Bowral. Bradman was aloof too and didn't subscribe to the team culture, spending his spare time writing a book rather than socialising with team-mates. Many noted the contrast between his dynamism on the field and his lack of exuberance off it.

In the first innings of the first Test both men scored just eight. Despite a second innings Bradman hundred England won the game. In the second Test Bradman scored 254, an innings he later said was the best of his career, to set up an Australian victory. In the third he made 334 and in the fifth another double century. Australia had regained the Ashes and Bradman had scored 954 runs, surpassing Hammond's record haul of the previous series.

Hammond wasn't even close, amassing less than a third of his rival, scoring a solitary century and coming behind Sutcliffe and Duleepsinhji in England's run aggregates. Bradman was a revelation and returned home to the level of public adulation only ever seen in sporting circles for W.G. He was uncomfortable with it, referring to himself as a reluctant hero. Hammond nursed his ego and coming out second best in press comparisons with his rival saw him develop an obsession with beating Bradman.

The Ashes rivalry, the pendulum swinging one way and then the next, had become the most compelling sporting contest of all and the stage was set for one of the most famous and written-about series of them all as England looked to nullify the threat of Bradman. Before we look at that series I'll introduce you to some of the supporting cast.

Australia's match-winner with the ball was leg-spinner and inventor of the flipper Clarrie Grimmett. Born in New Zealand and starting his first class career there in their pre-Test era he moved to Australia, married and became a first class cricketer. He didn't make his Test debut until he was 33 – they do say wrist spinners mature later – but made an immediate impression. He became the first Test bowler to take 200 wickets and one of the few to reach that milestone in fewer than 40 Tests. With discipline, consistency and skill he provided a foil for the quick bowlers and in his late forties formed a formidable partnership with fellow spinner Bill O'Reilly. Nicknamed 'the Gnome', Neville Cardus said he was a 'master of surreptitious arts'.

For England two young men had come into the team from very different backgrounds. Douglas Jardine was born in 1900 in India, son of a cricketer and barrister. Returning to live with family in Scotland he boarded at Winchester College, with a brutal approach to discipline and a proud sporting record. He went up to Oxford in 1919 and played first class cricket, scoring 96 against the touring Australians in 1921 that put him on the England radar. Leaving Oxford, he trained to become a solicitor and played as an amateur for Surrey. His amateur status did his chances of selection no harm, given the dearth in the post-war ranks. By 1927 his average was rising, his style becoming freer and more attractive and he made runs in the matches that caught the eye of selectors, such as the Gentlemen versus the Players. He made his Test debut in 1928 against the West Indies and toured Australia in 1928/29, impressing Bradman. The Australians took against him for what they saw as a haughty demeanour, not helped when he flaunted his privileged background by fraternising with Oxbridge contemporaries and wearing a Harlequin cap. He missed Bradman's heroics in 1930 due to business commitments but was made captain in 1931.

There were no such airs and graces about Harold Larwood. Born in a coal mining district of Nottinghamshire in a strict Methodist household, he worked in the pits at 13 leading a team of pit ponies. This hard labour gave him a strong physique and though relatively short he developed into a very fast bowler, impressing at a trial at Trent Bridge when he was 19. The county matched his mining salary of £1.60 a week. By 1925 he was a regular in the side and had the knack of taking the wickets of senior England batsmen. He wasn't confident in his ability at the top level and when selected by England told his county captain that he wasn't good enough. He went on to play a key role in helping England reclaim the Ashes in 1926 for the first time since 1912. On the 1928/29 tour he too faced abuse from the Australian crowd, though it was noted that that was just part of the combative, gritty atmosphere the Australian fans enjoyed rather than anything particularly personal.

Larwood and the rest of the England bowlers had been given a torrid time by Bradman in 1930 and the Nottinghamshire man's confidence was dented. But Jardine, looking for a chink in Bradman's armour, focused on a supposed weakness of the Australian to fast, rising deliveries. In the aftermath of the humiliating defeat Jardine called a meeting with Larwood, his fellow colliery school paceman Bill Voce and their Nottinghamshire captain Arthur Carr, where he convinced them to hone this hostile short-pitch tactic in advance of the next Ashes tour. The basis of the tactic, long known as leg theory, wasn't new, with English and Australians practising it. Though often effective it wasn't popular with crowds as it slowed down the game and was considered a negative tactic. Jardine wanted to add raw pace to the plan and consistently pitch the ball short. Later that winter Jardine's predecessor Freddie Calthorpe had made a complaint when Constantine employed this fast leg theory in the West Indies.

Jardine took further counsel, with Surrey captain Percy Fender agreeing that it was a potential weakness for Bradman and reports from Australia attested that he had struggled against pace in Shield cricket and against South African quick Sandy Bell. The combination of his own hatred of Australian fans following his experiences out there, a patriotic fervour to win back the Ashes and a determination as captain to do all he could proved a potent cocktail and outweighed any notion of a gentlemanly spirit. It was, to put it another way, an amateur taking a hard-nosed professional approach.

When the England touring party contained four quick bowlers it raised a few eyebrows, including from Bradman himself. Jardine used the sea passage to instruct his team on the plan, reportedly encouraging a hatred of Australians and a nicknaming of Bradman as 'the little bastard'. Quite how that spirit went down with tour manager Pelham Warner, still relishing a cricket tour even after hanging up his bat, is interesting to speculate given that Pelham's notion of an 'honour code' had permeated 20th-century cricket to that stage.

Jardine's prickly temperament and the historic ill-will between him and the Australian public provided a confrontational and hostile context to the tour. The first few games saw only occasional bouncers and no incidents, but against an Australian XI England unleashed the fast leg theory experiment. It worked against Bradman, who was forced to duck and weave and was bundled out for modest scores. The Australian crowd, not known for keeping opinions to themselves, thought it dangerous, disgraceful and spitefully intended to hurt the batsmen. They dubbed the tactic 'Bodyline'. Without helmets or other protection it undoubtedly presented a real threat of injury. In six tour games Bradman had only made just over a hundred runs. Jardine wrote to Fender to say their devilish plan was working and that he'd have to move all his fielders to the leg side.

It had the makings of a cricketing manifestation of a morality play. Warner objected to the tactic, believing it was underhand and not in keeping with the ideals the game represented, but he was not willing to say anything publicly. Some of the Australian press also began to question whether it was ethical. Bradman missed the first Test, ostensibly due to fatigue though Jardine later said he thought it was a mental breakdown. Bodyline was only used intermittently and England won easily, despite a lusty, hook-punctuated 187 by Stan McCabe. Gubby Allen, the amateur in Jardine's pace battery, clashed with Jardine over the tactic and refused to bowl to his captain's plans. There were no formal complaints but the situation was brewing to the concern of administrators. Some in the Australian camp wanted to fight fire with fire and call up their own pacemen but the captain refused.

Bradman returned for the second Test and on a slower pitch managed to nullify the threat, with a second innings century allowing Australia to draw level. The unfolding drama moved on to Adelaide. A sharp Larwood bouncer struck Australian captain Woodfull above the heart and he bent over, wincing in pain. Jardine, seeking to gain a psychological hold over Bradman, shouted 'well bowled Harold'. There was a delay before the first ball of Larwood's next over as more leg side fielders were brought in for deflected catches. Woodfull battled on, being hit several times, and finally getting out for 22. The crowd were at fever pitch and officials were concerned that a riot would break out. Warner visited the Australian dressing room to express sympathy to Woodfull but was told that 'one team out there is playing cricket, the other is not.

This game is too good to spoil'. This line of attack on Warner reduced this proud man and long-time defender of sportsmanship to tears.

After a rest day the tension increased further when Warner and Woodfull's conversation was leaked to the press. Some pointed to Fingleton, who was the only full-time journalist in the side, as the culprit, but Fingleton blamed Bradman. Although leaks are fairly common these days it was unheard of then and broke an inviolate code that shocked both teams. It was testament too to the level of public interest in the series and the broader national rivalry it represented. Cricket had moved to the front pages. This wasn't a cricket story, it was international news. Then a Larwood bouncer to a conventional field struck Bert Oldfield, fracturing his skull. He had to be helped off the field and the crowd were whipped into a frenzy again. Some England players grabbed stumps to protect themselves in case the crowd stormed the pitch. Larwood apologised and Jardine sent a telegram of apology to Oldfield's wife and a present for his daughter. But, the situation was about to escalate further.

The Australian board wrote to the MCC saying that Bodyline was dangerous and unsportsmanlike and unless stopped immediately it would harm the relationship between the teams. To accuse the MCC of unsportsmanlike behaviour was akin to a claim of high treason and their response was unequivocal, saying they deplored the cable and that there had been no breach of sportsmanship. They did, however, offer to consider a law change if proposed by Australia. Jardine was shaken and offered to withdraw the Bodyline tactic if the team did not support it, but without his knowledge the team released a press notice that they fully supported their captain and use of Bodyline. The Australian board replied to the MCC that they were content for the series to continue and that they could delay a response to Bodyline until after the series. But the MCC demanded that the 'unsportsmanlike' slur was withdrawn as a condition for continuing the tour. This took it into the realm of a potential diplomatic crisis. Politicians on both sides showed concern that the imperial relationship was at stake and feared the impact of trade embargoes. Under pressure from Australian Prime Minister Joseph Lyons, who outlined the devastating impact to lost trade and soured relations, the Australian board replied that the sportsmanship of the British team was not in question.

England won the series 4-1. Tactically Jardine had been vindicated but though winning on the field their moral authority off it had been a little tarnished. Being admonished for poor sportsmanship by a dominion was certainly not what the MCC ordered. Hammond topped the run charts and was the only player to make two centuries in the series, so got his wish in his personal duel with Bradman. He was, however, opposed to the use of Bodyline.

Jardine had feared the sack from the MCC but was retained as captain for the following West Indies tour. There he faced some of his own medicine when the West Indies employed the tactic. He proved resolute, making a five-hour century against a barrage of hostile, short bowling. It was said that he was perhaps the best player of the tactic he invented. To some extent the West Indian adoption of Bodyline, albeit as a reactive rather than pre-planned tactic, showed that other teams were willing to risk accusations of unsportsmanlike behaviour if it was within the rules. It wasn't just England on the naughty step. But this hardened attitudes against Bodyline and the public view was that while not prohibited it was certainly not pleasant. Jardine was subjected to a pep talk from the MCC on diplomacy before being offered the captaincy for the next tour, India's first home Tests. While Jardine remained ultra-competitive he was happier in India, the land of his birth, engaged positively with the fans and happily carried out the softer, diplomatic aspect of captaincy asked of him. But the tour wasn't without incident, with Jardine reprimanding an umpire for giving too many lbws and sending a telegram to London to ask that he be removed from the final games. Given the umpire was under the wing of Indian princes this was all a bit delicate. Spin dominated in the local conditions but Bodyline was used in bursts by both teams.

He played well too in a comfortable series victory. Meanwhile he had written a book to put his side of the story in the Bodyline controversy. This sought to justify his tactics and put blame on the rowdy behaviour of Australian fans and the abuse he and other players were subjected to. He even proposed suspending tours until the Australian crowds were dealt with. With Bodyline becoming a feature of all tours the MCC decided to act and with Jardine its progenitor his position was at risk. Politicians wanted to avoid another rift in empire relations and applied pressure for him to be removed. As it is he made it easy by announcing in the *Evening Standard* that he wouldn't tour Australia again, in effect ending his cricket career. As a batsman he had averaged 48 in 22 Tests, albeit with only a lone century. As a captain he had won an Ashes and blunted Bradman, but at what cost? His technique was described as that of an old-fashioned amateur. This was in stark contrast with his visceral desire to win, often thought of in amateur circles as a vulgar characteristic of the professional.

His character was complex and if he had charm and humour, which many contemporaries attest to, it was certainly not entirely open and innocent. He remained a pantomime villain for many years and in Australia represented the arrogance and snobbishness they love to hate in the British character. Bradman was certainly not a fan and snubbed him throughout life. In the credit column terms like implacable resolve have been used. England captains in the modern era have sometimes channelled his will to win as a positive attribute.

In the aftermath of the tour Harold Larwood was keen to put his side of the story too. His take was that the issues arose from technical deficiencies in Woodfull and Bradman and pointed to other batsmen, such as McCabe, who played Bodyline well. In other words the danger came from the batsman's weakness rather than his bowling. He showed solidarity with Jardine on deflecting any criticism on to the behaviour of Australian crowds. His ghost-written book *Bodyline* was serialised in a magazine. The tour had brought him fame and notoriety and despite an injured foot limiting his bowling, Notts played him as a batsman to keep the crowds coming. Meanwhile, the Australian Board changed their domestic rules to outlaw

Bodyline bowling and applied pressure on the MCC. They prevaricated on a formal law change but committed to not using Bodyline on the 1934 tour. They also put Larwood in a difficult position by requiring him to make an apology for using the tactic. They didn't ask Jardine to do likewise. Larwood refused on the grounds that he was only following the instructions of his captain. In effect this ended his Test career. *Wisden* thought he had been coerced by the press to make provocative statements that made his position in the team untenable, in the process ending the career of a very talented bowler. He played on in first class cricket until 1938.

Stung by his treatment by the MCC, he used his sizeable benefit to buy a sweet shop in Blackpool where he hoped to evade the public eye. Finding post-war austerity a strain on his business he emigrated to Australia and was employed by a soft drinks firm. He was often visited by English touring teams. In 1982 the 50th anniversary of Bodyline was marked and the old man received renewed hate mail. Bodyline had left its legacy. In his dotage he became very quotable on current cricket, decrying the use of protective clothing and dismissing Botham's bowling as not being able to burst a paper bag.

For Bradman it marked a turning point, if not in his seemingly unstoppable accrual of runs, then certainly in his technique and attitude. Many feel he lost some fluency after Bodyline, remaining an extremely capable runscorer but perhaps without some of the elan of his youth. He sought a refuge away from the public gaze and took a job as a stockbroker in Adelaide. His health suffered in 1934 and he didn't play all of the Tests, but a triple century and a double century, in world record partnerships with Bill Ponsford, helped Australia regain the Ashes. But after the tour he was diagnosed with peritonitis, a life-threatening abdominal swelling, and came close to death. A public appeal for blood donors was required and the response was extraordinary with the hospital overwhelmed by those wanting to help. It was touch and go and many papers prepared obituaries, but he made a slow recovery.

At the resumption of peace after World War Two Bradman became a national cricket administrator and juggled this with commercial interests and the twilight of his playing career. His doctor advised him not to play and with batting rhythm deserting him he was reduced to methodical but scratchy accumulation of runs. But it was still enough to score hundreds. His old rivalry with Hammond was resumed in 1946, with Bradman 38 and Hammond 43. When Bradman didn't walk after the umpire had judged a clean catch as a bump ball Hammond remonstrated with him and shouted 'a fine fucking way to start a series'. This ill feeling permeated the remainder of the tour, which didn't match the public mood of peace, rejoicing and unity. Hammond, in his last year of Test cricket, couldn't make the big scores expected of him and cracks also appeared in his decision making and captaincy. In contrast Bradman regained old form and averaged 97 in a 3-0 victory. Hammond played his final Tests in New Zealand at the end of the Ashes and retired, with 7,249 runs at an average of 58.45 and 22 centuries. He also took 83 wickets. It is a record that puts him in the very top echelon of Test players. But to him, in comparison with his great rival, it wasn't good enough. Bradman's farewell tour was against England in 1948. As he strode out for his final innings he was averaging 101. A second ball duck, deceived by a googly, saw it drop to one of the most famous numbers in cricket: 99.94.

The Bradman and Hammond rivalry had been one of the compelling narratives of the inter-war years and Bodyline its defining moment. New Test teams had been created, providing more variety to international cricket and laying the foundation for further growth in India, West Indies and New Zealand. The emergence of Bradman and Larwood demonstrated that cricket had spread from private to grammar and state schools and therefore a greater proportion of society were being introduced to the sport, with opportunities to play at a range of different levels. Seen in a vacuum, therefore, cricket had experienced another Golden Age and defied the post-war nerves about its viability as a mainstream sport. However, it was a Golden Age for sport more broadly with football, rugby in all its variants and tennis all rapidly gaining in popularity, in football's case becoming dominant in Europe and South America. This wasn't a binary situation of course, with many happily combining a love of football, cricket and other sports especially if they could alternate in the seasons. Hammond, after all, could have been an international footballer. Growing and maturing economies meant more people had leisure time to either play or watch their chosen sport. And this drew money into sports. Cricket wasn't yet under pressure to retain its share but a few warning shots across its bows had been fired.

Chapter 9

Heroes of resistance and heroes of peace

I N Europe cricket had missed an opportunity with football soon surpassing it for participation and cultural cut-through. Its link with Englishness was both its weakness and its strength. A weakness because its definitive cultural context made it hard to cultivate universal appeal and be embraced as a national sport. But a strength in the level of commitment of a certain class in the Netherlands and Denmark who sought its reflection of honour and sophistication. By 1928, when Warner toured with an MCC side, there were around 1,200 players in the Netherlands. By 1932 there were over 50 clubs, not comparable to football but perhaps staking a claim to be more than a marginal pastime. Dutch cricket even had its own magazine. The 1930s are sometimes referred to as the Dutch Golden Age of cricket. In 1933 they defeated an MCC side on the 50th anniversary of the formation of the national board. They may not have been in the ICC but they had sufficient profile to lure national teams touring England across the North Sea to play, such as South Africa in 1935. Although no Dutch players had emulated the great Posthuma in plying their trade in England, some such as Terwiel and Glerum arguably had the ability to.

In Germany cricket attracted more local players between the wars, Berlin at least providing a large enough community to service a growing league. The linchpin of German cricket was Felix Mendel, a jeweller and gem of a niggardly medium-pacer. In 1930 Mendel and his brother Guido were part of a German cricketers' tour of England. Coinciding with the visit of Bradman they were always going to struggle to generate interest and media but it was further evidence that there were some green shoots of life beyond the empire. Mendel took 24 wickets at an average of 6 on the tour. While in London he took the opportunity to lobby the MCC to run a tournament for developing nations on the continent. This never came to fruition. Another missed opportunity, perhaps.

Soon after their return Hitler came to power but Mendel's personality and passion helped galvanise the cricket community in the face of the Nazi party's aversion of cricket due to its lack of physical contact. The Fuhrer clearly hadn't seen Larwood bowl Bodyline! The game was actively discouraged but remarkably, thanks to Mendel's resolve, it kept going.

On a bombing raid of Rotterdam in May 1940 the only shop selling cricket equipment in the country was razed to the ground. This should have spelt the end for continuation of the cricket league. But, perhaps through a sense of defiance and solidarity with English allies, the cricket community refused to stop play. They covered their remaining balls in boot polish to extend their life, in the process giving swing bowlers the time of their lives. With private cars banned and rail severely restricted, some clubs fashioned home-made tricycles to get the kit to the grounds, and others cycled 30 miles to play. Despite poles placed in grounds to stop them being used as allied landing strips and pavilions and sight screens requisitioned by the Nazis for firewood there were 300 fixtures played in the Netherlands in 1944. It is a plausible theory that this psychological defiance helped cricket gain in popularity after the war.

In Denmark, too, cricket was a form of resistance. As in the Netherlands cricket had continued despite curfews and travel restrictions but when naval blockades stopped the supply of bats and balls from England it looked like they would have to draw stumps. But cricketer and businessman Frederick Ferslev refused to give up, learnt how to make bats from an article in *The Cricketer* and secretly scoured the country for timber. In 1943 his first batch were pressed into service, though being made from poplar they were too heavy and soft. He placed adverts in newspapers for willow and finally found some. Then, in surely the most remarkable display ever of cricketing bravery, he defied the Nazis and risked death in establishing a bat press in the basement of a Nazi-commandeered workshop. By Christmas 1943 his willow blades were in production and distributed to clubs. Thanks to this heroism the game continued throughout the war.

After the liberation of Berlin in the rubble of the war-torn German capital an allied officer was amazed when he was approached by a German citizen and asked if he wanted to play a game of cricket. Mendel had seen potential cricketers marching into his city.

Cricket boomed in the euphoria of victory with record attendances in county cricket despite a wretchedly wet summer in 1946. Cricket had been part of the green fields of home image used to prop up national spirits in the war years. Although victory was won Britain was tentatively finding its place in a new world order as the sun was setting on the power and moral authority of traditional imperial powers. They were supplanted by the contrasting ideologies of the new superpowers America and the USSR. This was to have an impact on the empire game but a glorious peace was no time to wrestle with such weighty themes. Not when Denis Compton was batting.

Born in the London district of Hendon in 1918, Compton became a prolific schoolboy cricketer and footballer, joining Middlesex and Arsenal respectively in the years preceding the war. A dashing batsman and useful chinaman bowler, he was soon courted as the bright young thing of the English game and became one of the youngest debutants ever when he was selected against New Zealand in 1937, having just turned 19. He scored his first Test century at 20 against Bradman's touring Australians and was one of the leading lights in the first class game when the war started.

The winter of 1946 was cold and bleak. In a London still strewn with rubble and bomb craters people hibernated with their meagre rations to ride out the long winter. The summer that followed was glorious and Compton was in irresistible form. He scored five centuries against the touring South Africans alone. In all he scored over 3,800 runs with 18 centuries, both records that stand to this day. But it wasn't just the volume of runs, it was how he scored them, with a cavalier style and sense of adventure that made him a household name. Cardus observed 'there were no rations in an Innings by Compton'. In his obituary in *The Observer* Scyld Berry noted: 'It is no exaggeration to say that Compton brought back a feeling of gaiety to a ravaged people as no propaganda film, or Churchillian speech, could have done.' He added that his style combined 'the classicism of Wally Hammond and the eccentricity of Derek Randall'. That the sporting hero of the year was a cricketer was testament to its standing in the country. He made the most of his fame, lucratively becoming the 'Brylcreem boy'. His partnership with Middlesex and England colleague Bill Edrich was legendary, setting unbeaten Test and county records. And they lived it up on tour, too.

During the war Compton had played a handful of games in the Ranji Trophy where he played against and befriended tall, strapping Australian fighter pilot Keith Miller. Born in Melbourne in 1919, Miller and his brothers were taught the game by his father and after showing early promise he came under the tutelage of Bodyline captain Bill Woodfull, who was headmaster at his school. With a terrible academic record but burgeoning sporting talent he left school to play both Aussie Rules football and cricket. He made his debut for Victoria in 1938, scoring 181 on debut. In his early career he was a steady, technically correct accumulator much in the mould of his headmaster, who had been dubbed 'The Unbowlable' in his career. At this stage he was also playing football to a high level, in a parallel with Compton's career. By the outbreak of war he had established himself in the Sheffield Shield side and scored his first century.

Miller had a lively war. Posted to England, he trained as a fighter pilot, had a few Biggles-like near-death experiences, faced reprimands for drunken nights of revelry and duelled with Messerschmitts in bombing raids to Germany in his Mosquito. Later in life when asked how he coped with pressure on the cricket field he responded that 'pressure is a Messerschmitt up your arse'. In between the derring-do he played cricket for the Australian services, his batting becoming more expansive and his bowling developing to the extent where he finished the war a genuine all-rounder. At the end of the war he was a star of the so-called Victory Tests, organised by, yes you guessed it, Pelham Warner. In the last fixture of the Victory Test programme Miller played alongside Learie Constantine in a Commonwealth XI against England. Though he didn't take his bowling very seriously he could be somewhat slippery and with the bat he regularly planted balls into the roofs of pavilions. It was in the following services tour to India that he played against Compton and cemented their friendship.

Following the war Miller made his Test debut and represented his state side in football. After his discharge from the RAF in 1946 he returned to his pre-war job in an oil company, but found himself far more junior than those who hadn't served in the war. He was tempted to come to England as a professional in the Lancashire League where the salary was considerably higher than what he could earn at home. But the Australian Board would not select players serving as English professionals for Test duty. He decided to sign for Rawtenstall anyway for the 1947 season, flew to the States to marry his wartime sweetheart and played in the Ashes on home soil. Though he was Bradman's go-to man with both bat and ball he felt a kinship with fellow servicemen, such as Bill Edrich, and resented his captain's hard-nosed approach to victory by all means. His relationship with Bradman was complex and has been much written about. It was certainly based on deep mutual respect but there was a clash of styles. Miller didn't like to take things too seriously and this carefree approach gave him a certain swagger that the crowds loved. During the series he cancelled his contract with Rawtenstall and moved to Sydney as a liquor salesman. Australia dominated England in a 3-0 victory with Miller the star, averaging 71 with the bat and 21 with the ball.

This was the prelude to the 1948 Ashes tour. Compton fresh from his summer of summers, Miller the dynamic Australian all-rounder and Bradman in his Ashes swansong. The record crowds of 1947 perhaps masked the threat that modernity was posing to the game. An increase in car ownership after the war saw greater mobility and leisure options contributing to a halving of County Championship attendances from 1946 to 1956. A series of committees were established to identify how to arrest the decline, with shortened boundaries introduced to boost excitement. The general consensus was that tactics were too negative, scoring too pedestrian and draws too common. As gate receipts significantly reduced the game became reliant on Test matches for income, establishing a pattern cricket authorities have wrestled with to this day. To what extent can domestic cricket be economically self-sustaining?

The MCC, as ever, invested most of their energy into defending the amateur ideal, with its perceived inextricable link with the spirit of the game. But the age of the amateur was an anachronism by the 1950s with only a few quality amateurs emerging each year and these making a living from the game whether termed professionals or not. In a desperate last stand the MCC broadened the definition of amateur to the point where it became a nonsense, with just the technicality of whether payment was made from wages or expenses separating the two. They'd also been forced begrudgingly through a dearth of talented amateurs to make a professional, Len Hutton, the England captain. The annual Gentlemen versus Players game, traditionally the most prominent fixture in the calendar, was played for the last time in 1962.

Chapter 10

The fear of decline and the threat of innovation

THE state of the game debate, a staple of cricket fans' discussion through the ages, intensified in the late 1950s. The decline in young people taking up the game saw the creation of organisations to encourage cricket in schools. The new comprehensive schools didn't adopt cricket as readily as public and grammar schools, partly due to expense of equipment and facilities. Studies showed that cricket was generally a sport played in youth and cherished throughout life. It was not common for people to take up the game in adulthood.

English counties were increasingly forced into innovative money-making ploys in order to balance the books. These included running lotteries and other fund-raising events. By the 1960s most counties were propped up by donations from their supporters' clubs. A radical solution was needed and it came in the form of limited-overs cricket. The notion of one-day games had been recommended in a 1956 state of the game report but hadn't initially gained traction with administrators as many thought bowling teams out was an essential element to the game. But the game had become outmoded. In Birley's words:

'County cricket had become a national monument rather than a popular modern attraction.'

The press made the case for a one-day cup competition and with the emergence of sponsorship in sport in the late 1950s cricket finally embraced a commercial lifeline. In 1962 the Midland Counties Knockout Cup was run as a pilot and the following year the MCC sanctioned a 65-over knockout cup for first class counties sponsored by American razor company, Gillette, who were apparently amazed at how little they were asked to contribute. Although 130 overs in a day was very ambitious it nevertheless proved popular with a crowd of 24,000 attending the final at Lord's. The press, who had championed shortened games for years, were encouraging and it was felt that cricket had found its equivalent to the FA Cup and in so doing a popular, modern format that could arrest its decline. Initially it was seen very much as a financial expedient to safeguard the counties and first class cricket. While its popularity was a commercial success many traditionalists were disparaging about the kind of fans it attracted, with an unsavoury association with the populism of football. This would become engrained as one of the themes of cricket in the modern age, protecting its traditions while seeking relevance in changing times.

In parallel with wrestling with its conscience over limited-overs cricket England was also adjusting to the post-war, increasingly post-empire world. India had become independent in 1947 with Pakistan and then Bangladesh created. In the 1960s West Indian states also started to break away. There remained a bond and kinship through the Commonwealth but Britain's direct influence beyond its shores was beginning to wane. This presented a challenge for cricket, but also an opportunity. A challenge because cricket had grown with the empire and therefore there was a risk it could decline with it too. An opportunity because cricket had become defined by imperial ties rather than universal appeal. A depoliticisation of the sport could remove a constraint to its further growth.

Timing is everything in cricket and the sequencing of the gradual retraction of the British empire was important. Had, for instance, it happened after the First World War rather than the Second cricket may not have had sufficient interest or embedded structures to remain a mainstream sport in India, the West Indies or New Zealand. In the case of the West Indies, by the time Jamaica became independent in 1962 the West Indies side was very strong and cricket a very important national and cultural institution. In the 1950s the so-called 'Three Ws', Clyde Walcott, Everton Weekes and Frank Worrell, all born within a few miles of each other in Barbados, had come into the side and forged reputations as world-class batsmen. Together with talented spinners Alf Valentine and Sonny Ramadhin and fast bowler Wes Hall they made a formidable team who were the equal of England and Australia. The real star of the era was Bajan Garfield Sobers, widely considered the best all-rounder to play the game.

Sobers made his Test debut in 1954 as a 17-year-old against England. Primarily in the side as a spinner he took four wickets but also made some useful runs at number nine. His batting ability was soon recognised and he was sent up the order. In 1958 at just 21 years of age he scored his maiden Test century, against Pakistan, in Kingston. He batted on and on, finally making 365 not out to break Len Hutton's world record score made 20 years earlier.

Traditionally the West Indies had always had white captains and this convention continued after the war. However, by the early 1950s this was being challenged by the public and the press and there was widespread approbation in 1954 when leading player Frank Worrell was overlooked in favour of the white Gus Atkinson. The noted historian C.L.R. James championed a black captain and in 1960/61 Worrell was made captain following sustained media pressure and more progressive appointments to the selection panel. Worrell proved an excellent captain and cricket strategist.

Cricket was also prospering in India, who far from jettisoning the English game once they gained independence embraced it wholeheartedly. Although they had played Tests before the war these had been limited to occasional short series against England. After independence they played Bradman's Australia, were narrowly defeated by the West Indies and then recorded a historic first Test win against England in 1952 in their 24th match. They followed this with their first victory over new Test nation Pakistan.

While withdrawal of Britain's direct imperial influence proved a springboard for cricket in India, West Indies and Pakistan, in other parts of the Commonwealth it saw the core of the cricket community, typically British administrators and traders, depart leaving the future of the game vulnerable. This was particularly the case in countries where cricket had remained a British pastime and had not been widely adopted by local populations.

In 1961 South Africa had left the Commonwealth over its apartheid policies and therefore no longer qualified for the ICC. They had, you'll recall, been the original instigators of an imperial conference. With India now an independent nation, West Indies becoming stronger and Pakistan joining in 1952 there was a potential threat to the stranglehold on power and the moral authority the MCC held, along with founder member Australia. It was Pakistan who in 1964 made a proposal for the body to become more inclusive and international in focus. A year later the body was rebranded the International Cricket Conference and the USA, Ceylon and Fiji were admitted. But these new countries were not given equal membership and Test status.

A new 'associate' member category was created for them. In the case of Ceylon cricket was firmly established as a mainstream sport but there was no objective assessment of whether they could play Tests. Instead there was a continuation of the old informal process whereby the MCC made their own judgements of whether teams were strong enough to play Tests. The ICC had originally been established solely to schedule fixtures. Its new associate members didn't have any. In 1966 Bermuda, the Netherlands, Denmark and East Africa joined as associates. They didn't have any fixtures either.

As with its founding, the reconstitution of the ICC in 1965 is fascinating for its lack of ambition. Given its switch to an international body you would have thought it would seek to survey the extent and quality of the game across the world and proactively invite those countries that played cricket or wanted to develop the game to join the organisation. They may even have thought of producing a development plan for the global game or tournament structures for those teams not playing Tests. Or even just allow all teams to play Tests. The fact they didn't do any of these things reveals a lot about how those running the game perceived it. The aims remained to organise fixtures between the leading cricket nations and to ensure the laws were consistently applied. The MCC by convention still provided the president and secretary. The global body of world cricket was run by a couple of Englishmen in a small office at a gentlemen's club in London.

Although there were more members there was an enormous gulf in status and opportunity between the associates and full members. The system was almost designed to prevent the two classes from mixing (that old gentlemen's club analogy works well again!). In 1964 though they did, when the Australian Ashes team stopped off in the Netherlands during the tour. For the Aussies it was a gentle warm-up and the chance to see some sights and sample some advocaat. Or so you'd have thought?

At the picturesque Hague Cricket Ground in front of 3,000 spectators Bill Lawry strode out to open the batting. The tourists struggled on the matting surface that was livened up by a shower of rain. They were pinned down by accurate bowling fully utilising the conditions and despite a late flurry were all out for 197.

It was a disappointing total on a small ground but they'd still expect to defend it. However, they couldn't use their studs due to matting and rubbers took some venom out of their bowling. Opener Marseilles made a solid, well-crafted 77 with the veteran Van Arkel making 45. They'd set a very strong platform but a flurry of wickets saw the game back in the balance. It was then that the free-flowing batsman Rudi Onstein came to the crease and rather than feel the nerves drove Cowper for six. He then scored two boundaries when needing nine off the last over to secure a memorable victory. There followed jubilant scenes as the local crowd savoured this notable feather in the cap. It is a victory still spoken of in Dutch cricket circles to this day. It showed that given opportunities the associates could compete against full members. The sadness is associates were given so few opportunities to do so.

The first limited-overs international match came about through accident rather than design. When the third Test was washed out on the 1970/71 Ashes tour an ODI was arranged for what would have been the fifth day. The organisers were surprised by the level of public interest with 46,000 turning up to watch, enjoying the greater urgency of run-scoring and the athleticism in the field required to counter it. Following this ODIs were added to tour schedules. But the ICC missed an opportunity to extend this status to its growing number of associate nations, enabling them to play recognised international tournaments that could help them raise profile and recognition for the sport in the game's hinterlands.

In 1971 the ICC first discussed the formation of a World Cup and it was eventually staged in England in 1975. Participants were limited to the six full members and two associates, Sri Lanka and East Africa, invited to join. It isn't clear on what basis the decision to include two associates or to exclude the rest was made, beyond perhaps a feeling that Sri Lanka and East Africa may have been the most competitive. This lack of forethought or transparency on decisions impacting associate nations and global development more broadly was to prove a hallmark of ICC governance in the coming decades.

The World Cup, although arguably far too long in coming, provided an opportunity for the game to increase its global profile. The searing pace of Australians Dennis Lillee and Jeff Thomson, who had held sway over England in the preceding winter's Ashes, helped attract the crowds as did the long, uncommonly hot summer days. Prudential, the sponsor, contributed £100,000 and the aggregate attendance was 158,000 with the Australia versus West Indies final being the most profitable one-day match ever staged. The profits were distributed amongst ICC members, including those associates who were not invited to participate.

The inaugural World Cup is also an opportune moment in the history of the game to consider the tradition of cricket broadcasting and the impact it has had. Cricket's ideals of sportsmanship and its nuanced, cerebral appeal proved a good fit with the BBC's founder John Reith's philosophy of public sector broadcasting. Despite the challenge of describing the complexity of cricket on radio, there were simple broadcasts in Australia from 1922 and the BBC made their first cricket broadcast in 1927 and have given the sport considerable air time ever since. In 1930 they covered the Ashes for the first time and in the thirties cabled ball-by-ball updates were used to create remote commentaries. One such, in 1932, was broadcast from the Eiffel Tower.

Radio commentary gained a very loyal and devoted following, especially since the creation of *Test Match Special* in 1957. Cricket is appealing from a broadcast perspective as it can fill daytime schedules where it is often difficult to draw in regular listeners. By the 1930s cricket was the most broadcast sport in England and the extent of media coverage has undoubtedly helped cricket retain a higher profile and cultural significance than indicated in direct participation. The interest in following cricket and the opportunity provided by broadcasters to do so has given cricket a considerable remote audience even though attendances at games has dwindled. This high level of interest has translated into revenue that has become more and more critical to the game.

Initially, cricket authorities did not see broadcasting primarily as a money spinner. The fees paid by the BBC were ostensibly compensation for the lost revenue from their facilities, such as camera platforms. Before the 1950s these payments were only a fraction of the revenue from gate receipts.

Television broadcasting had begun in 1936 and although television sets were very expensive and a signal could only be received in London, the BBC began to plan sports broadcasts. In 1938 they showed Wimbledon, football internationals and the Lord's Test. It was a simple three-camera set-up featuring the batsman, bowler and general crowd, field and atmosphere shots. Teddy Wakelam, the established voice of cricket on the radio, was the commentator. It proved popular, although this was all relative with only around 7,000 sets in the country and the broadcast only accessible within 20 miles of the transmitter on Alexandra Tower. The press welcomed the innovation not only for enabling viewers to watch the match remotely but also to feel part of the atmosphere in the ground. Later in the year Len Hutton's world record score of 364 was televised.

During the 1950s revenue from television rights exceeded those from radio. By 1965, by which time one-day cricket was being played, the BBC paid £50,000 to broadcast the summer of cricket. This was not only a source of revenue in its own right but also critical in securing sponsorship deals, with Gillette and the tobacco companies wanting their branding to be seen in the nation's homes. Sponsors and broadcasters proved the stimuli for further tournaments to be added to the county roster, such as the John Player League on Sundays from 1969 and the Benson and Hedges Cup in 1972. The cricket schedule was beginning to be shaped by commercial considerations. BBC Test coverage in the early 1960s often topped five million viewers for the evening session although this had declined by the end of the decade.

Chapter 11

Kerry Packer and the threat to the establishment

THE commercial potential of cricket demonstrated by healthy broadcast audiences and the marketability of the new limited-overs formats brought tensions into the game following the first World Cup. If cricket was getting wealthier, who were the beneficiaries and were they making the most of the opportunity? The status quo and the control exerted by the game's traditional power brokers was about to be threatened by a larger-than-life Australian entrepreneur by the name of Kerry Packer. Australian cricket had introduced a one-day tournament in 1968 and a sponsorship deal with British American Tobacco. This included greater consideration of payments for players rather than all profits being redistributed back to state boards. At the time players' wages were relatively low in comparison with other sports and certainly as a percentage of the growing money in the game. The mid-seventies was also a time when there was a growing divide between wizened, old-school administrators, like Donald Bradman, and young, aspiring players. On the pitch the almost absurd disparity between old and new was symbolised by the encounter between 42-year-old gent Colin Cowdrey and abrasive young quick Jeff Thomson, who, when offered a hand by the esteemed veteran, told him to 'Bugger off, Fatso.'

Leading cricketers struggled to make a decent living and looked on enviously at other sportsmen enjoying the fruits of celebrity. Packer, the son of a media mogul, was in his late thirties and looking for opportunities to grow his portfolio. Encouraged by the viewing figures for the World Cup, he offered the board a bumper $2.5 million deal for exclusive TV rights to Australian cricket, but was told the rights had already been acquired by state broadcaster ABC. Assuming money would prompt a reconsideration he said, 'Come on gentlemen, we're all whores. What's your price?' and offered many times the value. But there was not a deal to be done. It wasn't that commercial stations hadn't shown an interest in cricket before – Ashes and West Indies tours had been shown on occasion – but rather that in ambition and exclusivity Packer's offer was a game-changer.

Incandescent but undeterred, Packer had the resolve to go his own way and with the help of Dennis Lillee's manager, Austin Robertson, the recently retired Ian Chappell and England captain Tony Greig, formed World Series Cricket. Greig signed up leading players from the West Indies, Pakistan and South Africa with the promise of higher wages and high-quality cricket. The fact so many signed without hesitation to what was at the time such a speculative venture reveals how discontented they were at their stake in the growing business of cricket. Naturally such a bold concept gaining such wholehearted endorsement from the leading players of the day aroused the suspicions of cricket authorities. To what extent would the World Series wrest control of their cricket schedule? Would it pose a threat to the traditions of the game and tear cricket itself?

Packer met the ICC and was conciliatory but confident, limiting his desire to securing broadcasting rights rather than overturning the game. His request for exclusive rights was again rebuffed and furthermore those that had signed his contracts were blacklisted from international cricket. The authorities had taken a stand and with it an almighty gamble. Packer's resolve hardened further and he moved the dates of his Supertests to coincide with Australian Test matches in the coming summer. He also took the ICC to court and won, with the judgement that the banning of players was unreasonable and that players had a right to be beneficiaries of the profits the modern game was capable of generating. It was a victory for player power over the establishment. Sydney Barnes would have been very proud.

While Packer had scored a notable victory on behalf of players that was to have far-reaching consequences, his Supertests only attracted modest crowds in the first summer, despite the star quality on display. Staging the games was a colossal undertaking, having to lay drop-in pitches in other sports stadia and launching an unprecedented marketing machine. For cricket it was a glimpse into the future with coloured clothing, floodlights, a white ball and the glitz and glamour of an entertainment event. It helped popularise the one-day format which despite the World Cup the year before was still not fully entrenched in the cricket public's psyche. Unburdened by the stipulations of authorities, he was free to innovate and he threw money at the spectacle, employing multiple cameras, the latest replay technology, graphics, on-field microphones and the works. A simple innovation was to always show coverage from behind the bowler's arm, rather than just from one end. This wasn't replicating being sat in a fixed position at the ground but a new immersive televisual experience for cricket fans. Advertising and sponsorship were maximised at every opportunity. It cost a hell of a lot of money but such was the size of Packer's empire it wasn't a commercial risk. The whole enterprise was insulated from failure.

The relative failure of the first season had been put down to the distaste amongst many fans that it was all for the money. Many, so the logic goes, wanted their cricketers inspired by pride and sporting valour. Realising that star quality alone wasn't enough, in its second season Packer launched a marketing campaign that tapped into Australian patriotism, pitting their all-stars against the world. With this attractive pitch and access secured to the SCG it worked and the crowds came in droves. Australia lost six Tests that year in front of dwindling audiences while Packer staged game after game. Packer was primed to take over world cricket. But knowing he was in a position of strength to achieve his objective of exclusive rights he signed a ten-year deal. The Board, with an almighty sigh of relief, got control of the game back and Packer got a long-term deal at an excellent price.

The players returned to the official fold but animosities remained for years to come. Packer's deal saw basic wages rise but he took control of image and merchandising rights, ensuring players remained servants to the cause. As Gideon Haigh, author of a book on the Packer revolution, noted: 'World Series Cricket precipitated more innovation and experimentation in two years than establishment cricket had in probably the entire three decades since the Second World War.' Even a casual follower of the game would recognise the Packer reforms as the foundations of modern cricket in the sports entertainment age, but though he left a legacy to the game it didn't fully materialise for several decades. Establishment cricket had been given the shock of its life and its distaste for the vulgarity of profit over spirit, of fan spectacle over the sport's traditional rhythms was confronted with what must have seemed, to many, the death of cricket as they knew it. But, seen another way, cricket had been shown how it could compete for relevance, audience and financial might in the modern era of sports business.

Despite the challenge and resultant impetus provided by Packer, cricket entered the consumerist decade of the 1980s slightly uncertain of itself. In Britain the government's social survey of 1965 showed cricket as the most popular outdoor sport. By the end of the decade it had slipped to tenth behind golf, tennis and bowls. In 1979 cricket was second behind football as a spectator sport, albeit falling increasingly far behind its winter competitor. By 1983 it had slipped behind horse racing and rugby. Football had received a boost from the World Cup win in '66 and the profile of international heroes such as Pele. The Football League saw headline-grabbing million-pound transfers. Golf and tennis were soaring in popularity too and seemed to fit with the image of the times, with Ballesteros, Faldo, Edberg and Borg becoming household names and the darlings of advertising. You could imagine Faldo in a polo neck driving a Porsche in a Sunday magazine glossy. Harder to do with Boycott or Emburey.

In the Thatcher era aspiration was everything and time was money. The grind of Test cricket didn't quite fit the mould. By 1980 the leisure industry was worth £600m, a growth of 42% since 1970 and an incredible 76% from 1960. Packer showed that cricket could claim its share but did it have the will and the dynamism to throw off an increasingly staid image? With cricket an increasingly marginal sport in state schools and local cricket's pastoral charms not chiming with increasingly urban-focused trends, the sport was in urgent need of inspiring idols. Two young Somerset colleagues were to step into public consciousness.

Ian Botham had been born in Cheshire in 1955 but moved to Somerset as a young boy, where he excelled at sport as a schoolboy and as a 16-year-old was offered professional contracts as a cricketer and footballer. While serving on the ground staff at Lord's he learnt how to swing the ball and broke into the Somerset team in 1973 and then the England side in 1976. His youthful exuberance and dynamism were a counterpoint to the dour style of Boycott, who returned in 1977 after a self-imposed four-year exile, and the impact of Greig's absence at World

Series Cricket. He won the *Wisden* Young Cricketer of the Year award in 1977. But to judge Botham by statistics, however good they were, is to underestimate his impact. It was his will to win, his lust for life and his strength of personality that pulled up English cricket by its bootstraps.

In 1980 England captain Mike Brearley had announced his retirement and the selectors chose Botham to replace him despite his youth and lack of leadership experience. It proved to be a disastrous tenure, with the team losing and his personal form deserting him. The press rounded on the ECB for saddling their enigmatic all-rounder with the burden of captaincy with predictably disappointing results. Botham resigned rather than be sacked after bagging a pair in the Lord's Ashes Test of 1981. Brearley was brought back from retirement to steady the ship. But Botham's redemption was to be the story of the summer and the Leeds Test one of the most celebrated in history. Botham had bowled with a point to prove in Australia's first innings but despite his six-for the tourists still posted over 400. Botham then scored a half-century but England were bustled out for 174 and, following on, were on the brink of defeat at 135/7. Bookmakers put odds of 500/1 on an England victory. But Botham refused to roll over and with resolute support from the tail hit a swashbuckling 149 not out, leaving Australia a modest 130 for victory. Botham took the first wicket and then fast bowler Bob Willis took 8-43 to claim an improbable, remarkable victory by 19 runs. His miraculous return to form continued in the following Tests to see England win the series.

The result propelled Botham to stardom and national treasure status. He was the talisman of the side and his lifestyle off the pitch hit the front pages as his performances on it dominated the back. The media followed his often stormy private life, his prodigious capacity for revelry on tour and his outspoken views with relish. His profile was more akin to a football star or film icon than a cricketer. Despite declining performances after the age of 30 the strength of character remained and his presence alone gave English cricket a cache and profile that belied signs of decline. In challenging the establishment he joined a long line of anti-heroes that won the public's heart, such as Sydney Barnes and more recently the straight-talking Yorkshire fast bowler Fred Trueman. Botham enjoyed the trappings of fame and his conspicuous consumption was very on trend in the 80s while his no-nonsense, fiercely competitive approach helped break through cricket's stuffy image.

A player that emerged at the same time as Botham and who also played over a hundred Tests for his country was David Gower. Perhaps the most graceful batsman ever to play the game, his ethereal looks, effortless style and understated charm made him a darling of fans and in some ways a throwback to the more easy-going, amateur spirit of the past. As Britain became more multicultural after waves of post-war immigration so the team evolved too. Roland Butcher and Gladstone Small were selected from the growing West Indian community, who helped add numbers and vibrancy to the crowds, and South African emigres such as Robin Smith and Allan Lamb came to England to play Test cricket while their home team remained in the international wilderness due to apartheid.

By the late 70s the West Indies were the best side in the world. The heroes of earlier eras had inspired the next generations and the islands became a production line of world class players. Not only was cricket the predominant sport, despite often rudimentary facilities, but there was a very strong sense of national and racial pride that underpinned their dominance. There was a point to prove to their former colonial masters of course, beating them at their own game. But this period also coincided with the apartheid era in South Africa and the West Indian team saw themselves as the champions of black identity and equal rights. Being champions of the world in the white sport meant more than just personal and national pride.

The West Indies were famous for a seemingly endless supply of fast bowlers. The tallest of them, Joel Garner, was a team-mate of Botham at Somerset. Tourists to the Caribbean not only faced the technical challenge of playing the best team in the world but the physical and psychological battle of taking guard against their battery of quicks. It was not for the faint-hearted and many returned home with bodies and egos bruised and nerves in tatters. For all their bowling strength it was a batsman that embodied the confidence and swagger of West Indian cricket, the Antiguan Viv Richards. Antigua is a small nation in the Leeward Islands, away from the main centres of Jamaica, Barbados and Trinidad. It was over 40 years after the West Indies first played Tests that a Leeward Islander has been selected. The selectors started to scout the smaller islands and in 1974 Antigua celebrated as their fast bowler Andy Roberts was picked. This gave cricketers on the island hope they could follow in his footsteps.

Richards had learned cricket in the streets and recreation grounds of St John's, his father pushing him hard to work and improve at his game. By 19 he was playing for the island team and in his early twenties his talent was spotted by the vice chairman of Somerset who invited over for a trial. His expansive style of play was just the tonic required in England, where cautious accumulators were still the stock in trade in county cricket. He made his debut in the same match as Botham and shared a flat with his team-mate in Taunton. A Test debut followed in 1974 against India in Bangalore, where he admitted to being a bit overawed by the crowd and distracted by the small mirrors some in the crowd used to put him off as he prepared to face each delivery. But he made 192 in the second innings to announce his talent to the cricketing world.

In 1975 Richards was part of the World Cup-winning team at Lord's, his athletic fielding proving a particular highlight. The following year the West Indians returned to England for a Test series. It was one of the hottest summers on record and the outfields were golden and grassless. The team enjoyed huge, passionate support from the West Indian diaspora and there was a carnival atmosphere at the grounds, especially in London. The England captain Tony Greig charged the atmosphere further with an ill-advised interview before the series in which he said, 'The West Indians if they get on top are magnificent cricketers, but if they are down they grovel. And I intend to make them grovel.' Coming from a man with a strong South African accent in the height of apartheid the racial undertones were unmistakable. The West Indian team watching the interview bristled with anger and it fired them up even further to prove a point. Greig himself took a battering in the series, targeted with particular hostility by Roberts, Holding and Croft. In the fifth match at the Oval Richards scored 291 to round off a personal triumph and a comprehensive victory for the West Indies. Greig saw the funny side and got on his knees to grovel himself. In four Tests Richards scored 829 runs at an average of 118. It was his summer and at times it looked like he was playing a different game to everyone else. Richards also acknowledged the duty the team felt to give the West Indian population something to believe in. The tour was of socio-cultural as well as sporting importance.

It was Richards's fearless style and swagger that made him one of the greats. He had free-flowing shots all around the wicket and often played audacious strokes that showed disdain for the bowling. He couldn't be subdued and never backed down from any stares from a bowler. If he got hit by a short ball he'd hook the next ball for six. When he walked out to bat, casually chewing gum, he looked like nothing could phase him. After that series the team just got stronger and stronger as talented players were introduced. There were fast bowlers that in any other era would be world beaters that couldn't force their way into the squad. During Richards's match-winning century in the World Cup Final of 1979 Richie Benaud on commentary noted after a slap through the covers 'there was a certain air of contempt about that'. That was how he played. The statistics demonstrate that too. In an era when a strike rate of over 60 was considered fast scoring even in limited-overs cricket, Richards's was over 90. In his own way he was as distinctive statistically as Don Bradman. When asked whether this was a deliberate tactic he replied simply: 'Us Caribbean folks like to hit the ball.' The West Indian brand of cricket was simple, uncomplicated and passionate.

The unity of the West Indian team was to be challenged when players were offered huge money to play in rebel tours in South Africa. The sporting world had shunned South Africa due to the apartheid racial policies of the white supremacist government of De Klerk but the regime was desperate to lure rebel tours to the country and many, putting principles aside when large cheques were presented, took up the offer. The West Indies public stood in solidarity with the oppressed black community and saw any even indirect support for the apartheid regime as a betrayal. Richards and most of the team stood by their principles and refused to go. The most high-profile West Indian to take part was fast bowler Colin Croft. As a result not only did he face exclusion from the national team, a price he knew he'd pay for joining the rebels, but more significantly he was disowned by many in the Caribbean and chose to settle instead in the USA to avoid the enduring social stigma of his decision.

Many fans and players of the modern era point to the West Indian team of the late 70s and 80s as instilling in them a passion and joy for the game. But their dominance also saw a shift in cricket's fulcrum away from traditional, established old order to newer, fresher cricketing nations. England were playing catch-up.

Chapter 12

The rise of India

WHILE the West Indies began to dominate, India too became a greater cricketing force. By the late 70s they had a world-class opening batsman in Sunil Gavaskar, who would go on to be the first to score 10,000 Test match runs, and a formidable spin quartet of Chandrasekhar, Bedi, Prasanna and Venkat. They had established a reputation for being hard to beat at home in the 1960s and were also becoming more competitive away. They'd beaten England away in 1971 and at home in 1972/73. But the real turning point for Indian cricket came at the World Cup of 1983.

India went into the tournament as an unfancied side playing in English conditions that were very different to those they faced at home. They had a few quality players in Gavaskar and Amarnath but most of the squad were relatively unheralded and they lacked the superstars and high-impact players of the West Indies and Australia. The West Indies had been world champions twice and had won a remarkable 38 out of 52 ODIs since the format was introduced. In comparison India had won only 12 of 40. They had flopped at the previous World Cup in 1979 and their only victory in the two tournaments had been against associate side East Africa. The bookies had them at 66/1 to lift the trophy.

The captain was 23-year-old all-rounder Kapil Dev, an outswing bowler and destructive batsman. He had been picked by India as a teenager and quickly became the leading fast bowler in the country and a national star for his heroics in a series win over Pakistan in 1978/79. By 1980 he had become the youngest player to reach the milestone of 1,000 runs and 100 wickets in Tests. He played through pain-killing injections in the 1980 tour of Australia to help draw the series. But there followed a few fallow years and India turned to their enigmatic all-rounder to rejuvenate the team. It was a situation reminiscent of Botham's promotion to captaincy, but Kapil proved better suited to the responsibility.

The captain aside, India relied on canny medium-pacers bowling to disciplined plans to apply scoreboard pressure. They weren't going to blow a team away like Holding, Marshall and Roberts. In the group stages the plan worked with a disciplined win over the West Indies. But they then lost two of their next three games and were an improbable 9/4 against Zimbabwe at the unlikely venue of Royal Tunbridge Wells when Kapil came to the crease. They were soon 17/5. What followed was one of the most remarkable innings ever seen in limited-overs cricket as the captain led a recovery, finishing on 175 not out off 138 balls taking his team to a total of 266.

They won the game and made it into uncharted territory, the semi-finals of a World Cup. They beat England at Old Trafford and faced the West Indies in the final. Put into bat at Lord's India struggled against the pace attack with no batsman making a half century, but the tail wagged a little and took the total to 183. It didn't seem enough against a strong West Indies batting order. After all, Richards had memorably toyed with the bowling in the 1979 final. But the morning sun had given way to afternoon cloud cover by the time of the West Indies reply and the medium pace of Madan Lal and Sandhu choked the scoring rate and offered little to break the shackles. The pressure told as the West Indies fell to 76/6 with the captain taking a superb over-the-shoulder catch to dismiss Richards for 33. Dujon led a recovery with sensible, disciplined batting but Madan Lal returned to clean up the tail and India were champions.

Wisden's notes in the 1984 almanack that followed called the win 'unexpected' and noted that the team were 'feted the length and breadth of the land' on their victorious return. Given its anglo-centric viewpoint it didn't chose to reflect that the tournament marked a broader rise of Asian cricket, with Pakistan also appearing in the semi-finals. On the field India didn't capitalise on the victory straight away, with a humiliating series loss against the West Indies leading many to see the World Cup win as an aberration in the general order of the game. But the population had been gripped, the younger generations enthused and the still relatively young nation had become a world champion. This undoubtedly helped ingrain cricket further into the country's soul and in so doing laid the foundations for future success. Kapil Dev and Pakistani Imran Khan were to enjoy long and distinguished careers and were classed alongside Botham and New Zealander Richard Hadlee as the great all-rounders of the era.

Chapter 13

An expanding game

BY 1984 the international game had opened up further to give more opportunities to countries beyond the Test match nations. The addition of new members since the mid-sixties had seen a broader range of voices in committee meetings, albeit influence and governance was tightly controlled by the founding members. Associate nations were not permitted to play Test matches or bilateral ODIs (outside of a World Cup) and unlike full members didn't automatically feature in World Cups. Pakistan had been very encouraging to new members and sought to fight their corner for increased opportunity. This helped establish a qualification process for the World Cup in 1979. This took the form of the ICC Trophy, which all associate members were permitted to enter.

The ICC Trophy was the first ICC-endorsed tournament for its non-Test countries introduced 14 years after the creation of the associate member category. The announcement of the tournament had an immediate impact with countries like the Netherlands, Denmark and Bermuda creating international tours to prepare for the tournament. The first tournament featured Argentina, Bangladesh, Bermuda, Canada, Denmark, East Africa, Fiji, Israel, Malaysia, the Netherlands, PNG, Singapore, Sri Lanka and the USA. Wales, part of English cricket jurisdiction, were added as a guest team.

These countries fell into several categories. Firstly there were Sri Lanka and Bangladesh, where cricket was the national sport. Sri Lanka had a structured national tournament from 1938, played biennial tournaments against India and was a regular staging post for touring teams. In 1964 they had beaten a Pakistan A team and in 1965 had beaten India in a four-day first class fixture. Following these victories the Sri Lankan board were keen to further their case for Test status with a tour to England in 1968 but troubles generating finance and arguments between the selectors, some of whom were very keen to select themselves, saw the tour cancelled. But they found an ally in the Pakistan board whose president, Oxford-educated Abdul Kardar, who had represented India prior to partition and is widely credited with popularising the sport in his homeland, was so impressed with the quality of Sri Lanka in 1972/73 that he petitioned the ICC for their elevation. His plea may have been instrumental in the ICC's invitation to Sri Lanka to play in the 1975 World Cup. During that tournament they drew witness to their calibre by running Australia close. The following year their domestic tournament was remodelled and provided a ready-made basis for a first class structure.

Being part of greater India, cricket had been played in Bangladesh for centuries before the area was hived off on religious grounds as East Pakistan after partition in 1947. Although geographically distant from so called West Pakistan, where the seat of power lay, Bangladesh teams were incorporated into first class competitions. They also played touring sides such as India and the MCC in the fifties and Dhaka hosted Pakistan Test matches through the 1960s. Tensions between West and East came to a head in 1971 after what was perceived to be a lax response to the civil emergency caused by cyclone Bhola. The ensuing nationalist movement led to a bloody and bitter liberation war that finally led to independence in December 1971.

The new nation endured a difficult infancy with famine, unrest and a succession of military coups. Nevertheless, cricket was prioritised and an official cricket board created in 1972 with a domestic structure put in place. By 1977, with the country finally finding some much needed stability, an official national team was formed and hosted the MCC. This led to Bangladesh being made an associate member that year. Sri Lanka toured in 1978 but a series of innings victories by the visitors showed a gulf in ability and accordingly Bangladesh games were not awarded first class status. The ICC Trophy presented an opportunity to gauge their quality against other associate nations. Whatever the quality cricket certainly had the interest, visibility and political support to flourish.

The second category consisted of former colonial outposts where cricket was long established but had remained a secondary sport with limited cultural capital when the British had withdrawn. This group included

Singapore, Malaysia, Papua New Guinea and East Africa. Of these the most established team was East Africa, who had been invited to participate in the inaugural World Cup. East Africa consisted of Kenya, Uganda, Tanzania and Zambia. Cricket had first been organised on the colonial model but locals had adopted the game to a degree and economic migration from India, initially to build the railways but then settling as merchants and traders, had created a multi-ethnic cricket community and a network of clubs, especially in Kenya and Uganda. The collective became an associate member in 1966 and India and the MCC toured, with the separate constituent members playing their own quadrangular tournament in between. In 1972 they were invited to tour the UK by the MCC and played 18 one-day fixtures, including some against county sides. It was perhaps a Commonwealth paternalism that saw such proactive support, that three years later saw East Africa invited to join the World Cup.

Cricket in Malaysia had grown in popularity after the war and a national board was created in 1948 (that included Singapore until its independence in 1965) but there was not a competitive domestic tournament and although they hosted an MCC tour the establishment didn't adopt their cause in the same way as East Africa. In Papua New Guinea cricket was a mix between expats in the capital Port Moresby and locals in the outlying villages, where it was a major pastime for young and old alike albeit on a relatively small scale. Cricket in Fiji hadn't sustained its strength from its Golden Age around the turn of the century but was relatively established with a core of local, indigenous players. The British had introduced cricket to Israel but it had almost died out in the 1950s before emigrants from England, India and South Africa had helped revive the game in the late 1960s.

The next category was the long since independent North American countries of Canada and the USA. As we've seen, both played to a relatively high standard earlier in the century but cricket had been pushed to the sporting fringes by baseball, American football and in Canada's case ice hockey. Club cricket had survived and become a socio-cultural magnet for increasingly multicultural communities. The Canadian squad was made up largely of West Indian emigrants, a Ugandan and a few local players. Sadly, the Philadelphian legacy hasn't lasted in the USA and the team comprised emigrants from the West Indies and the subcontinent. This multicultural make-up reflected broader American society and clearly marked the US as an exciting potential growth area for cricket. But it was also testament to the fact that cricket hadn't entered the socio-cultural landscape of the country as a whole and its appeal was largely confined to communities with their own cricket heritage.

This leaves countries without any historical connections to empire or the Commonwealth. Argentina, who you'll recall had played at first class level early in the century, did retain a devoted, albeit small-scale, local cricket following based on several historic clubs and cricket-playing schools. It was a marginal sport in comparison to football and rugby, but it was local. Though football had come to completely dominate the sporting scene in Europe there had been encouraging signs of growth in both Denmark and the Netherlands.

A relatively small but proud and committed club structure had survived the war and in both countries cricket had begun to reach out beyond its traditional upper-middle class, private school player base.

An outlier to this categorisation was Bermuda, still a British overseas territory, where cricket was a national passion but where the player base was tiny in comparison to its competitors.

With such a mix of teams with different backgrounds and histories the first ICC Trophy proved a fascinating barometer of the strength and characteristics of global cricket beyond its main centres. Denmark, Bermuda and Sri Lanka topped their respective groups, with Canada the last semi-finalist. Sri Lanka's quality shone through with a demolition of Denmark, when they made 318 and bowled out the Danes for 110. Canada came through quite a close game with Bermuda but were well beaten by Sri Lanka in the final. The finalists qualified for the World Cup played directly afterwards in the English summer. It had confirmed Sri Lanka as the heir apparent to full member status but also showed that some of the stronger teams at associate level came from beyond the Commonwealth. The ICC's faith in East Africa hadn't been repaid.

Canada really struggled in the World Cup itself, making an excruciating 45 off 40 overs against England at Old Trafford. Sri Lanka fared better, securing a historic victory over India that helped secure them elevation to full member status in 1981. With sponsorship and gate receipts the tournament made over £500,000, with £350,000 surplus distributed to members. This was undoubtedly an invaluable source of revenue for the associate boards to develop cricket in their regions. Though not mentioned in the *Wisden* review in 1980, a key factor in the first two global tournaments was audience and broadcaster opinion on whether the tournament should be exclusive to ensure close matches or be inclusive to bring further teams to the global stage and global TV audiences to raise profile and serve as a springboard for development. The fact that the tournament did not enlarge despite an increasing number of associate nations indicates that the ICC remained squarely focused on the leading nations. The competitiveness of the tournament itself was the primary objective rather than its potential role as a vehicle for growth of the global game.

This is seen by the fact that the following ICC Trophy, held in England in 1982, had 16 teams but only one qualifying spot available. Although Sri Lanka now didn't need to pre-qualify their place was taken by newly independent Zimbabwe, an established cricket-playing culture with a first class structure. Unsurprisingly they went on to win the tournament and claim the World Cup spot. This lack of opportunity must have been dispiriting for teams with such a slim chance of qualifying. This included Bangladesh, making their debut in 1982, who made the semi-finals but lost to Zimbabwe.

The second ICC Trophy in 1982 saw several teams make their debut in official ICC tournaments. Along with Bangladesh and Zimbabwe, West Africa, Hong Kong and Gibraltar participated for the first time, with Kenya playing in their own right alongside an East Africa composite team. Gibraltar and Hong Kong followed a similar template to Singapore, small British colonial outposts with a long cricket history but a small player base. The West Africa team consisted of Nigeria, Gambia, Ghana and Sierra Leone. By the early 1980s cricket had 25 teams, covering 30 countries, competing in officially endorsed tournaments. It had gained strong new cricket centres in Sri Lanka, Bangladesh and Zimbabwe that increased the level of competition. Asia with three Test nations had the most of any region, with two in Australasia and one each in Europe, Africa and the Americas. Amongst associates there was relatively good global coverage, albeit largely covering a Commonwealth blueprint. There were gaps in North Africa, South America, Eurasia and the Gulf. It was hard to argue it was a global game.

In 1984 as Viv Richards led the West Indies to a blackwash, Simone Gambino, a passionate champion of Italian cricket, was in London drumming up support for his idea to broaden the global cricket community still further. A great admirer of the MCC as the guardians of the game and seeking official recognition for the embryonic cricket community in Italy, he had been thwarted by the governance and scale requirements for associate membership. Lacking government endorsement in Italy and unable to meet the thresholds for numbers of teams, he proposed a new emerging cricket category of membership. With influential backers and a steely determination he succeeded and Italy became the first affiliate member. In the next four years Switzerland, the Bahamas, France and Nepal became fellow affiliates. Beyond recognition it wasn't immediately clear what Simone and the affiliates had gained. There were no voting rights, no funding and no fixtures.

※ ※ ※

One of the ball boys at the 1987 World Cup was a young lad from Bombay called Sachin Tendulkar. He had been a bully as a young boy and was introduced to cricket in the hope it would channel his energy and focus, and it certainly did. He spent countless hours at the Shivaji Park on the island of Dadar, often referred to as the cradle of Indian cricket as many greats of the game, including Gavaskar, had learnt their cricket there. He was taken under the wing of famous Mumbai coach Ramakant Achrekar and trained at Shivaji before and after school every day. His coach encouraged him to switch to a noted cricket-playing school where he fast became a schoolboy prodigy. To encourage toiling bowlers at net sessions in Shivaji, Achrekar put a coin on the top of Tendulkar's stumps, which they could claim if they dismissed him. Tendulkar would keep the coin if he survived the whole session. Sachin often took the coin home.

In 1988 in a schools competition named after Lord Harris, still part of the game's narrative long after he passed, Tendulkar compiled a world record 664-run partnership with his friend and future India team-mate Vinod Kambli. It is said that the two boys reduced the bowlers to tears in the Herculean feat which was widely reported and gave them early celebrity. It cemented Tendulkar's reputation as a future star. Despite being just 15 years of age, Tendulkar was selected for his first class debut for Mumbai after selectors witnessed him getting the better of Kapil Dev in the nets. The years of constant practice was paying off and his rise was simply irresistible. He duly became the youngest Indian to make a century on first class debut in the Ranji Trophy and went on to make a century on debut in the Deodhar and Duleep Trophies too. He was India's darling son and the whole country was wondering how soon he would win international honours. After averaging 68 in his first season it was clear he was good enough and for the selectors it was just a case of when to introduce him. He was discussed for the West Indies tour but the selectors were wary of exposing a schoolboy to the barrage of West Indian quicks. Later in the year, at the tender age of 16 years and 205 days, he made his debut against Pakistan in Karachi. He was India's youngest Test cricketer and arguably the most talented, complete schoolboy cricketer the world had ever seen. If Boris Johnson had written about the young cricketer he would have surely described him as 'oven ready' to dominate the international game. Though only making 15 he impressed with his maturity, temperament and technique, and showed courage in playing on after getting a bloody nose from a spell of Waqar Younis chin music.

It was clear to all that the young prodigy from Mumbai would be a star of the game as the 1990s dawned. In August he made a famous maiden century at Old Trafford, the second youngest to do so, a precocious 17-year-old with the world at his feet.

Meanwhile, on the other side of the world another young cricketer was making a name for himself. Brian Lara was born in Santa Cruz, Trinidad, in 1969, four years before his Indian counterpart. One of 11 siblings his father enrolled him in Sunday coaching clinics at the age of six. By his early teens he was a class above his contemporaries averaging a frankly absurd 127 in the school league. At

15 he was selected for the West Indian Under-19 team. In 1987 he broke the run scoring record at West Indian youth level that had been recently set by Carl Hooper. The following year, at 18, he made his first class debut. He came into the game when West Indies were at their peak with the domestic tournament containing enough quality quicks to fill half a dozen international attacks. In that environment you had to have something special to stand out, and he did. In only his second game he made 92 against a Barbados attack including the legendary Malcolm Marshall and Joel Garner. The innings that really announced his talent to the wider world was a 182 against the touring India team. This saw him selected for the West Indies in 1989 and he was set to enter Test cricket in the same year as Tendulkar but fate intervened and he withdrew after the devastating loss of his father. He made his debut a year later against Pakistan.

Lara and Tendulkar had broken into their national teams at a similar time with their respective countries at different stages of their journeys. India had been on the rise since their World Cup victory and were beginning to flex their financial might and exert more influence on the global game. On the pitch they were competitive but not yet a dominant force in all conditions. In contrast the West Indies had dominated the game in the 1980s with a golden generation of established stars and a psychological grip galvanised by unity and passion to champion black power in the face of apartheid. Lara and Tendulkar were part of a new generation including Atherton, Younis and Warne that were coming into the game at a pivotal point it its history. It was set to lose its carefree innocence in a bitter power struggle between its traditional guardians and the new power brokers of the game and in the process vie with other sports in the business of entertainment.

※ ※ ※

The 1990s was to be a pivotal decade in the history of the game and it began with the emotional release of Nelson Mandela from prison after 27 years. This accelerated negotiations to end the oppressive apartheid regime that had seen them frozen out of the ICC for 20 years. Cricket had continued in the country thanks in no small part to Ali Bacher's South Africa Cricket Association that organised cricket on a multi-racial basis. A series of controversial rebel tours by 'de facto' international touring sides had also provided impetus and enabled South Africa to keep pace to a degree. The formal boycott of South African sport meant the rebels were rebuked and suspended by their boards, even though SACA sought to distance cricket from any tacit endorsement of the racially motivated political ideology of the country. Fast bowler Colin Croft, one of the highest-profile West Indian rebels, was vilified back home to the extent where he chose to resettle in the USA. Mike Gatting's tour of 1989 drew a huge public outcry and angry crowds protesting at the matches. At press conferences Gatting was lambasted for leaving his morals aside for a lucrative pay cheque.

When apartheid legislation was repealed the year after Mandela's release, Lord Cowdrey as chairman of the ICC acted swiftly to welcome South Africa back into the fold with just enough time for them to feature in the 1992 World Cup. It was too late for legends of an earlier era such as Barry Richards and Mike Procter to grace the international game again but it did see the likes of Kepler Wessels, who had moved to Australia and represented them, Clive Rice and Peter Kirsten realise a lifelong dream. Forty-year-old spinner Omar Henry became the first non-white player to represent South Africa in the post-apartheid era.

The 1992 World Cup, the first to be played in the southern hemisphere, was a jazzed-up affair featuring coloured kits, white balls, black sight screens and floodlit matches. It was cricket with a modern sheen and embracing the entertainment age and the rich rewards this brought. England could still not manage to be crowned champions in the sport they had invented, losing a thrilling final to Imran Khan's Pakistan. Despite the growth in membership it remained a small, elite tournament. The ICC may have been welcoming new members but they weren't enabling them to dance on the global stage. It is a tournament still fondly remembered by many as the classic World Cup and its success brought pressure on two traditional tenets of the game: England's guardianship and the primacy of Test cricket. Zimbabwe, who had been dominant at associate level, performed with credit at global events and had an established first class structure, were admitted as the ninth full member shortly after the tournament.

Chapter 14

England loses its grip

WHILE cricket was expanding its membership and beginning to take advantage of the financial opportunities of the sports business age its governance had remained virtually unchanged since 1909. The MCC had feudal overlordship and had run, or at least sought to run, the ICC as its imperial branch. But with new members bringing new votes and financial power shifting to Asia it could not go on as it had. It came to a head in an infamously fractious annual meeting in February 1993. The substantive issue was confirming the location for the 1996 World Cup. It had previously been agreed it would be hosted in England but India wanted it themselves and requested multiple adjournments of the meeting to consult India's Lord Chief Justice on how to amend ICC voting laws to reverse the decision.

ICC voting had become more complex with the increase in its associate members. Although full members had two votes each they could theoretically be outvoted by the 19 associate nations who had one vote each. This had led to a rule change where two-thirds of full members were needed to pass a majority on a binding decision and one of these had to be a founding member, England or Australia. This veto for founding members had been agreed by India but they then contended that the destination for the World Cup should not be categorised as a binding decision and therefore a simple majority vote should apply. Given World Cup hosting was the principle reason for calling the meeting it seemed churlish in the extreme to claim it wasn't a binding decision. In preparation for taking this stance India and its subcontinental supporters had courted favour with the associate nations by offering a bigger cut of funding and they applied pressure on Zimbabwe who they had championed for elevation to full membership. The meeting went on long into the night and in the end England's Test and County Cricket Board capitulated on the proviso that they would definitely host the 1999 World Cup.

A decision had been reached but the ramifications went much further than merely who would host the next World Cup. It was announced that David Richards, chief executive of the Australian Cricket Board, would become chief executive of the ICC later that year, signalling the end of the MCC's influence. England had also ensured that the profits from the 1996 World Cup would be reserved to fund the ICC secretariat. TCCB head, A. C. Smith, pulled no punches in describing the meeting as the worst he had ever attended with no talk of cricket whatsoever. It was a watershed moment in the game. Many in Britain lamented the politicisation of the game and the capricious effect of profit over principle that signalled a loss of innocence. It had all worked perfectly well, the argument went, on the basis of goodwill and focusing on the spirit of cricket. Cricket had always pursued purity and the ugly spectre of profit and politics had conspired to pollute the game. Even the term purist is used far more in cricket than any other game. 'I make no apology for being a purist,' many cricket fans will declare. But this view came from a country that had run the game, had ensured they were protected with a veto and ran cricket like the Commonwealth. It was understandable others may question this hegemony and want a share of the power, even if their methods lacked, what more fitting word, grace. Understandable too that management of a multi-million-pound global sport may have outgrown leadership by an 18th-century gentlemen's club, however honourable and paternalistic their intentions.

For England only time would tell whether this was just a sentimental wound or would seriously limit their progress at home and influence abroad. The Test team were at something of a low ebb, domestic cricket was stale and participation levels dipping year on year. Symptomatic of this malaise was Gatting's dismissal by Warne later that summer. It is a delivery so famous that it has the sobriquet 'Ball of the century' and a dedicated Wikipedia page. It certainly left an indelible mark on the consciousness of every English cricket fan. England's portly, battle-scarred veteran was utterly bamboozled by young, cocky Aussie leg-spinner, Shane Warne. I'll pass over to Neil Hannon, the Irish pop genius, to describe the action through his 2009 tribute to the delivery 'Jiggery Pokery':

'I took the crease to great applause
And focused on my dinner.
I knew that I had little cause
To fear their young leg spinner.
He loosened up his shoulder
And, with no run-up at all,
He rolled his right arm over
And he let go of the ball.

At first the ball looked straight enough
I had it in me sights
But such was its rotation
That it swerved out to the right
I thought 'well, that's a leg break.
That's easily defended.'
So I stuck my left leg out
And jammed my bat against it.

But the ball it span obscenely
And out of the rough it jumped,
Veered back across my bat and pad
Clipping my off stump.
It took a while to hit me.
I momentarily lingered.
But then I saw old Dickie Bird
Slowly raise his finger.

It was jiggery pokery, trickery, jokery,
How did it open me up?
Robbery, muggery, Aussie skull-duggery.
Out for a buggering duck.

What a delivery,
I might as well have been
Holding a child's balloon.
Jiggery, pokery, who was this nobody
Making me look a buffoon.'

An image of Gatting's bewildered expression was all that was needed to tell the story of that cricketing summer. English cricket, old but fragile. Punch drunk from blows on and off the field. English cricket fans were locked in a dizzying spin of anguish and hope that in a perverse way emboldened our commitment to the game. We may have invented cricket but we had the maniacal zeal of the underdog. The Premier League had brought glamour and glitz to football. The Benson and Hedges Cup felt rather pathetic in comparison. Botham bowled in the low 70s for Durham.

In contrast Shane Warne was one of the most dynamic discoveries in recent decades, practically single-handedly reviving one of cricket's greatest arts (with a nod to Abdul Qadir of course) and turning Australia from a decent side to a dominant one. How on earth could we win the Ashes now?

Cue existential crisis, watching old videos of Gower and scouring the land for anyone even theoretically capable of landing a leg break. Terrible man management and a selection policy blessed with the farcical attributes of a Norman Wisdom film saw rare young talent like Ramprakash and Hick fail to reach their potential. Middle-order collapses were like painful, predictable initiation ceremonies for anyone foolish enough to divert their attention from Matt Le Tissier scoring wonder goals game after game.

In Warne, Lara and Tendulkar the international game had superstars every bit the equal of those of earlier eras. Tendulkar was fast becoming a national icon amid predictions he'd surpass Alan Border's Test runs aggregate, while Lara's brilliance went some way to masking the end of the West Indian Golden Age and the early, worrying signs of decline. Warne was spellbinding to watch returning to the game the artistry of wrist spin, the drama of close catchers and that delicious game of cat and mouse between a master of spin and a quality batsman. In 1994 England fans still reeling from Warne watched Lara stroke a world Test record 375 against a toothless attack. Later the same year he made 501 for Warwickshire, which remains the highest first class score. He was playing a different game.

※ ※ ※

The ICC, meanwhile, began their existence as a distinct organisation. David Richardson moved from Australia to a converted staff canteen in the Lord's clock tower, where he was ably supported by a comprehensive new team of three people: a PA, receptionist and officer. The initial focus was on scheduling umpire appointments, after Pakistan amongst others pushed for neutral appointments, and standardising playing conditions. Previously such details had been left to the countries themselves.

With associate member support key in securing a subcontinental World Cup in 1996 and non-founding members keen to earn capital from them for future support the tournament was extended to 12 teams. Whatever the political machinations that led to the more inclusive approach it was the beginning of a more expansionist policy by the ICC, who had previously shown little interest in giving associate members a global stage and a platform to raise profile and develop. This gave far greater context and competition to the preceding ICC Trophy with more teams having a genuine chance of making their World Cup debut. In turn this provided impetus to the leading associates to push for a genuine breakthrough and seek to prove competitive against the world's leading teams. *Wisden's* report of the tournament briefly lauded this 'missionary' role before expending vastly more words on lambasting logistical difficulties, the preponderance of group games and the fact there was an official chewing gum provider.

The associate nations had mixed fortunes. The UAE were thumped by South Africa with Gary Kirsten making a World Cup-record 188. The image of Emirati captain Sultan Zarawani, who had raised a few eyebrows by coming out to bat against the ferociously quick Allan Donald in a floppy hat, being painfully struck first ball instilled a feeling amongst some that full member against associate was men against boys: uncompetitive and potentially unsafe. The Netherlands endured a few one-sided games too but performed with credit against England. But the associate cause was boosted by the performances of Kenya, who defeated the West Indies in what was billed as the biggest upset in World Cup history. Despite only making 166 after losing the toss the African nation bowled out the West Indies team for just 93. There were lots of patronising references to 'minnows' and 'amateurs' in press reports but in truth the team played with vibrancy and adventure and in Tikolo and Odoyo they had players of considerable natural talent.

The associates also would have taken heart by Sri Lanka winning the tournament so soon after being promoted from associate status themselves. From ICC Trophy to World Cup winners. Countries could develop quickly and traditional cricket powers didn't have a monopoly on success. The expansive opening partnership of Jayasuriya and Kaluwitharana was an innovation that laid the foundation for their triumph and changed the tactics of one-day cricket for good. It was no longer good enough simply to accumulate and pick up the run rate in the last ten overs. Limited-overs cricket was beginning to diverge from its Test elder brother. Global development also had a stake in the tournament's commercial success, with money promised for an expansion in ICC activity. There was of course no chance that the subcontinent hosts, having gone to such lengths to secure the event, would leave any rupee unclaimed. Remember that the event was owned by the hosts and beyond the contributions offered to all teams the profits were theirs. They had sold the media rights for $14 million, with the UK rights increasing seven-fold from four years earlier. They got more money for the drinks sponsor than the title sponsor got in 1992. Wills, the tobacco firm, paid $12 million for naming rights, a four-fold increase on what Benson and Hedges paid for the Australian-hosted 1992 event. Overall, India made a profit of $50 million.

Despite Sri Lanka's victory, the legacy of which was to turn the country cricket mad, and the encouraging performance of Kenya, most took more interest in the entertainment of the tournament itself rather than how the tournament could help the global game. A one-sided encounter may not enthral the crowd and of course everyone would prefer a competitive game but if the very fact the fixture is played supports development of the sport beyond its traditional centres then that surely justifies inclusion. Numbers of teams, formats and the balance between maximising revenue and supporting development would become contentious themes in all subsequent global events.

England endured a limp, chastening World Cup that capped a disappointing year. By the mid-nineties it was customary for England to hold a state of the game autopsy on at least an annual basis. *Wisden* editor Matthew Engel did not hold back in his notes in the 1997 almanac.

'Amid the general global public mood of cricketing expansion, England is a spectacular and potentially catastrophic exception. In England, football has always been more popular than cricket. Ten years ago, when Ian Botham and David Gower were more instantly recognisable than any footballer, and soccer was struggling against the ravages of hooliganism, the gap was a narrow one. It is now a yawning chasm.

'The consistent failure of the England team is the biggest single cause of the crisis, but it is not the crisis itself. The blunt fact is that cricket in the UK has become unattractive to the overwhelming majority of the population. The game is widely perceived as elitist, exclusionist and dull.'

Engel could write more eloquently than most but expressed a commonly held view, born of a deep love of a suffering game and a simmering frustration at the lack of a positive response to a mounting challenge. There was a real fear that cricket, in England at least, was sleepwalking into a future as a minority sport.

That year *Wisden* also carried a manifesto for English cricket by the supremo of the newly formed ECB, Lord MacLaurin, still at the time the chairman of Tesco. His message was that success was defined as not declining further in an increasingly competitive marketplace. Hardly a rallying call. His mantra was that all would flow from a successful England team and the structure of the game should be designed with that goal in mind. Football analogies were clearly all the rage that year and MacLaurin spoke longingly of the impact on the nation and a generation of impressionable children of England's performance in Euro 96.

With money coming into the game and enabling a belated interest in development the country best placed to benefit was Kenya. The victory over the West Indies at the 1996 World Cup made them the next full member elect, following, they hoped, as the next African Test nation after South Africa's re-entry and Zimbabwe's promotion. Kenyan cricket had been an exclusive expat sport until the mid-1970s when local families like the Odumbes, Tikolos and Obuyas progressed from eager ball boys who had learnt their cricket watching matches and playing with makeshift bats in the street to league players. Significant investment from the Kenyan-Asian community had seen Indian Test players signed up by clubs in Nairobi, ensuring competitive cricket and crowds in their thousands. The African players raised their standards in this context and regular, high quality domestic cricket gave Kenya an advantage over many of the other leading associates. Future captain and coach Steve Tikolo, a stylish batsman often compared to Mark Waugh, made such an impression that he gave up his job as a courier to play first class cricket for Border in South Africa.

After the 1996 World Cup Kenya were given ODI status as a stepping stone to becoming a full member. A few months after the tournament they hosted a quadrangular tournament featuring Pakistan, South Africa and Sri Lanka. In 1998 they made their national squad professional and arranged a competitive international schedule. For the likes of Tikolo and Maurice Odumbe it represented not just recognition of their talent but also an escape from poverty. The ball boys were now professional cricketers playing against the best players in the world. Professional contracts enabled a full programme of matches and regular training and fitness. Unsurprisingly, this increased their competitiveness and they defeated India twice in ODIs.

Emboldened by these high-profile victories and confident in their new professional structure, Kenya formally applied for full member status, proposed by the West Indies and seconded by Zimbabwe. But while their competitiveness and results on the field were impressive, arguably more so than Bangladesh who were granted full member status that year, there were concerns both within the ICC and among Kenyan cricket fans that there had been too much emphasis on the national squad and not enough focus on development. There was undoubtedly a talented, golden generation of Kenyan cricketers but who would replace them? Were the foundations for sustainable growth in place? The presence of professionals from the subcontinent had masked deficiencies in the domestic structure, there was no significant investment in youth development and no domestic multi-day tournament to prepare them for Test cricket. Although high-profile results had piqued the interest of the nation cricket remained a minority sport in the country. There was also the small matter of Bangladesh having a population of 100 million. But, as we shall see, Kenya were to make an emphatic case again in 2003.

Theoretically ICC full members had a responsibility to develop cricket in their region. This was casually acknowledged rather than a stated commitment against which they would be judged. It was a paternalistic sentiment retained from the ICC's colonial roots. In practice any support to emerging nations in the vicinity was generally occasional or accidental. Nevertheless, one development model for the sport was to spread from its various regional centres. In the UK, for instance, Scotland had a long and proud cricketing heritage and had become an associate member in its own right in 1994. Despite a comparatively large player base by associate standards it had remained an amateur sport with only a handful of representative games a year, against the MCC, Ireland and some English counties. The notorious Scottish weather often put paid to many of these. Efforts to strengthen the international schedule were constrained by the need for employers to grant players time off. In 1980 Scotland were admitted to England's Benson and Hedges Cup competition, in effect playing as an additional county. This gave the team more fixtures but financially it proved difficult to make a profit from hosting touring sides, especially when the rain fell, as it inevitably did.

Scotland's emergence from under England's wing was an opportunity to put the game on a more professional footing with a director of cricket employed and a proper training programme introduced. This paid dividends with Scotland qualifying for the 1999 World Cup with a third-place finish in the ICC Trophy. They had not only qualified for a World Cup at their first attempt, making them the envy of many associates, but it provided a platform to raise the profile of the sport north of the border not only through their first ever televised games but hosting games too. This generated interest from the media and Scottish cricket was thrust into the public eye. After losses in England to Australia and Pakistan they hosted full member elect Bangladesh at their home ground, The Grange. With a masterclass of seam bowling they reduced the tourists to 26/5 but then failed to close out the innings, enabling Bangladesh to make 185. Despite Gavin Hamilton's fluent half-century they collapsed and an opportunity to inspire the nation and attract money to the sport had passed them by.

Domestic cricket was reformed too with a national league replacing the traditional regional model, providing higher levels of competition. Though the initial results as a separate ICC member were disappointing, it was clear that they had the domestic structure and profile to be a leading associate in years to come. Unlike many fellow associates, leading Scottish players also had the prospect of making a career out of the game with the potential of professional contracts over the border. In all-rounder

Dougie Brown they were even deemed good enough to play for England. Long before there were, of course, Douglas Jardine and Mike Denness. There is a school of thought, supported by the testimony of some former players, that the tribal loyalties that give football encounters between the auld enemy such visceral passion do not apply to the same degree to cricket, where England is seen as the representative team for Britain. This is reflected in the pride of the Scotland camp when Hamilton's World Cup performances (he scored 217 runs at 54) saw him selected for the England team. We won't mention the fact that he got two ducks and went wicketless in his sole Test. This feeling may have been a factor in constraining widespread public support for Scotland's distinct cricket identity. The issue was they didn't meet on equal terms, England having Test status and Scotland not.

Although culturally very distinct, continental Europe was also within the orbit of the ECB and those that shared a North Sea coast were so close geographically that they could watch cricket on the BBC. The availability of free to air cricket was a significant factor in the growth of the sport in the Netherlands in the seventies and eighties. Participation levels increased steadily to a peak of around 8,000 players, becoming more inclusive and socially diverse. An established club culture certainly helped and the best players began to interest English counties. Seam bowler Paul-Jan Bakker was the first, joining Hampshire, and others followed in his stead including Somerset and Glamorgan all-rounder Roland Lefebvre and the legendarily quick Somerset paceman Andre Van Troost. Van Troost, though at times erratic, is often cited by county players of the era as the quickest they faced. Such was the power with which he drove through his delivery stride he reportedly once broke his knuckles on the ground on his follow-through. On the back of his accomplished performances in the 1996 World Cup, batsman Bas Zuiderent played a few seasons for Sussex. The ECB invited the Netherlands to join their domestic one-day tournament in 1995, giving the team high-quality opposition and the players a shop window. With no regular international fixtures for associates it also gave the national team a few fixtures between ICC Trophies. Denmark were also invited into the Sunday League, offering county cricket fans the exciting prospect of away games in Copenhagen. They too had stars who broke into the English professional game with pace bowler Ole Mortensen a fans' favourite at Derbyshire for many years.

This regional development model could also be seen in Southern Africa where Namibia, who became an associate in 1992, were incorporated into South African domestic competition. Players in Papua New Guinea could turn the dial and enjoy the delights of Channel 9 commentary.

In 1998 the football World Cup went back to its origins for its 16th edition and was hosted by France. A record 174 countries had embarked upon qualification, demonstrating the unparalleled global reach of football compared to rival sports. FIFA had been actively courting new markets and would have been delighted that Japan and Jamaica qualified for the first time. The sublime skills of host hero Zinedine Zidane were beamed to 200 countries. The next tournament would be hosted by Japan and Korea, part of a strategy to conquer Asia. Football had broken the USA in 1994 when the World Cup was held in Los Angeles with sponsorship revenue for the final eclipsing the profits from the Super Bowl. This laid the platform for the growth of the American Major League Soccer that would later lure David Beckham over the Atlantic. Football had embraced the opportunities of satellite television, providing a balance in most markets between access on free to air and ever-lucrative contracts for live matches on premium channels. This increased revenue, that could then be invested in developing further markets. It was a commercial juggernaut that looked unstoppable. Unlike cricket the game at club level was growing in business potential year on year, with clubs like Manchester United becoming global brands at the birth of the new millennium. They didn't just host a match in Manchester, they served a global fan base. A few years into the noughties Manchester United opened a training camp in Goa. India was perhaps the one market, alongside China, where football had struggled. Cricket looked over its shoulder anxiously, with Jamaica playing World Cup football and India being courted.

Rugby union had professionalised in 1995 after years of fending off lures from rugby league for its best players. This enabled the sport to fully capitalise on the opportunities of the entertainment age and the World Cup in South Africa in 1995, featuring an emotional Nelson Mandela and a country visibly uniting around sport, was a breakthrough and announced rugby as a major modern sport. While remaining in the shadow of football, rugby generated interest from major broadcasters and won lucrative contracts. At club level regional tournaments like the Heineken Cup provided high-quality events to complement international schedules. The International Rugby Board were actively looking at global expansion, with Argentina and Italy breaking through as major teams. In sevens they had a traditional, shorter format that was naturally suited to emerging nations and festival atmospheres.

US-focused sports such as basketball and baseball were past masters at monetising their brands and had expansion plans of their own. Not to mention motor sport, where F1 had an eye on lucrative new markets, too.

Where did cricket stand in this increasingly competitive sports entertainment age on the verge of a new millennium? Well, cricket was noticeably different in several significant ways. Firstly, the money and profile were all invested in the international game. Club sides, though many had a rich heritage, just fed international cricket and had virtually no presence commercially. Certainly not in comparison with Champions League sides. This put power in national boards rather than club chairmen. The lure of unprecedented profits saw members jostle for decision-making power in the global game, exposing the antiquated and desperately inadequate governance structure of the ICC. Cricket had stumbled upon new-found wealth, making its members more financially stable and its World Cup hosts extremely wealthy. But there was no strategy. International teams played each other if they mutually agreed to. It was as simple as that.

Chapter 15

A new millennium and a recruitment drive

O NE'S perspective on the game at the birth of the new millennium largely depended on where you were from. As we have seen, England had suffered a difficult decade both on the field and off it. While they still had considerable influence on the global game their feudal authority had been wrestled from them by Asian members who controlled the game's purse strings.

Was it still an English game? Could they still shape how it was played? These fears were compounded by an embarrassing run of results on the field that saw them plummet to bottom of the Test match rankings and suffer a humiliatingly limp early exit from the World Cup they hosted. They had failed to replace stars of the calibre of Botham and Gower; one callow debutant followed another in a seemingly futile search for quality from an ailing county game.

The powers that be knew that a boost in profile and participation would flow from strong international results but these proved consistently elusive. Inevitably this all triggered the latest soul-searching state of the game debate. Commentators appeared torn between calling for profound root and branch reforms and being fearful of losing the last vestiges of a simpler, more graceful game everyone harked back to. The truth is that for most followers of English cricket success is judged purely and simply by winning the Ashes. Other international series are often seen as mere warm-ups for the next tussle over the urn. In 1999 Australia was building the strongest side ever to play the game. England had far less talent and the talent it had was being poorly managed. While there was a fascinating debate to be had about the state of the global game, column inches in England rarely ventured beyond the fear that the Ashes would never return. If the Ashes was the purest embodiment of cricket and they ceased to be a contest then that was the mortal wound for cricket as a whole.

An extension of this Ashes anxiety was the fear that cricket would decline in its historic heartlands. English cricket fans of the nineties liked nothing better, aside from confirming the impossibility of winning back the Ashes in their lifetimes, than lamenting the end of the West Indian Golden Age. Legends retired and were not replaced. A once unbeatable side now rolled over rather too easily rather too often. Young West Indians prefer basketball, it was said; the old clubs were no longer central to their communities. This perceived decline was given far more weight than any potential counterbalance, like the rise of Sri Lanka or a resurgence of cricket in Africa. For many, success was staving off decline in the sports heartlands and protecting the primacy of Test cricket. In this world view, financial growth and the catalyst this could provide to development was often seen as a threat rather than an opportunity. It was a threat to the spirit of the game, its charm and its historical context. It was a depressingly defensive mindset.

Elsewhere in the world the perspective was different. In Asia the money in the game was an opportunity for growth. Clearly for those in positions of power growth translated very happily to greed, but to the majority in India or Pakistan it simply meant following a team that could stake a strong claim to be the best in the world. Power also helped make the game theirs in a post-imperial world. It was their sport and it was right that they increasingly called the shots.

For associate nations the new millennium was approached with a heady mixture of hope and frustration. Hope because they were set to be one of the beneficiaries of money and opportunity flowing into the game, yet frustration that they were restricted in status, fixtures and recognition.

※ ※ ※

In 2001 the ICC created a new head of development post within an expanded executive team. This was a demonstration that development was a strategic objective for the first time in nearly a hundred years of governance. It marked a shift to a more hands-on, interventionalist role. Until that point national boards were largely left alone to develop cricket in their country and a competitive national team, but with money now earmarked for development the ICC wanted accountability and a return on investment. The primary focus was on bridging the gap between the leading associates and Test nations. To this end the High Performance Programme was created to help Kenya and the qualifiers for the 2003 World Cup become more competitive on the global stage. It was intended to inject professionalism into the leading associates to help them take the final step to become an established cricket nation: a finishing school if you will. There was also a clear and urgent commercial objective, to ensure the associates didn't disgrace themselves at global tournaments and in doing so devalue the product for broadcasters. If you were to take a cynical view of the High Performance Programme it existed as an insurance policy to protect the revenue-generating potential of the ICC's global events.

The ICC made a shrewd appointment in recruiting highly respected and innovative coach Bob Woolmer to run the High Performance Programme. He devised tailored training programmes for the four World Cup qualifying teams, Kenya, Canada, the Netherlands and Namibia. He stressed the importance of adopting a professional approach, meticulous preparation and matching the Test teams in fitness and fielding. Instilling self-belief was a critical part of his role and he sought to change the mindset from giddy excitement in merely playing alongside the world's best teams to having the skills and tactical nous to defeat them. It wasn't enough to turn up and do your best. You had to develop a game plan and hone your skills to execute it under pressure. The leading associates may not have had the funding and facilities of professional cricket teams but under his tutelage they'd certainly not be accused of having an amateur approach. Throughout his illustrious coaching career Woolmer was an innovator and he introduced scientific analysis and reflex tests. In practice this new, professionalised approach took some getting used to. For the players it was an insight into what was required to be competitive against the best in the sport. It was difficult for the national coaches to adjust to a new environment when they had to regularly pass their players over to Woolmer's care. It was still their team but now shaped to fit a blueprint provided by the ICC.

Woolmer became a passionate advocate of global development and saw his role in far broader, profound terms than merely avoiding embarrassingly one-sided games on television. He pushed for the development programme to provide a pathway for associates to become future full members and for cricket to become a professionalised sport across the world.

Woolmer's High Performance Programme was part of a broader development agenda under the leadership of New Zealander Andrew Eade. This saw a greater role for the five regional development offices that had been created in the 1990s, often from earlier decentralised bodies. Their principle function was to implement and oversee regional tournament structures that would serve as qualifying pathways for global events. They also provided advice and support to national boards in their region, promoting more robust, accountable and professional approaches to accounting, governance and youth development. As time went on they were to take a more and more prominent role, increasingly providing the blueprint that national boards were expected to follow. Global development had become an ICC project and regional development officers were the project managers. This investment and support was helping cricket to develop outside its heartlands but the increasingly prescriptive top-down approach was also seeing it become more homogenised. Competitiveness and professionalism became the bywords of development but the extent to which this would help emerging cricket nations break through into the sporting consciousness was less easy to calculate or assess.

There was a lot riding on the 2003 World Cup for the development programme. Whether rightly or wrongly the validity and return on investment for the programme would be judged on just a handful of World Cup fixtures. For all those within the programme and the wider cricket community that wanted the associate sides to thrive there were just as many who expected them to falter. The tournament and by association the game as a whole would be debased and devalued by one-sided games, the logic went. People would lose interest and switch off. The image of the sport was best served by the best playing against the best. The stakes could not have been higher at this key juncture. Development was in vogue and had influential backers but the development programme was still in its infancy and a few bad results could yet see it consigned to history as a brief experiment. Cricket could once again narrow its horizons. All eyes were on Woolmer's charges.

On 24 February 2003 the cricketing world's gaze was focused on a historic ground for a World Cup game. The venue was the evocative Nairobi Gymkhana ground, where the hosts were facing an in-form Sri Lanka side. A win on home soil would not only help their progression in the tournament but also strengthen their credentials for promotion to full membership. Perhaps it would inspire the next generation of Kenyan cricketers eagerly watching their heroes from under the shade of the jacaranda trees encircling the ground. The signs of recent investment in Kenyan cricket were clear for all to see, a new press box and large imposing stands. Kennedy Otieno, the burly opening batsman, eschewed tentative accumulation for bustling assault, dispatching the normally metronomic Chaminda Vaas to all parts. Others stumbled against the magic of Muralitharan but Otieno's 60 saw them to a 200-plus score. The captain, Steve Tikolo, feared it may be 30 runs light. Sri Lanka started purposefully and looked well set but then 21-year-old Collins Obuya bowled the spell of his life. The tall, angular leg-spinner varied his pace intelligently and extracted bounce and, bowling his ten overs unchanged, took 5-24. It wasn't even close in the end, Kenya winning by 53 runs. The Kenyans sauntered a lap of honour and the country went cricket crazy. Woolmer, who had spent considerable time with the Kenyan squad, was delighted and even pulled a few strings to get Collins a contract with Warwickshire.

A few days later New Zealand were due to play but withdrew over security concerns, giving the hosts a walkover win. A victory over Bangladesh secured their place in the super six stage. In Bloemfontein they defeated Zimbabwe and with points carried over from the super sixes qualified for the semi-finals. For champions of global development it was a seminal moment and proof that emerging teams could develop the quality required to challenge the best. For romantics it was a stirring story of the underdog challenging the status quo. For Woolmer and the development programme it was a feather in the cap and proof that with investment and specialist support the gap between Test nations and associates could be bridged. For the ICC it was a gamble that had paid off and it was ready to raise the stakes.

※ ※ ※

The development programme buoyed by producing a World Cup semi-finalist expanded after the 2003 World Cup. With the decision taken to increase the 2007 World Cup to 16 teams, there was an even greater spotlight on ensuring the associate qualifiers would be competitive. Regional offices got more staff and resources and busied themselves organising a packed schedule of tournaments. By 2006 the European region had four senior divisional tournaments, A team fixtures and youth tournaments at Under-13, Under-15, Under-17, Under-19 and Under-23 level. With a giddying succession of tours European cricketers were rarely at home. It was the age of the development pathway and those who progressed through the age groups to senior representation clocked up more air miles than your average foreign secretary.

For established associates it was a fundamental change in how they operated. For decades they had been left to their own devices focusing on domestic leagues, spending their grant as they wished and once every four years meeting up for the ICC Trophy. Even leading associates like the Netherlands had very little by way of structured governance. An elected board would oversee domestic cricket, including fixtures, umpire appointments and arbitrating on squabbles between clubs. International fixtures were few and far between. The board would work with employers to grant leave of absence for national players. It was in stark contrast to the professional set-ups of full members who had invested in psychologists, data analysts and centres of excellence. Left unchecked this widening gulf in professionalism would surely render any attempt to make associates competitive futile. And if they weren't competitive it would be impossible to make the case to include them in global events and invest in their development. If the ICC were to deliver development objectives they had to instill professionalism in cricket administration. It was an extremely ambitious goal but with the ICC board behind them and funding flowing into the programme they set about it with unbounded energy.

Each member was assigned a development officer tasked with helping to shape their objectives and development programmes. The central philosophy was to create development pathways all the way through the cricket community. Young talent discovered at outreach events would develop through a school and club and then be integrated into age-group national sides and high-performance camps before graduating to a semi-professionalised national squad. Schools, clubs and the board would work in an integrated approach towards this common goal. The detail of development pathways would be enshrined in five-year development plans, signed off by regional development leads. These plans would include on-field targets such as improving rankings, promotion through regional divisions and qualification for global tournaments. They would also cover rise in participation levels, increase in clubs and schools programmes, links with central and local government, expanding revenue sources and professionalising governance. Development officers would then oversee bids for targeted development grants to deliver these plans. Progress would be constantly monitored and assessed in annual reports by the regional office. On top of this the development officers would run coaching clinics, high-performance camps and a host of workshops covering accounting, leadership and marketing. It was soon a very different world for associate boards. Older players must have looked on with awe at the level of support and opportunities offered to young players in this era.

It must have been like a small start-up business having a team of management consultants constantly leaving memos in the boardroom. Stagnation and inertia were anathema. Associates and affiliates were on the march, with regional development managers the drum majors. It was the same in the Americas, Africa, Asia and East Asia Pacific regions. The cream of each region were taken under the wing of the High Performance Programme.

※ ※ ※

Bob Woolmer had long advocated that in order to be truly competitive players needed to hone their skills in longer formats. It was only in multi-day fixtures that solid techniques could be developed that were needed as the foundation for competitiveness in any format. Although Woolmer was lured back into top level international coaching by Pakistan he got his wish and the Intercontinental Cup was born.

Launched in March 2004, the Intercontinental Cup provided the leading associate sides in each region with four-day fixtures awarded first class status. This would provide a dual purpose of developing techniques and concentration levels amongst leading players and serving as a proving ground in assessing suitability for promotion to Test status. Bangladesh had suffered a chastening entry in Test cricket following their elevation, losing most games by an innings. This not only provided an uninspiring, one-sided spectacle that did little to boost the confidence of the newest full member but also in some people's eyes devalued the Test format itself. There was a general belief that it led to an inflation of averages that made comparison across ages of Test cricket impossible. This was a little over-dramatic given that many a poor Test side has taken the field over the years. Quality hasn't been consistent. If Bangladesh had never played regular longer-format games how could they be expected to be competitive? The Intercontinental Cup would give teams a grounding and allow their suitability for Tests to be carefully considered.

The Intercontinental Cup was a significant show of faith in the associate nations. For players, being able to regularly represent their country at first class level was a huge source of pride. It gave shape and meaning to their careers as cricketers, even if their day job was in IT or marketing. For years associate cricketers who had not had the opportunity to play in World Cups had toiled away with very little recognition or profile, their deeds largely invisible in the statistical record. But now they would have first class records and could compare themselves with first class cricketers across the world. Furthermore, there was the significant motivation that success in the Intercontinental Cup would open the door to Test cricket, the ultimate form of the game.

It was a significant financial commitment by the ICC to stage the tournament and there wasn't an obvious short-term benefit in either marketability or increasing World Cup earning potential through increased competitiveness. In this sense it was a genuine development initiative to support growth of the game. But the nature of ICC governance meant there were some significant qualifications. Although billed as a second division of Test cricket it wasn't awarded Test status. Tests were, after all, one of the privileges of full member status and full member status came with financial rights too. Existing full members may have been content to support development in an abstract sense but when it came to potential erosions of their privileges or reductions in their grants they were less communally minded. This meant that promotion from and relegation to the Intercontinental Cup was not considered. It stood rather awkwardly askance in the cricket firmament, important and yet dislocated. Although still broadly welcomed it was in essence a league without a prize. The tournament was popular with fans and generated a good following through scorecards and reports. It didn't, however, generate interest from broadcasters and therefore there was little hope it could be financially self-sustaining.

The inaugural year saw Ireland, Scotland and the Netherlands in the Europe group, Kenya, Uganda and Namibia in Africa, the UAE, Malaysia and Nepal in Asia and Canada, USA and Bermuda in the Americas.

Teams played others in their regions before group winners competed in a semi-final and then final. Scotland emerged victorious with the longer-form experience of their county-based players proving instrumental. Encouragingly, scores were generally high and games for the most part competitive. Kenya's stylish batsman Ravindu Shah made a couple of centuries including a mammoth 187 not out against Namibia and averaged 122. Scotland's Fraser Watts made over 400 runs in four games.

The tournament marked a breakthrough opportunity for two Asian sides who were yet to make a mark on the global scene but had considerable potential. Malaysia had a long cricketing heritage in the colonial age that had bequeathed the country several excellent grounds. The sport's recovery after the devastating Japanese occupation in the Second World War was aided by it being attractively located for touring sides. Sri Lanka, the MCC and several county sides toured in the 50s and 60s and although they meted out heavy defeats to their hosts their presence gave the cricket community focus and impetus. In 1970 they inaugurated the Saudara Cup against Singapore. This competition was for citizens rather than expats and gradually helped standards improve. With a state of the art ground and a strategic geographical location Malaysia promoted themselves as an international venue, hosting the ICC Trophy in 1997 and Asian Cricket Council Trophy in 2004. With first rate facilities, a growing, affluent, multicultural population and a cricket tradition they had great potential. This had yet to translate to on-field success but the Intercontinental Cup presented a further opportunity. Their leading player was Selangor-born all-rounder

Suresh Navaratnam, who broke into the senior team in 1993. On the international stage he had averaged 18 in the ICC Trophy and made useful lower order runs and by the end of his career held the national record for both runs and wickets. They also developed some promising young players. In 1999 15-year-old Arul Suppiah had taken 6-48 against Singapore, announcing his considerable promise. Unfortunately he was lost to Malaysian cricket when he moved to England, first to Millfield School and then Exeter University. After representing England at age group level he went on to a career with Somerset as a stylish opening batsman and occasional spinner. It was his occasional spin that found him fame, taking a world record 6-5 in a T20 game against Glamorgan. He was forced to retire at the age of 29 due to a serious knee injury.

Without Suppiah's county pedigree Malaysia struggled to be competitive, losing heavily to both UAE and Nepal. Their potential remained but this was to be another opportunity missed.

Nepal didn't have the colonial legacy and infrastructure of Malaysia. Their potential was to be found in the passionate support of their fans. In many associate nations cricket was a minority sport that had struggled for recognition and profile in the national sporting consciousness. This tended to constrain playing numbers and opportunities for sponsorship, government support and widespread media coverage. But Nepal was different. Cricket had been brought to the country by the ruling Rana dynasty in the 1920s, who had learnt it at English and Indian public schools. The country was insular and isolated and cricket remained a game for the privileged played behind palace walls for much of the 20th century. After the overthrow of the house of Rana the country remained a feudal society but gradually outside influence was felt. The game was popularised by Indian traders that settled in expanding urban centres. Cricket was incorporated into the National Sports Council, providing funding and political backing. Nevertheless, cricket remained an occasional sport and the Cricket Association of Nepal parochial in its ambitions. Nepal did not become an ICC member until 1988. Cricket grew as the country modernised and a national communications network was implemented. Cricket was introduced to schools and regional tournaments were established. Nepal faced the opposite challenge to Malaysia. While Malaysia had the facilities but struggled to generate the demand, Nepal had ignited the demand but didn't have the facilities to cater for it. In the land of the Himalayas, flat ground for pitches was very much at a premium. There was a risk the interest would be temporary and fans and players would be lost to other sports if starved of opportunity.

Nepal's elevation to associate status in 1996 saw an increase in grant funding and Sri Lankan legend Roy Dias was contracted as coach in 2001. Dias sought to identify and develop talented youth players through a series of local and regional trials. At youth level they excelled, claiming notable scalps in South Africa, Pakistan and New Zealand at Under-19 World Cups. Their strong, indigenous player base was an asset they enjoyed over other associates but the lack of facilities and a professional development programme saw this advantage lost by senior cricket, much to the frustration of Nepal's fans. Under

Dias their performances improved and they gained greater consistency. Their bowling was well disciplined and ruthless and they quickly asserted themselves as one of the leading teams in the Asia development region. Their elevation to the Intercontinental Cup came before the introduction of an organised domestic league. Players, however talented, tend to struggle with only a handful of occasional, sporadic games to prepare them. Without a strong domestic game or a viable career path in cricket many of the stars that lit up Youth World Cups were lost to the game, favouring security and income over the lottery of playing cricket. For all the potential, Nepal, as with other associates, were faced with must-win games to retain momentum, to stay on their development pathway. Surprising losses to Fiji and Qatar meant they missed out on qualification for the ICC Trophy. From first class cricket to outsiders in the course of a year. It would be a long road back.

As well as marshalling their established members into a more professional approach and coordinating delivery of five-year development plans, the regional offices turned their attention to new members. It wouldn't be accurate to call it a recruitment campaign because, oddly, the ICC have never had a proactive role in identifying new members even at the height of their development mania. It would seem a constructive use of time to visit countries where some cricket, at whatever scale, is played to provide advice and support to attract new members. But the process has always been a reactive one. The initiative has to come from a board to check they fulfil the minimum eligibility requirements and make an initial application. Only upon receipt does the regional office review the application and make a visit to judge for themselves. This may lead to recommendations needing to be implemented before applications are approved. This policy carries with it the risk that early promise, enthusiasm and momentum are lost without a guiding hand and an opportunity to broaden the global cricket community is also lost. Many have called for the ICC to create a new category of prospective members that they actively assist in meeting the minimum requirements. Perhaps their advice and support could have its greatest impact at that earliest embryonic stage.

The rate of successful applications had been steadily increasing in the final years of the millennium. By 2000 there were 42 associate and affiliate members. It was a growing game and the cricketing map was expanding, often in surprising locations well beyond old Victorian surveys of empire. Was it that through extending the reach of television coverage cricket was finally inspiring countries that had hitherto shown little interest? Well, that may have played a minor contributing role but the major factor was economic migration. As we've seen in countries like Hong Kong, Kenya and the UAE, expat immigration had always played an important role in establishing and sustaining cricket communities. Affordable travel, improved communications and a globalised job market meant that by the 1990s the level of economic migration was unprecedented. This was changing culture and sport more broadly but had a particular impact on cricket due to the huge increase in migration from cricket-mad South Asia.

Seeking employment, security and improved prospects for their families, many left the region for the West. As well as having a significant demographic and cultural impact on the countries they chose to call home it also introduced a large number of cricketers keen to play the sport they loved and retain a cultural link to home. Those who arrived in countries where cricket was established found it relatively easy to join a club. But if they settled in a country where cricket wasn't established it only took a few friends, some rudimentary equipment and a piece of open ground to start playing. Add perseverance, will-power and networking and a cricket community could be formed. Once established a community could become a fledgling cricket nation.

A good example of a new cricket nation created this way was Norway, one of a number of new affiliate nations that joined in the year 2000. There was no cricket at all before a first wave of economic migrants arrived from the subcontinent in the 1960s. At first the cricket was sporadic and unorganised until a group of Pakistani emigrants formed the Oslo Cricket Club in 1972, closely followed by the Indian cricketing diaspora forming the Kampen Cricket Club. The clubs were without a ground until 1996 when the Oslo Sports Council provided a facility. As further waves of immigration saw the Indian and Pakistani communities grow and cricket became available through Asian TV networks, interest in cricket increased. By the early 2000s there were 14 clubs in Norway. I say clubs but these were more groups of friends and acquaintances who had formed teams rather than sporting clubs in a traditional sense. They had no grounds, facilities, coaching on Saturday mornings or mid-week bingo nights to raise money to fix a pavilion roof. All 14 teams were reliant on a single ground. The fixture congestion was, as you can imagine, considerable and if the pitch was waterlogged then all cricket in the country was postponed. The challenges in Norway were typical of those facing the new cricket nations: enthusiasm and demand was constrained by infrastructure and facilities.

Drawing players exclusively from immigrant communities provided both an opportunity and a challenge. It was an opportunity as it provided a growing community who knew and loved cricket in a nation that without their arrival would be unlikely to play the game at all. Socially and culturally cricket became an important factor in ensuring cohesion and stability in increasingly ethnically diverse cities like Oslo. Cricket's role in providing recreation, enjoyment and cultural affinity to ethnic groups facing the inevitable tensions of relocation in an alien land and culture was recognised by local and central governments. Settled and content communities integrating smoothly into broader society was a political priority in Norway and the rest of Scandinavia and investment was targeted at cricket to help deliver this objective.

As the cricket community grew so clubs became savvier in how to access support to overcome their frustrations, such as a lack of playing facilities and equipment. In Norway, for instance, a critical step in development was getting cricket formally recognised by the National Sports Council. This was achieved in 2007 and provided cricket with the resources and government endorsement to enjoy a sustainable future in this Northern European frontier. As an official sport Norwegian Cricket got an office adjoining the 25,000 capacity national football stadium in Oslo. It had access to lawyers and a marketing department, an open door to local governments and municipal organisations that could help identify land for grounds, and a revenue stream that was both larger and more secure than that from the ICC. Norway was to become one of the richer affiliates with finances the envy of many an associate.

While many cricketers in continental Europe make do with impromptu tape-ball games in parcels of waste land between housing blocks, Norway's cricketers can be found taking a bus to a nondescript, light industrial estate in an outer suburb of Oslo. They haul their kit bags past rows of stark 1970s office blocks until they reach an old printing works. The smell of ink and whir of machines has long since faded to be replaced by perspiration, sweetly struck drives and anguished appeals. For this is the unlikely setting of Norway's Cricket Academy, a facility boasting state of the art nets, a gym, canteen and seminar rooms. It provides a hub for the country's cricketers and a base for training sessions and development days. It cost 400,000 Euros and was paid for from government ethnic integration grants.

Although hamstrung by inclement weather and a dire shortage of grounds, Norwegian cricket had far more resource and support than other fledging members. Cricket may have remained a mysterious unknown to the vast majority of the population, hidden from sight in old printing works and a single, cramped, over-used ground but suddenly, from nowhere it seemed, it had an international cricket team. As the Pakistani and Indian expats had played club cricket before they emigrated many played to a decent standard and approached the game with the confident, bat-swirling approach of heroes like Shahid Afridi and Virender Sehwag. This meant that when they entered affiliate-level tournaments in Europe they did rather well, winning their first ever tournament, the 5 Nations tournament in Vienna. In some ways it wasn't surprising; after all, although they were on their international debut they had far greater cricketing experience than some of the eager but tentative teams they faced who had only recently been introduced to the game.

Inevitably this raised a few eyebrows. A Norwegian team comprised exclusively of subcontinent expats speaking Urdu in their wicket-taking huddles rubbed many up the wrong way. It wasn't that the team wasn't legitimate. The players met the qualification requirements set out by the ICC, requiring seven years' residency in the country. The Board was official and had government endorsement. It was all above board. But for many it didn't feel like a team representative of Norway. Could you really claim Norway was a cricket nation if there were no indigenous players, many asserted? Wasn't it all just a sham? An alternative, more positive perspective was that it was wonderful that cricket was now being played in Norway, a country that would surely never have echoed with leather against willow were it not for modern migratory trends. These pioneer immigrant communities could provide a catalyst to spread cricket beyond their community and into mainstream culture. Or at least that was the hope.

Another country to become a member in 2000 was the Czech Republic. Like Norway it wasn't a country you'd naturally think of as a cricketing outpost. It was one of many examples of a cricket nation being developed by English residents keen to establish their summer game. The first recorded fixture, in 1997, was arranged by a worker in the British embassy. This sparked some interest and regular fixtures were arranged at a makeshift square in a Prague park. A handful of locals were intrigued enough to pick up a bat and once cricket was established Asian expats swelled the ranks as levels of migration slowly increased. There wasn't the scale of migration from Asia that Oslo had seen and therefore unlike in Norway there wasn't a rash of teams formed.

Like many of the new members the Czech story was one of surviving rather than thriving, relying on a small band of dedicated enthusiasts to overcome hurdles and setbacks to play the game they loved. There were challenges at every turn, from finding somewhere they could play, to getting equipment and being taken seriously by local and central government. Czech cricketers reached out to other new members in the region such as Slovenia and Austria, both for moral support and fixtures. You could argue that in granting them membership the ICC took them more seriously than their own town council. In such circumstances it was difficult to consider potential. It is difficult to focus on five-year strategies when you are struggling to get 11 on the field and stay solvent on a month-by-month basis. The fact that the Czech Republic could even meet the eligibility criteria showed just how open the ICC now was to welcoming new members, however early they were in their cricketing journey. The Czechs were seeking to play international tournaments before they even had a stable, sustainable domestic league.

That isn't to say there wasn't commitment and passion in spadefuls, it is just to serve to put this new cricketing world into perspective.

The following year Croatia became the latest European cricket nation. There the story wasn't of Asian immigrants or busy Brits but of returning Croats who had emigrated to Australia but returned after the break-up of Yugoslavia and brought a passion for cricket back with them. They assembled a side to play a team in neighbouring Slovenia and a core of cricketers arose from a regular cross-border touring team. In 2000 they formed a club in Zagreb, albeit one without a ground. The nearest was actually in Austria and the team joined the Austrian league, with players driving four hours to turn out for their club. Despite such fragile foundations and without any further ado they entered European competitions. This was an era when hundreds of club players a year were becoming international cricketers. It made for a fantastic anecdote and a great, expenses-paid weekend away. What it would all lead to only time would tell.

The appearance of these new members changed the nature and balance of power of cricket within regions. In Europe traditional teams based on local, home-bred players, like Gibraltar and Greece, found it difficult to compete on the field with expat-focused teams. It was a clash of cultures too, with the technical orthodoxy of countries inspired by the English game and the crash, bang, wallop of six-hungry expats from Pakistan and India. A veteran seamer known for an impeccable line and length being smote to all corners by an Afridi-inspired whirlwind certainly upset the applecart. It was a different brand of cricket from a different cricketing culture. These two cultures were not always the easiest of bedfellows. The culture clash wasn't just confined to the pitch either. Off the pitch the approach to governance and development also tended to be divided along cultural lines. There were tensions, inevitably. Sometimes this led to entrenched views and prejudices while in some cases it dissipated over time as cricketers got used to the new reality of cricket below Test level. The new members brought new players, more destinations and more fixtures. They also made cricket more complex. Some didn't like change and resented complexity. They would henceforth hark back to an age of MCC tours, gentlemanly handshakes and pedestrian run rates.

Another new member in 2000 was Oman, a sultanate in the Middle East that like its neighbour the UAE had attracted a culturally diverse population through a burgeoning economy. Cricket's origins in the country has many parallels with Norway. Indian expats established clubs in the 1970s and a national board was established in 1979. The player base grew steadily and the board made an effort to encourage local players to take up the game. This resulted in three all-Omani teams being formed. Within three years of gaining affiliate status there were 60 teams playing in eight divisions in Muscat. The board stipulated that all teams must play an Omani national or play with ten players. This emphasis on developing home-grown players was admirable and in contrast to some other teams in the region.

Despite a lack of facilities, no government funding and a seeming lack of interest in local businesses sponsoring or supporting cricket, the national team nevertheless developed quickly after making its tournament bow in 2002. By 2004 Oman was the strongest affiliate in Asia and had closed the gap on neighbours UAE. The clement weather and ability to play cricket all year round was certainly an advantage and with economic vitality assuring a constant stream of expat players, Oman had a lot of potential. In 2001 another Gulf country, Bahrain, became an ICC member. The oil industry had seen expats form the Awali Cricket Club as early as the 1930s. By the time of its accession to membership most of its players were of Pakistani origin although the board had started a school programme with a quota system to encourage Bahrainis to play. With Kuwait having joined as a member in 1998 the Gulf was slowly developing into a strong cricketing sub-region within Asia, with wealth, weather and a high proportion of expat immigration.

Further east Bhutan joined the membership ranks in 2001. This was a different proposition indeed to the Gulf states. The Himalayan kingdom had been closed to the outside world, developing in isolation and at different pace to the rest of the planet. There were no expats to introduce the game there. It was only once television was permitted in 1999 and cricket games were shown that some interest was sparked. Its champions saw it as a healthy pursuit for their countrymen and a national board was established in 2000. Having no national ground was a constraint on development although they have regularly played in Asian regional events, albeit with very little success. Young, callow Bhutanese with no formal training were hardly likely to be competitive against Indian and Pakistani expats. Some of the mismatches have been embarrassing. But while some countries have continued with an almost exclusive reliance on expats, achieving on-field success if not development accolades, Bhutan has taken its own path. That cricket survives in such a remote part of the world without any outside influence is a heart-warming story in itself. It is testament to the unique appeal of cricket that it can capture the imaginations of so many from such different cultures.

The Africa region had been boosted by the rise of Kenya, the successful reintegration of South Africa and the recent elevation of Zimbabwe to Test cricket. In the south of the continent the concentration of teams was augmented by Botswana. Although there were references to games in Botswana from the late 19th century and it was played in some prestigious public schools it wasn't until immigration from the subcontinent began in the 1970s that cricket became a regular recreation, at least amongst expat communities. In addition to club cricket the game was played in around 30 schools by the new millennium.

In contrast cricket had never gained a foothold in the north of the continent. In 1999 Morocco had become an affiliate member courtesy of teams established by members of the British and Pakistani embassies in Rabat. Sufficient interest was roused amongst the locals for a Moroccan club to be established by 2001. Over time the game spread from Rabat to Tangier and Casablanca, albeit on a modest scale. Playing numbers didn't reach the critical mass to ensure a competitive national team but an entrepreneur helped put it on the cricketing map with an ambitious plan. Abdul Rahman Bukhatir was a wealthy Emirati who had fallen in love with the game on a visit to Lord's in the 1980s. He took the game back home to Sharjah and helped establish the city as one of the principal destinations in world cricket. But there was a problem. Sharjah became synonymous with match fixing and the ground was banned from hosting international games. Seeking an alternative venue Bukhatir came to Morocco, saw cricket being played, asked questions and offered support. He then invested $4 million on building a state-of-the-art cricket stadium in Tangiers. With the help of eye-watering prize money he lured Pakistan, South Africa and Sri Lanka to play a triangular tournament in 2002. The pitch played well, the weather was very conducive to cricket and it was strategically located as a neutral international venue. With a lack of cricket culture in the country the crowds were modest, although amongst them were the Moroccan national squad.

Bukhatir was keen to honour his commitment to Moroccan cricket and contracted his friend and Indian World Cup winner Mohinder Amarnath to help develop the game there. Amarnath arrived in 2000 with bats, balls and an open mind. It was a blessing for the small core of national team players but it proved a struggle to attract a significant number of locals to the game. While attempts to popularise cricket in the country were being frustrated, Bukhatir sought to schedule a further triangular tournament in 2004. However, suicide attacks in Casablanca could not have come at a worse time and international sides were reluctant to tour. The Morocco Cup was never played again. Internationals in

Casablanca were fated to be a brief and intriguing footnote in cricket's history. Local cricket, however, had a brief moment, reaching a peak of 600 players in the middle of the noughties with Bukhatir providing considerable investment. But sadly it was to turn sour, Moroccan players were banned from the international stadium and the country drifted out of international competition amid wrangling between the board and players and an unexplained financial black hole that saw the players have to beg for kit and equipment from opposition teams.

The Tangier Oval, that once drew the eyes of the cricketing world became a forgotten, dilapidated stadium of ghosts. Moroccan cricket is a story of what ifs. What if the suicide bombings had not taken place and North Africa had challenged the Gulf as an international cricket hub? What if the administration had been well run and the local talent had been given an opportunity to thrive? What if English counties had provided investment and impetus by using Morocco as an affordable, short haul winter training destination? As it was the whole of the Maghreb was destined to remain an unconquerable region for cricket.

Another region that cricket had struggled to colonise was South America. With the exception of Argentina, who had played to a high standard in the twenties and where the game had continued through being played at a network of public schools, it was a continent obsessed by football. As with Argentina a healthy community of English expats had seen cricket played regularly in Brazil in several of the major cities in the 19th century but as English influence waned cricket tended to become marginalised and then disappear from the sporting clubs where it was once played. Unofficial international fixtures continued to be played against Argentina late into the 20th century and club sides toured and hosted teams from Montevideo. There were some encouraging signs of revival in the 1990s with several clubs apiece in Sao Paulo, Brasilia and Curitiba. This saw a national cricket board being created in 2001 and Brazil joined the ICC as an affiliate member in 2002. Momentum was helped by the establishment of the South American Championships in 1995. This provided not only regular fixtures but crucially a regional support network for fledgling cricket nations facing an uphill battle for recognition and acceptance in football's heartland. Initially the Brazilian team was almost exclusively Western expats but gradually some local players were attracted to the game and competed for the national team.

Chile had a similar historical context to Brazil with the ebb and flow of the game's fortunes largely dependent on the presence of expat communities. As with Brazil there was a gradual recovery for the game late in the 20th century and Chile joined as a member in 2001, with ten teams spread across two divisions. ICC funding was targeted at a schools programme to take the game to the local population.

Every year in the early noughties ICC meetings announced the latest crop of recruits. Gaps in the cricketing map were shaded in and there was a constant stream of new charges for the legion of regional development officers. For a few giddy years it seemed there was no stopping the development dream that cricket would conquer the world. In 2008, to great fanfare, the ICC proudly announced its 100th member. They may have been very late to the development game but you couldn't argue with a doubling of membership in a mere decade. Cricket had gone global and cast off its colonial past to embrace a truly international future. But did this confident press release with the jubilant tone stand up to scrutiny? It showed endeavour, undoubtedly, and provided a foundation to grow the game way beyond its historic footprint. But they were fragile foundations. Very fragile indeed. The majority of these new members only just complied with the most generous, untaxing of qualification criteria. A handful of players comprising a couple of teams was enough to be a cricketing nation. If a few expats decided to go home or a key volunteer saw his job take him abroad the whole dream was in jeopardy. If a local park banned the game due to breakages to nearby windows cricket could be stopped overnight. The ICC hoped to insulate and overcome this fragility through the support of its development offices and riding a wave of confidence and self-belief they believed all these countries could not just survive but flourish. It was certainly ambitious; only time would tell whether it was also naïve. Those of a cynical disposition would argue this expansion was a mirage of growth, merely reflecting global migratory trends rather than genuine new cricket centres.

Chapter 16

T20 and the development dream

WITH new affiliate members being founded every year the percentage of members playing Test cricket was rapidly diminishing. The original format had become a niche offering within the sport. The reality of cricket in the new millennium was limited-overs matches. Only one in ten teams was permitted to play what most consider the purest form of the game and which many feel is the only form worth playing. If only the majesty and cerebral delights of Test cricket elevated the game above other sports then cricket had devalued itself. With multi-day cricket ruled out for the vast majority, 50 overs was the longest format. And although in cricket 50 overs represents a significantly contracted game, in general sporting terms a seven-hour fixture is ludicrously long. It is nearly five times longer than a professional football match. It made cricket a very hard sell in countries where it was virtually unheard of beyond immigrant communities. Cricket needed an enticing, accessible, shorter format.

Short forms of cricket were nothing new. Single wicket games between star players had been extremely popular in the 19th century, often attracting bigger crowds and larger bets than 11-a-side encounters. In the modern era expediency and logistics had often dictated shortened games beyond the professional sport. For those who could only spare the occasional evening a shorter format was essential if they were to play the game at all. The first country to professionally market a shortened form was Hong Kong. Their sixes tournament was launched in 1992. It consisted of six players per side with all except the wicketkeeper bowling an over each. Wides and no-balls counted as two runs and if five wickets fell before the end of the five-over innings the last batsman would bat on, retaining strike until they got out. With only a handful of overs and a shortage of fielders it made for frenetic action. With games only lasting 50 minutes or so it was possible to hold a tournament with multiple teams in a weekend.

It was cleverly marketed as a sports tourism event with a carnival atmosphere, much like the very popular rugby sevens circuit. It attracted most of the top international teams who sent their big-hitting stars, that is as long as they could bowl! The six-hitting extravaganza was the ultimate antidote to what thrill seekers may have perceived as the turgid pace of Test cricket. Spectators could see a host of international stars in a weekend and have a jolly fun time to boot. It was also tailor made for television coverage just at a time when sports broadcasting was being revolutionised and premium sports channels were looking to keep subscribers entertained. For the Hong Kong Cricket Association, it was an opportunity to put Hong Kong on the cricket map and generate investment for development of the game in the colony.

Its mix of international stars, power hitting and relaxed, jovial atmosphere proved a hit and the tournament flourished, becoming a fixture of the international cricket calendar, a favourite with players and earning official endorsement by the ICC. Naturally it attracted considerable interest and investment from sponsors. Pakistan won the inaugural tournament and then England enjoyed a run of victories in the mid-nineties that provided a diverting tonic from their lacklustre performances in Tests. Sixes went from strength to strength into the new millennium and by the late 2000s plans were afoot to take the format international through 'isixes'. The plan was to establish a series of sixes tournaments organised on a franchise model, taking carnival cricket global. Broadcasters were on board and the finance in place but the dream was ultimately scuppered by a lack of support from the Asian Cricket Council.

Four years after the creation of the Hong Kong Sixes another new format was born in New Zealand. It was the brainchild of Kiwi legend Martin Crowe, who wanted to replicate the challenge of Test cricket but in much truncated form. The 'Max' format saw each team bat for 20 overs split across two innings. Players were encouraged to play technically correct shots through the 'V' rather than agricultural swipes across the line through the creation of a trapezoidal 'Max zone' where runs counted double and a batsman could not be caught out. A fourth stump was added to provide a compensatory balance for the bowlers. Each team was allowed a 12th man as an interchangeable replacement fielder and field restrictions were in place to boost over rates. Follow-ons could be imposed. With straight sixes worth 12 runs the scoreboard could fairly rattle along and there was an incentive for clean, orthodox hitting in front of the wicket over contrived nurdles behind it. Games lasted for around three hours.

Following a trial in 1995 the format was fully integrated into the New Zealand domestic programme in 1996/97. The following year a Max roadshow was launched that took the format across the country, reaching out beyond the major cities and Test venues. The aim was both to attract new fans and players to cricket and to sharpen the skills of the country's talented young players. It wasn't intended to replace existing formats, in fact quite the opposite; it was intended to sharpen skills for them. Cricket Max was quickly added to the international schedule too with New Zealand facing an English Lions side in October 1997. Phil DeFreitas took to the new format rather well, claiming a format-best 5-38. Two years later the so-called Max Blacks hosted a West Indian team branded the Caribbean Calypsos. The last Cricket Max international was played in 2002 with Sachin Tendulkar, who else, making the highest ever Max score with 72 off 27 balls.

Despite committed backing by the New Zealand board the Max format never truly found its place in domestic cricket, despite the excitement of several Max centurions and the drama of a single over being struck for 50 runs! Not a record Otago's Nathan Morland would have told his grandchildren. Ultimately, despite its backing Cricket Max was never taken to the hearts of cricket fans and its short, ebullient life came to an end in 2003 when another shortened format came on to the scene.

The New Zealand board weren't alone in seeking an innovative new format to reinvigorate the game, arrest decline in match attendances and inspire a new generation in a new millennium. The ECB were deeply concerned by declining interest year on year and had come to the conclusion that cosmetic tinkering with their existing formats to make them more exciting and youth-friendly simply wasn't going to work. Many counties were on their knees financially and insipid performances by the national team were hardly inspiring the next generation of cricket fans. The game was stale and the fear was it was contracting in popularity to an aging, socially exclusive rump. In response the ECB spent a quarter of a million pounds on the most comprehensive consumer survey ever. This probed all ages and sectors of society to understand why people were not attending cricket and concluded that the game was not accessible enough. In short, games were too long and too boring. People didn't have enough time to spare to watch cricket and there were plenty of other forms of entertainment that were more exciting and appealing.

The survey results must have been a sobering read for the ECB but it confirmed their fears that without a significant change of direction cricket was destined to become an increasingly marginalised game destined for a limited shelf life once its current acolytes grew old and infirm. The research wasn't all doom and gloom though. It revealed a 19 million strong target market that had potential interest in the game if it could be tailored to their busy lifestyles. This meant a format of three hours' duration that could be played at evenings and weekends. Such a format already existed at recreational level throughout the country and 20-over cricket was poised to turn professional.

With the ECB's minds made up the next challenge was to convince the county chairmen, whose majority vote was needed. While some came out in favour others of a more traditional bent were wary and unconvinced. Was this short confection of a format even cricket? In seeking quick thrills would they unwittingly remove all that was good and precious in the game? And, critically, how could they look their aging county members in the eye and justify their support for this betrayal of all that they held dear? In the end an appeal to not let fear of the novel stand in the way of the future prospects of the game won the day. T20 had begrudgingly been endorsed. For all those excited by its potential to revive the game there were others who were willing it to fail. Cricket had always been especially sensitive to reform and reincarnation as for many its unique appeal was born from its traditions and timeless immutability. For traditionalists any change was a further wound inflicted on its delicate soul. For pragmatists the game had to evolve to stay relevant and survive. The debate over T20 mirrored that over the birth of one-day cricket almost 50 years before. Many prophesied doom while progressives urged them to open their eyes to a greater cause: survival.

In order to retain credibility and allay some of the concerns of the doubters the decision was made to resist the gimmicks of Max Cricket. There were 11 players, an over was an over and no runs were doubled. The first professional T20 fixture was played in Hove, Sussex on 13 June 2003. Both players and fans didn't quite know what to make of it but glorious weather, intrigue and lusty blows saw crowds flock to grounds across the country. Even larger stadiums like Lord's saw sell-out crowds for a domestic fixture for the first time since the 1950s. Commercially the tournament was a godsend to the counties and even chairmen who had concerns had to concede that financially the gamble had saved their business. Whether fans liked it or not it had saved the professional game in England. County cricket could be propped up by subsidisation but what if its benefactors one day tired of the financial millstone of a romantic, cherished but hopelessly uncommercial national game? Seeing the success in England, other countries wasted no time in establishing their own domestic tournaments. Naturally expansive players revelled in the risk-free format though it soon became clear that clever shot selection and tactics brought greater rewards than trying to hit every ball out of the ground.

By 2005 T20 had achieved sufficiently widespread endorsement to be elevated to an international format. When New Zealand played Australia in the first ever T20I the Kiwis wore retro kits and amusing hairstyles and the general approach was one of comic light relief after the Tests rather than a serious contest in its own right. Ricky Ponting smashed 98 but wasn't convinced T20 internationals were there to stay. Nevertheless, the ICC, fearing losing control of the game and its profits to a next-generation Packer, moved quickly to create a T20 World Cup as one of its flagship events. Given what has transpired in the last decade it may be surprising to learn that the most vehement opposition came from Pakistan and India. Both boards dug their heels in and exclaimed that their teams would never play T20. Efforts were made to placate them and eventually they agreed to a World T20 in 2007 as long as their attendance was optional. In the end they agreed to participate on the understanding they could host future events, if it proved a success.

As T20 became established and it became clear that it wouldn't be a flash in the pan like Cricket Max the sport began to recalibrate accordingly. English counties who had little prospect in the County Championship remodelled themselves with a T20 focus. As the format started to display its commercial potential players adjusted their outlook and techniques accordingly, hoping for bumper paydays and realise at least a fraction of the earning potential footballers were receiving. Those with the highest profile, and most eye-catching statistics made sure they got an agent and presented their credentials to franchise owners around the world. An average in the 20s was suddenly OK if it came with a strike rate of 200. Players like England's Owais Shah racked up the air miles with a succession of lucrative, short-term contracts around the world, proudly wearing whatever shirt invested in them. As with World Series Cricket, T20 was to prove a game-changer for players, providing them with a greater share of the sport's burgeoning profits. These profits also gave cricket in its heartlands a financially sustainable business model that in turn enabled investment in youth development and facilities. In an increasingly competitive sports entertainment business this was critical in cricket being able to compete.

With T20 quickly establishing itself as a popular and lucrative format the question then became the extent to which it could happily coexist with more traditional version of the game. Would T20 fans develop a passion for Test cricket? Or conversely would T20 draw interest and audiences from Test cricket and ODIs and leave those elder siblings vulnerable? For a sport that liked nothing better than peering into its soul, the media obsessed over whether T20 presented a threat to Tests or would completely transform the game. They weren't interested in the less provocative angle of appreciating the shortest format as a novel, supplementary form in an evolving game. It was a period when you would often overhear at a match someone proclaim that T20 would see the death of Test cricket within a decade.

Many people revelled in hating it. It was a marketing invention, they said, that had none of the hallmarks of cricket and was an empty and vacuous spectacle. Where was the artistry in a cow corner six compared to an elegant caress through the covers? Where was the nuance and beauty in a smash, bang, wallop under floodlights? For some it was not only a completely different sport but an imposter that would spell the death of the one and true sport they adored. But thinking back to the ECB consumer survey, the role of T20 was to access an as yet untapped market, not to please traditionalists. Counties, national boards and the ICC were all very quick to offer reassurance that Tests were still the ultimate form of the game and were not under threat. But inevitably commercial drivers saw Test series shortened to accommodate T20 fixtures, much to the disgust of many. It also saw the improvised and contrived shots created for T20 creep into the Test arena. Reverse paddles and switch-hits caused many a set of dentures coughed up in disgust by traditionalists. Loose strokes, batting collapses and vapid cameos were all blamed on T20 cricket.

But there was an alternative school of thought. If T20 could rejuvenate the game and bring a new generation to it then that meant discovering new talent and developing new audiences that could ensure the continuation of Test cricket. The revenue it attracted could insulate the risk of longer-format games domestically making a loss, thereby ensuring a continued supply of cricketers into Test match cricket. Once fans got the T20 bug it would surely only be a matter of time before they developed an appreciation for longer formats. T20 could be the saviour of cricket and rescue Tests from irrelevance and extinction. Whatever your view it was clear that T20 was here to stay and national boards and the ICC would need to ensure an appropriate balance with other formats.

Having taken the decision to adopt the format to head off any dastardly entrepreneurs at the pass the ICC were quick to christen T20 as its global development vehicle. It was feared that traditional formats were perceived as a bit pedestrian and impenetrable by would-be players in cricket's global outposts and that this was proving a constraint to boosting numbers and building profile in cricket's new nations. In contrast T20 provided a fast-paced, short duration package that promised instant excitement for thrill seekers. It helped that it was simpler and cheaper to stage and guaranteed a result within a few hours. As the basis for competition it offered the flexibility to offer evening leagues rather than asking players to give up their whole weekends. Cricket had the commitment to development and it now had the format to truly become global, or so the theory went. At international level T20 was thought to give emerging cricket nations the best opportunity to be competitive against established sides, providing the tantalising prospect of exciting, closely contested tournaments featuring teams from across the world. T20's emergence at the height of the ICC's development craze seemed propitious.

The rise of T20 had created a renewed nervousness around the future of Test cricket. The ICC's attempt to provide more context to the seemingly random succession of bilateral series, through formation of a Test championship and each team playing each other in an equal number of fixtures, had been resisted as too interventionist by a number of boards. What was needed was a classic icon series to remind everyone just how thrilling, engrossing and resonant Test matches could be. As fate would have it, after almost 20 years of meek, one-sided contests the Ashes was starting to bubble up again. England's introduction of central contracts, a longer-term approach to development and a grown-up selection policy had seen the national team become more competitive. The brittle, fractious defeatism of the nineties had been replaced by a new-found self-confidence. The Nasser Hussain era had given the team backbone and pride in performance and Michael Vaughan had added confidence and a will to win. In Trescothick,

Flintoff and Pietersen they finally had some world class players. Grievous Bodily Harmison could wreak havoc and mete out psychological blows on his day. For the first time in living memory there was genuine hope amongst English fans in the summer of 2005 that the Ashes could finally be regained.

What followed has since been labelled the greatest series ever. Australia arrived in England with a team of superstars bred in a culture of winning hard-wired into the team over the previous decade of unparalleled success. Winning had become a habit and ruthlessness had ensured that complacency had not set in. England had steadily built a strong squad and in Kevin Pietersen had unearthed a freakish talent who was refreshingly free from the hesitancy and self-doubt that had plagued previous English sides. The hosts entered the series on the back of a successful year and Vaughan ensured that the tone and rhetoric was confident bordering on the confrontational. When talismanic seamer Glen McGrath, for so long the scourge of English batting orders, got injured when treading on a ball during fielding drills the media and the public sensed that this could finally be England's year. Mark Nicholas, fronting the Channel 4 coverage on terrestrial TV, used all his charm to raise the tension and expectancy as the drama began to unfold. Steve Harmison reared an early short-pitched delivery into Ponting's nose. The Aussies knew they were in for a contest. The combination of cricket of the highest quality, tension, hope, attack and counter-attack, personality and respect held the nation captivated.

Cricket tragics like yours truly found that suddenly everyone wanted to talk cricket, in the office, on public transport, even at the football. With the media sensing the national mood and splashing cricket all over the papers the excitement built and built as the contest ebbed and flowed. Some of the passages of play were nothing short of breathlessly scintillating. Pietersen dismantling Shane Warne in one of the most testing spells he had ever bowled on his way to 158 was viewing of the very highest calibre. It made a mockery of those who said Test cricket was dull and pedestrian. It was the symphony to T20's ring tone ditty: depth, pathos, tension, drama, skill, courage. As Michael Vaughan lifted the Ashes in emotional, spine-tingling scenes there was a general consensus that Test cricket had to be preserved at all costs. It had been the ultimate advert for the ultimate sporting contest.

When strong teams were evenly matched Test cricket could reach a level no shorter format could get close to. Seeing how much it meant to the country, politicians rolled out the red carpet with an open top bus parade, an audience with the Queen and MBEs all round. For a brief period cricket felt central and triumphant rather than peripheral and apologetic. Nine million people watched the series on Channel 4. This didn't fit the narrative many wanted to force on the game, one of apathy, disinterest, creeping inertia and inevitable decline. But as the country glowed in cricketing triumph many asked the critical question: could cricket capitalise on this opportunity?

The 2005 Ashes showed how incredible Test match cricket at its best could be. But it also emphasised the painful reality that it was rarely at its best. Many encounters were hopelessly one-sided and lacked the context, tradition and vibrancy that makes the Ashes so special. Sides were generally dominant in home conditions but stuttering abroad, giving the Test programme a predictable, sometimes almost jaded feel. Test cricket had the ingredients to generate widespread interest, even devotion, be commercially lucrative and produce levels of drama other sports envied. But how often did these ingredients combine successfully? It didn't help that the quality of Test cricket varied markedly. Meek capitulations by Zimbabwe or Bangladesh and increasingly fitful and frustrating performances by the West Indies saw many games played to near-empty stadiums. While Test cricket retained a strong following in England and Australia where demand remained high and stadiums were packed, elsewhere interest in the longer form was ebbing. That is not to say there was not widespread interest in the results, as attested by the enduring popularity of live scorecards, but that there was less interest in witnessing the spectacle behind the statistics.

The 2007 World Cup was a vital one for the ICC for several reasons. Firstly, it was held in the West Indies in the hope that hosting a global event would reignite the region's love affair with the game and arrest the worrying decline in Caribbean cricket. The international cricket community were genuinely saddened that the West Indies were not the force they were and fans, commentators and administrators all desperately hoped the World Cup could unleash the passion and the magic once more. Secondly, the 2007 World Cup was to be the showcase for the new development-focused ICC. With an unprecedented six associate teams participating it promised to show the strength and breadth of the new cricketing world.

For the 2007 tournament the traditional qualification method of all teams vying for a berth via the ICC Trophy had been replaced by a more complicated structure of pre-qualification. This reflected the fact that with 97 members it was impossible to run a single tournament as in the past and also acknowledged that there was an increasing disparity in quality between all the associates and affiliates. This meant that the journey to the World Cup became a dream for all and gave a competitive focus for the years leading up to the tournament. The World Cup itself was just the crowning showpiece of a much longer qualifying process that began as soon as the previous World Cup had concluded. The process hardly registered with the vast majority of cricket fans but helped give shape and purpose to cricket at associate and affiliate level. However improbable it may have been, in theory Luxembourg could begin a miraculous ascent to the World Cup at the European Cricket Council Trophy in August 2003, or Sierra Leone through the Africa World Cup Qualifying Series in March 2004. These tournaments eventually provided 12 qualifiers to the 2005 ICC Trophy, hosted by Ireland.

These teams represented the strongest associate nations and it wasn't just a prized World Cup spot they were competing for. In addition to coming under the wing of the High Performance Programme to ensure their competitiveness for the World Cup, the qualifying teams would also be granted One Day International Status for the next World Cup cycle. They'd also get a share of a $2.5 million development fund earmarked to increase competitiveness of the leading associate nations.

The stakes had never been higher and it was critical for aspirational associates to qualify for the ICC Trophy in the first place and then finish as one of the top five teams (Kenya were already guaranteed a berth by virtue of their special consideration following the 2003 World Cup). This presented a huge opportunity for the leading associates but also a real risk that under-performance could set their development back by a decade and see them look on enviously as others pulled away from them through increased funding, higher status and more matches. For every jubilant winner there would be a despondent loser. This was the fate of Nepal, who despite playing first class international cricket failed to qualify for the qualifier.

Ireland, Bermuda, Scotland and Canada claimed their spoils by making the semi-finals and they were soon joined by the Netherlands, who defeated UAE in the last-chance saloon, the fifth-place play-off. With the tournament representing such a seminal moment for all competing nations Ireland had a distinct advantage as hosts, as did other European nations in seaming conditions. It was a stiffer challenge for Asian qualifiers like the UAE and Oman, who had spin-centred attacks.

The elevation of a handful of new ODI nations brought more variety to top level international cricket and brought marketable, statistically visible cricket beyond the Test nations. The experience was meant to harden the qualifiers before the World Cup itself. When the teams landed in the Caribbean they weren't just playing for their own pride but for the cause of all associates and a vindication of the development programme.

The tournament was meant to be a carnival of cricket but organisers did their best to snuff out any joy by banning musical instruments and pricing out local fans. This ensured a sterile atmosphere in oddly sanitised stadiums. The format was designed to give broadcasters what they wanted, which was the maximum possible number of guaranteed fixtures featuring India and other lucrative markets. This commercial driver saw a contrived, elongated preliminary stage that seemed to go on forever and saw the tournament struggle to generate enthusiasm and momentum. Wrongly, this perception of a bloated tournament was blamed on the inclusion of more associates. This led many to feel that a more inclusive tournament was diluting the spectacle and therefore compromising the sport's ability to showcase the virtues of the game to the world. Despite the efforts of the High Performance Programme there were a number of very one-sided encounters.

Bermuda had performed well to qualify for the tournament but once there their small player pool and seemingly amateurish approach was exposed. It had one of the longest cricketing heritages of any of the associates with games played regularly from the 18th century. Cricket was an important part of island identity and the sporting scene. But it only had a handful of clubs and leading players lacked exposure to higher-quality opposition. The recruitment of Warwickshire stalwart and England A player David Hemp added experience and quality but the core of the team were laid-back island club cricketers and in many games it showed. One of their most talented players was left-arm spinner Dwayne Leverock, who bowled with admirable control and guile. However, weighing over 20 stone he was somewhat cumbersome in the field and a photograph of him diving, and wobbling in strenuous motion, to take a decent slip catch became one of the images of the tournament. It was an image that presented associate cricket as amateurish and a source of fun, which was unfair given the quality of the catch and the player. The media made much of him being a policeman by profession, a bit of colour for the coverage emphasising the romance of the underdog but serving to feed the view that there wasn't a place for such a supporting cast at the sport's showcase event. The optics weren't ideal for the development programme. A comprehensive qualification process to select the best of emerging cricket nations hadn't seen the emergence of a potential new cricketing super-power but a tiny British overseas territory. Was cricket still essentially an English game after all?

Bermuda lost by 243 runs in their opening game, bundled out for 78 by Sri Lanka, then conceded 413 runs to India. It made for chastening viewing for the High Performance Programme and champions of development. But in another group there was a ray of hope. Ireland, who had qualified for their first World Cup, had managed to wrestle a tie in their first fixture against Zimbabwe. Next up was Pakistan and no one gave them a chance. Their bowling was spearheaded by a trio of expats who were professionals in the Irish League and had qualified through residency. The pitch was tacky and slow, making the lack of pace a virtue rather than a hindrance. Australian Dave Langford-Smith had opener Mohammed Hafeez caught behind early and South African émigré Andre Botha then bowled some of the slowest, canniest seamers ever to grace a World Cup to have Pakistan in trouble. His eight overs only went for five runs and he took the wickets of Imran Nazir and Inzamam-ul-Haq.

They bowled Pakistan out for a meagre 132. Ireland not only had a chance for a historic, headline-grabbing victory over a full member but a win would see them progress to the super eight stage, at the expense of their opponents. Pakistan weren't willing to succumb without a fight and Mohammed Sami unleashed an intense 90mph spell that threatened to blow the Irish away. At 15/2 indefatigable Northants wicketkeeper, Niall O'Brien, came to the wicket. He turned around a spell of bad form in spectacular fashion, playing fluently to reach a half century, pulling his team-mates along with him. With only 20 runs needed they had a wobble with O'Brien holing out and two other wickets falling. But Niall's younger brother, Kevin, and captain Trent Johnston saw the Irish home. The Irish celebrated as only they can the most famous victory in their cricketing history, a victory that could change everything for them. Cricketing romantics across the world celebrated too, with many adopting Ireland as their second team. The Irish heroics had given the tournament the lift it needed.

While the victory filled many with joy and hope the narrow-minded view that expansion would dilute what they held dear in the game still prevailed. Those of this view put the success down to the handful of Irish expats who had played a starring role, belittling any claims of genuine development in the country and any talk of the victory marking the emergence of another top-level cricket nation. The result split the ICC too. The development wing celebrated a success for the HPP and a vindication, in part at least, for an expanded World Cup with a development focus. But the money men watched the drama unfold with utter horror. For them the result was a disaster. The elimination of one of the leading nations and strongest markets at the first hurdle saw broadcasters fuming at a significant loss of revenue. They had paid a premium for the rights package only to see the return on their investment devalued. The ICC were anxious, for if broadcasters had their profits constrained would they bid as much next time round?

Ireland's success saw them stay in the Caribbean for another month, emulating Kenya's achievement of progressing from the group stages. It gave the Ireland camp, journalists and fans a lifetime of anecdotes. Even now mere mention of 2007 will see Irish cricket fans commence an hour or more of blissful nostalgic reverie. After their Caribbean adventure the Irish squad returned to a heroes' welcome and renewed expectation. But the Irish Cricket Union remained resolutely amateur. This was the context for the appointment of Warren Deutrom as CEO, an astute businessman determined to bring professionalism and progress to the Irish game. With Kenya's promise being undermined by maladministration and corruption Ireland were the new development darlings. Deutrom asked awkward questions of the ICC, wanting to know what criteria needed to be fulfilled to gain full member status. After back-to-back Intercontinental Cup championships he asked what further proof was needed that they were ready. He met with prevarication and vagueness. Although the ICC couldn't admit as much to a fired-up Deutrom, the process was deliberately subjective as ultimately it was the full members rather than the ICC who would sanction another joining their club and they had a vested interest in not diluting their share of the game's profits. Deutrom would not be fobbed off. For his part he slowly professionalised the Irish game and attracted top level fixtures. He systematically addressed any weakness or shortcoming he felt the ICC would use against Ireland in their bid for elevation.

Following the World Cup the development programme was given the green light for a further expansion of the qualifying structure. The regional-based qualification process was replaced by a multi-divisional World Cricket League. This would provide a so called 'meritocratic pathway' to World Cup qualification for all associate and affiliate teams and in the process offer regular, competitive fixtures. There were five divisions sitting atop a regional qualification process. In each division the top two teams would be promoted and the bottom two relegated. In this way even the lowliest ranked team could progress through to the ICC Trophy and from there to the World Cup itself. It marked a fundamental shift in global cricket. For the first time it wasn't just the world's leading teams playing regular international cricket. The international cricket calendar was suddenly a lot fuller and richer.

On a glorious summer weekend there may be not only an Ashes Test and a bilateral T20 or ODI series between full members, but an Intercontinental Cup game and World Cricket League fixtures. And unlike bilateral series the World Cricket League had context. Finally, context, that evasive concept for cricket. Every result mattered, every victory or loss was part of an unfolding journey for an emerging cricket nation. With the vast majority of cricket's fanbase having a myopic, top-heavy view of the sport the WCL sadly only had a niche profile. Those fans who were brave enough to look beyond the Test teams were in for a treat. Most, regrettably, remained ignorant of its existence and its many virtues.

A meritocratic pathway was a commendable reform but the imbalance in the ICC's approach remained. Where did the pathway lead and how many could tread its path to the end? Its introduction signalled a further commitment to development but if the ICC were making development central to its strategy then there would be a further expansion of World Cup opportunities, a more even distribution of funding amongst members and a fundamental review of status in the sport. Why wasn't the whole of the WCL given ODI status rather than just its top league? What an incredible opportunity to market cricket in all its emerging nations. An opportunity missed. Why not extend the meritocratic pathway all the way through the sport and allow elevation into full membership, or demotion for weaker full members down into the WCL? The historic rights of full members prevented these exciting, potentially game-changing (pun very much intended), reforms. It meant that for all its virtue the WCL was only ever a partial solution to democratising the global game. Or seen another way, the dream of one part of the ICC was being undermined by another. Dr Jekyll and Mr Hyde were at work.

The World Cricket League was revolutionary in many ways and should have been heralded far and wide by the wise and wizened as the structure cricket needed as a 21st-century sport. The sad thing is not that people didn't agree, it is that it didn't even register sufficiently to generate a debate. This wasn't helped by the withholding of status that consigned the vast majority of games to be statistically invisible. For all the promise of the league the reality remained that the lower reaches of international cricket would pass the vast majority by until an associate appeared at the World Cup. It was only then that most fans would remember countries beyond the traditional full members played the game. However far the world game expanded it was still for fans to decide what levels they wished to engage with.

As the World Cricket League was implemented the work of the regional offices redoubled. Promotion through the league provided mini milestones for the five-year plans. The approach became even more interventionist as key performance indicators (KPIs) were introduced. Boards completed detailed surveys of number of players, coaches and grounds with their allotted development officer looking over their shoulder. Over time more and more detail was requested: the number of turf and artificial pitches, the percentage of league players locally produced, the number of outreach initiatives run and their success in player identification and retention. Within this top-down approach the spectre of funding raised its head. Traditionally funding was allocated solely on the basis of membership category. Associates would get more than affiliates, an incentive in itself to secure promotion of status. It soon became obvious that this was not the most equitable or targeted way to distribute the war chest. Countries with small player pools and limited potential to develop, like Gibraltar, received the same as huge countries with significant potential like the USA. The solution was scorecard funding. The scorecard awarded funding based on fulfilling a range of specified KPIs. Performance-based funding ruffled a few members' feathers but certainly challenged any culture of complacency. The more members achieved the more resources they received for another push. The logic was it would incentivise the countries with a deeper commitment to growth and development and limit funding to members where there was limited potential for further growth. Big brother was watching and big brother held the purse-strings.

The initial WCL rankings were set by where teams finished in the ICC Trophy and the feeder tournaments that preceded it. This put the HPP teams like Bermuda, Canada and the Netherlands at the top of the tree, followed by others in the ICC Trophy like Denmark, Papua New Guinea and the UAE. The bottom rung of the ladder was perhaps the most intriguing. Division 5 comprised teams that were either near the beginning of their cricketing journey, and as we've seen there were plenty of those following the race to 100 members, or established teams that had not performed well in the qualification process for the last World Cup, be it due to loss of form, player availability or just good old-fashioned rotten luck. As ever in competitive sport there needs to be a cut-off and quite a few teams found themselves below the WCL structure. They still played in regional tournaments of course but they were disenfranchised in the new world order, at least until their next opportunity to qualify in four years' time. Most of the teams in this position were the new recruits who had become members in the last decade. They could have been forgiven for wondering where they sat in the ICC's view of development after they'd served their purpose in the race to 100 members!

In late May 2008, 12 teams arrived on the picturesque channel island of Jersey to contest WCL division 5, with the theoretical chance of qualification for the 2011 World Cup. Only two journalists had flown in to report on the tournament, the current editor of *Wisden* and yours truly. We were both assigned chauffeurs which was a lovely touch. The field comprised long-standing members such as USA, Singapore and Nepal, all looking to prove a point, a clutch of newer members with expat-dominated squads, like Germany and Norway, and teams with a local player base but little previous international exposure like Japan, Vanuatu, Bahamas and Afghanistan. There was considerable excitement as the teams mingled in the hotel prior to the tournament. Unlike top level international cricket, where analysts know the strengths of every team and every player, no one really knew what to expect. There was also a heady mixture of approaches. The hosts, Jersey, were disciplined and well drilled. The Bahamas in contrast looked like they were there for the ride. There was chatter too about the reliance many of the teams had on expats. The USA carried themselves with a degree of arrogance, clearly believing they were starting far too low in the pecking order. Japan, who to their credit had largely selected Japanese players rather than go down the expat route, looked sheepish and uncertain.

The team that generated the most interest was Afghanistan. Cricket had only started in the country a few years before thanks to the British embassy arranging fixtures and Afghans returning from refugee camps in Pakistan where they had learnt the game. Cricket had been the only sport the Taliban had permitted, partly as they preferred long trousers to shorts. They had made their tournament debut in the 2004 Asian Trophy, following which the MCC had toured under Mike Gatting and invited their two star players, all-rounder Mohammad Nabi and fast bowler Hamid Hassan, to come to England to play for the club. To the outside world Afghanistan was known for war and unrest. That they were seeking redemption and recognition through cricket made for a stirring, romantic story and had been picked up by a film-maker, Tim Albone, who arrived with the squad to shoot his story of the team's attempt to qualify for the World Cup. Even the off-field footage was compelling, as when the squad stood by the edge of a road by the hotel looking up in bewilderment at the traffic lights wondering what they were.

Watching the Afghans play was nerve-shredding. With the bat their tendency was to swing themselves off their feet to strike the ball not just over the boundary but over to mainland France. Ignoring conditions and the niggardly seam that the hosts used so cleverly, they tried to hit every single ball even when the required rate could comfortably be reached by sensible rotation of the strike. This naïve approach was seemingly encouraged by their coach Taj Malik, who stood in anguish by the boundary rope imploring them to hit big, collapsing to his knees and praying when the tactics saw wickets regularly fall. I witnessed this from the press tent, sat next to a very animated commentator for BBC Pashtu. Several times their bowling got them out of trouble with many of their opponents clearly having never faced hostile bowling at 85mph before. Their emotions and reactions sometimes overstepped the mark. It was raw, emotional and not always appropriate. But it made for excellent footage and won't be forgotten by anyone who witnessed their games. There was certainly a sense amongst all present that they were witnessing something special. In the end they rode a roller-coaster in securing promotion through a narrow win over Nepal in the semi-final.

The few spectators that came to WCL events were rewarded with exciting, dramatic cricket where every game mattered and each team were at a key juncture in their cricketing journey. Compared to a dead rubber in a full-member ODI bilateral series it was entertaining cricket. The quality was patchy and the tactics often unfathomable but you felt part of something special. The trick was to gain broader recognition and profile for cricket at this level, both to celebrate the new-found breadth of the global game but also to make a case for it being financially sustainable. For Afghanistan it was just the start of a remarkable journey, though Taj Malik's emotion was replaced by the experience and tactical nous of former Pakistan Test player Kabir Khan, who instilled a more professional approach. Kabir guided them through division 4 in Tanzania and then division 3 in Argentina. They made it through to the World Cup Qualifier, a rebranded ICC Trophy, in South Africa in 2009 but narrowly missed out on a World Cup place, though they gained ODI status for the next World Cup cycle. It had been a miraculous rise through the ranks and for a time every features writer worth his or her salt focused on the Afghan story. The raw talent in the squad had been moulded but under the surface of professionally coached players lay the explosive power with both bat and ball that had been witnessed in Jersey.

Afghanistan became the poster boys for the ICC, who capitalised on their extraordinary story to showcase that dreams could come true in their new structure for world cricket. This was great for Afghanistan and their passion, verve and skill had lit up associate cricket. But it had the unintended consequence of drawing attention away from other countries and development goals more broadly. As you'd expect the winners took the plaudits but there were some lower-profile losers too. Teams like Argentina found themselves slipping down the rungs and would eventually fall off the bottom of the WCL structure. A nation with cricketing heritage and huge potential failing to capitalise on opportunities. The structure was as brutal as it was compelling. A few bad results could see demotion and a loss of development momentum for another four years, not to mention a cut in funding. This naturally saw teams seek to pick the most competitive teams they could, which in practice often meant recently qualified expats over home-grown graduates from their development programmes.

WCL results and progression was the critical metric for performance but the ICC were also targeting participation milestones. This was an important element of scorecard funding and the ICC targeted a doubling in participants outside Test nations from 750,000 to 1.5

million. Development officers cracked the whip of the boards to reach out to new communities and institutions to grow the player base. In countries like Gibraltar, Malta and the Cook Islands it was difficult to achieve anything more than incremental increases. But these modest gains could be more than compensated if cricket could make a breakthrough in highly populated countries like Canada, the USA and Malaysia. All members increased the volume of school visits and outreach programmes to ratchet up the figures expected from them. The ICC's target was for participants and this could include anyone who had picked up a bat or ball whether they remained in the game or not. In this sense measuring participants was very different from measuring players. In countries like Germany increased levels of economic migration was in effect doing the job for them.

For a decade from 2005 participation levels in Germany ballooned from 800 to over 6,000. The board were overwhelmed with requests to be matched to clubs and new clubs were being formed across the country on an almost weekly basis. The origin of the players was invariably Pakistan and Afghanistan. This huge increase changed the nature of cricket in the country dramatically. Where once it had been a small cricket community based around grounds in British military bases now it was impromptu tape ball matches on waste ground up and down the country. The challenge for members like Germany was not recruitment, it was keeping the new-found players within their system and retaining control. When the board weren't matching players to teams and overseeing the registration of new clubs they were resisting coups by those who had a complaint about match fees, eligibility rules or tournament specifications. It was a similar story in Scandinavia where participant numbers rocketed from the low hundreds to several thousand.

Although new recruits were welcome and kept ICC development offices off their backs it presented some problems. In Denmark, for instance, where cricket had a rich and proud heritage albeit on a relatively modest scale, a tipping point was reached where the balance between white Danish players and economic migrants altered to such an extent that it came to be seen as a foreign sport. Freddie Klokker, Danish wicketkeeper-batsman cum development officer, recalled how parents would often take their kids out of training camps once they saw that the vast majority of participants were Asian. The impact of race on cricket development has seldom been written about but has been a crucial factor. While there are many cases of excellent ethnic integration across Europe and beyond there is no doubt that where the ratio of cricketers is considerably out of kilter with the society at large it has proved a blocker to attracting indigenous players. In turn this has impacted how the media has covered the game. Is it considered a Norwegian sport or a sport played by certain communities in Norway? In Denmark such potential tensions have eased as second and third generation players of subcontinental heritage have taken up the game. Born in and learning cricket in the country, they have greater cultural affinity with classmates and neighbours. Denmark now have an ethnically diverse national team, most of whom have progressed together through the country's development programme, which is very different from local players feeling aggrieved if losing their place in the team to recently qualified expats in their mid-thirties.

In France two distinct cricketing cultures sat uncomfortably cheek by jowl. British expat communities playing in traditional clubs outside the major cities and Asian immigrants in Paris wanting to play cricket in a different way and focus funding on different priorities. Eventually the tensions between these two communities resulted in a power grab in the board and considerable bitterness. It would be naïve to assume race wasn't a major talking point in associate cricket. In a sense this is only an amplified example of a general theme in modern society. The bottom line is that migration significantly increased playing numbers and went a long way towards the ICC meeting their target. In contrast with a few exceptions, such as Nepal and Nigeria, the contribution of new indigenous cricketers towards the target has been minimal. That has been an enduring challenge for all members in their outreach programmes.

Chapter 17

New markets, old problem

THE biggest success in boosting participation numbers has been a transformation in the women's game. Women had played cricket from the beginnings of the sport in England but social pressures and conservative values had proved a constraint. There were women- only clubs in the Victorian age both in England and the Commonwealth but these pioneers often faced prejudice and opposition. Traditionalists campaigned vehemently for cricket to be a male-only game and certainly for any matches played in public. This led many early women's teams to play discreetly away from disapproving eyes. In such circumstances it was difficult for the women's game to develop, either in scale or in quality. As social attitudes changed in the 20th century so women's cricket gained more momentum and confidence. Unsurprisingly perhaps, given the patriarchal society in which it was founded, the ICC did not take responsibility for women's cricket. Women's Ashes matches had been played since 1934, although it was bizarrely stipulated that those pioneering Test tourists could not be married. In February 1958 the national women's boards of Australia, England, the Netherlands, New Zealand and South Africa formed the International Women's Cricket Council with the objective of organising international fixtures. In 1973 the first women's ODI was played and since then this has become the predominant format in the women's game, with Test matches staged but at a much lower frequency. The first cricket World Cup was staged in 1973 by the women's board, two years before the ICC held the inaugural World Cup in the men's game.

A critical figure in the development of the women's game was Rachel Heyhoe Flint, who captained England from 1966 to 1978. As well as being a leading player in the history of the game, striking the first six in Test cricket and scoring a third more runs than anyone else, she was also instrumental in raising the profile of the women's game and gaining broader recognition and support. She played a leading role in establishing the World Cup in 1973 by personally campaigning for sponsorship and she campaigned for greater coverage, writing reports for newspapers herself if no others were forthcoming. Given this passion and commitment it was with great pride the so-called W.G. of the women's game led the England team in the first ever women's international to be played at Lord's, in 1976.

Despite Heyhoe Flint's feats on the field and boundless profile-raising off it, women's cricket remained a marginal, amateur game into the 1990s. While participation levels and standards were steadily increasing it remained firmly in the shadow of the men's game with very little recognition or visibility in its own right. When England batter Charlotte Edwards began her career she played in a skirt, paid for her own kit and had to beg employers for time off to play for her country. By the time she retired after a stellar career spanning two decades the women's game had been professionalised in several countries, was regularly televised and was extensively covered in the media.

By the mid-nineties more countries were supporting women's cricket and the World Cup saw 11 teams competing, including the Netherlands and Ireland. Women's cricket was brought under the auspices of the ICC following a merger with the International Women's Cricket Council after the 2004 Women's World Cup. Immediately a women's cricket committee was formed that was tasked with making recommendations for growth of the women's game to the development committee. The timing was propitious for women's cricket as it had come under the aegis of development at a time when development was a critical part of the ICC's mission statement and had increasing access to funding year on year. By 2006 the ICC proudly announced in their annual report that women's cricket was being played in 45 countries. Members were encouraged to establish women's teams and in the process participation figures got a boost. Another significant boost in profile came when the ICC incorporated women's events into the media rights bundle and brought the men's and women's World Cups together. This was an important show of faith and saw the women's game get equal coverage to the men's. This, along with commitment of members, saw women's cricket played in 96 ICC member countries by 2010. Emerging stars such as Australia's Ellyse Perry enjoyed a worldwide profile and sponsorship appeal unimaginable just a decade earlier. Though the sport as a whole faced challenges in the new millennium, women's cricket had been an unqualified success.

While the women's game was on a course for professionalisation amongst traditional full members it was also becoming more prominent within the associate world. Most members established a women's team even if the player pool was very limited and standards low. The carrot of qualification for global tournaments provided a spur, as in the men's game, and helped drive up standards and encourage a professional approach.

2009 marked the ICC's centenary year. Its modern incarnation was of course unrecognisable from the body formed with the sole aim of organising a Triangular tournament between England, Australia and South Africa. This isn't perhaps surprising after a hundred years. What is more surprising is that the ICC of 2009 was completely unrecognisable from just 15 years before when two men working from an MCC back office comprised cricket's global governance. Now it had gleaming new offices in Dubai, a budget of over £250 million on the back of the unprecedented sale of media rights and over 70 members of staff across the world. It marked its anniversary by taking a 'catch the spirit' flag across the world to demonstrate its new-found global reach. Three members had grown to 104, two of which, Chile and Kuwait, received the flag with fitting pomp and ceremony.

One of the flagship events of the centenary year was the World T20. The ICC's decision to adopt the shortest format early had proved shrewd and the inaugural World T20 in 2007 had been a resounding success, both on the field and commercially. A decision had been taken to reduce the next 50-over World Cup to 14 teams, a decision out of kilter with the rhetoric of expanding the global game. In compensation emerging nations got increased opportunities in T20. At the 2009 event England were expected to make a strong statement with a resounding victory over the Netherlands at the opening game at Lord's. But the men in orange had other ideas. The Dutch squad was a mixture of homegrown players like garrulous gloveman Jeroen Smits and batsman Tom de Grooth augmented by professionals with a Dutch connection, including Essex's Ryan ten Doeschate and future Australian international paceman Dirk Nannes.

It started well enough for the hosts with Luke Wright and Ravi Bopara racing to a century stand off only 66 balls. But they then let the Dutch back into the game with a series of limp dismissals and as their scoring rate fell away alarmingly they posted a modest 162. Dutch pinch-hitter Darron Reekers, converted from stingy medium-pacer to a boundary bully, smote a few sixes to keep the Dutch up with the rate before de Grooth and ten Doeschate combined to threaten an upset. England should have defended 16 off 10 balls but a botched run-out attempt by Stuart Broad off the final delivery allowed ten Doeschate and Edgar Schiferli to scamper through for two and claim a memorable victory. The scenes of Dutch jubilation will live long in the memory for all who witnessed them. What was more telling than the result itself was the ensuing reaction. The Dutch were a well-drilled, professionalised outfit that had benefitted from tailored support through the High Performance Programme. They had a few players with professional experience too. So although it was a significant coup for the Dutch it wasn't surely as the BBC reported 'the most ignominious cricketing defeat of all time'. The coverage demonstrated that the perception of associates in the mainstream cricket fraternity was not of countries closing the gap and professionalising but of oddities and outliers, the source of trivia questions in years to come and wearers of colourful kits. Even if the ICC were taking global development seriously the majority of the mainstream press weren't.

The reaction in the Netherlands was interesting too. The headlines and euphoria gave the squad a brief moment of fame, with leading players appearing on chat shows and cricket getting rare coverage in newspapers and magazines. The board hoped this would be a springboard for greater profile and interest. In truth though it proved a short-lived quirk, the media pouncing on a topical, feel-good angle. Cricket remained very much a minority sport in the country. An eye-catching victory and an impressive global ranking made little difference. It was a demonstration of the scale of the task facing the ICC in popularising and developing the game in regions like continental Europe.

The year 2009 marked something of a high-water mark in the development drive. The Intercontinental Cup had been joined by an Intercontinental Shield giving more teams first class exposure, membership was over 100 and a few members shy of its peak and levels of investment continued to increase. The World Cricket League had been expanded to eight six-team global divisions.

However, cracks were starting to appear. After five years of the Intercontinental Cup there was still no sign that a proper prize, elevation to Test status, was forthcoming. Deutrom and others were wondering whether talk of it being a proving ground for Test cricket was just hollow rhetoric. The ICC were very keen to champion Ireland and Afghanistan at every opportunity as development success stories but what about the other 90 or so nations below Test level? The growth of women's cricket and the steep increase in participation figures, albeit largely flowing from economic migration trends, were undoubtedly a success. But what was the return on investment for the $2.5 million a year ploughed into development?

Although the ICC's annual reports continued to give significant coverage to development successes and were littered with the 'meritocratic pathway' mantra, other references began to creep in that hinted at a change of approach. The percentage of non-ICC revenue became a critical development criterion. Were the ICC seeking to wean off over-reliance of members on their grants? Were they starting to wonder what they were paying for? Some of the references to members sometimes switched to references to markets. Outwardly they had a meritocratic approach but behind closed doors they wanted to back potential. An example of this was a major research project established to look into the prospects for growth in China and the USA. A hundred years after ignoring the USA's prospects it was now looking to see if it had any left.

Among the glut of new members in the noughties one in particular caught the eye. China's accession in 2004 provided the tantalising prospect of a step change in the global game. If cricket's global credentials were based merely on shading of a map this was a breakthrough moment. Was it just a handful of players in a few isolated local leagues? Or could it be something more transformational, like the Chinese government endorsing the game in a bid to make it a mainstream sport?

The Shanghai Cricket Club had been founded in the 1860s by British expats who soon busied themselves in arranging inter-port matches with fellow countrymen far from home in Hong Kong and Singapore. It was an exclusive club and exclusively for the British. In Hong Kong a few natives were drawn to the game but this was not the case in mainland China. Had they been the sport would have certainly been banned under Chairman Mao's cultural revolution as a symbol of the decadent West. In any case the ground was seized and the SCC consigned to history. Under the authoritarian regime table tennis and basketball were the games approved of and therefore they were games several generations of Chinese grew up playing.

Once Mao's regime finally came to an end in the late 70s and the country's attitude to the West shifted from outright disdain to caution cricket slowly returned. Expats in Shanghai reformed the SCC and in 1994 hosted a team from Hong Kong. The media pounced on a quirky angle and a short report featured in the national news. The article was from the not particularly helpful 'strange game played where you wouldn't expect it to be' school of cricket journalism but nevertheless it did serve to raise the level of awareness and intrigue of the game. Hong Kong, then still a UK territory, helped provide a catalyst for development.

With the Hong Kong Sixes proving a resounding success the concept was exported to Shanghai by Kiwi Scott Brown where it soon became a social highlight, attracting major sponsors and the likes of Botham and Viv Richards. The Sixes helped the game become established in comparatively multi-cultural Shanghai, with three divisions of clubs and regular tours to Hong Kong and Singapore. They even had access to indoor nets and facilities for training during the winter.

The ICC sensed an opportunity for a major new market and the chief executive, Malcolm Speed, led a delegation in 2006 to assess the potential. This led to a promise of a £5m grant to help China prepare for hosting the Asian Games. Cricket's inclusion in the Games and the wish to perform creditably as hosts ensured government interest and support. It was hoped that this would prove the catalyst for widespread growth. This was reflected in the Chinese Cricket Association setting extremely ambitious goals, including qualifying for a World Cup by 2019 and playing Tests by 2020. The Asian Cricket Council, also excited by the potential, invested six-figure development funds too. This largesse wasn't just a philanthropic punt. If China became a leading cricket power, it was argued, it could boost the sport's global revenue by 40%. It was a big 'if' of course, but then it was a big prize. They could also prove a useful counterpoint to Indian dominance of cricket governance and direction.

Rather than follow the typical model for emerging cricket nations of expat-focused clubs in China the centres of the game are universities and the players very much home-grown. Watching the Chinese team play it is immediately apparent what elements of the game most appeal to the Chinese psyche. The batting is studious and tentative, with a run rate of two an over not uncommon even in T20s. The emphasis is very much on batting out the overs if they can. But when it comes to fielding they are absolutely electric, demonstrating athleticism, supreme skill and searing intensity. A dive to save a run in the covers is greeted by exuberant cheers with everyone running in to give the fielder in question high tens. A lack of adventure with the bat has often led to some very comprehensive defeats indeed. A total in the 30s can and often does get knocked off within a few overs with a flurry of sixes. The players slowly develop skills and game awareness but it can be difficult and dispiriting to watch. It is difficult to imagine a team playing in that way being competitive in the near future. But then you remind yourself that these are not expats, they are young Chinese batsmen and bowlers. And that is still exciting, however modest their results.

Unfortunately the Asian Games did not provide the breakthrough for profile and participation that had been hoped for and by 2014 the funding began to slow as China's promise failed to bear fruit. The Asian Cricket Council turned their attention to more established cricket nations like Nepal. The feeling was that the opportunity had been presented but China had not capitalised on it. There was a sense that China had been worth a punt but wasn't destined to be the game's golden goose after all. What would be transformative for cricket in China is inclusion in the Olympics. If the ICC set aside their commercial fears of diluting their brand and ceding control of broadcast revenue the Olympics could be the answer to unleashing the potential of cricket in this huge market. What is potentially a game-changer is not the direct investment the IOC provide to competing countries but the fact that countries take Olympic sports seriously and introduce structures and investment to organise and develop the sport on a national level. Every province now has a rugby sevens team and 10,000 play the sport in universities. This directly flows from inclusion in the Olympics. The decision for the ICC is simple: if they want cricket to take off in China they need to put short-term financial targets of full members to one side and embrace the Olympic dream.

In the absence of the Olympics the development model has been to coach schoolteachers and hope they then inspire a generation of Chinese to play the game. But limited resources are spread too thinly in such a vast country to make a difference. The number of players in the national championships has flatlined over the last decade. The state-of-the-art Guangdong International Stadium has not been used for international cricket since 2012 and has now been leased out for an expat league, a sad symbol of the shattered dreams in Chinese cricket. China may be a major potential market but it remains a small, uncompetitive cricket nation.

The prospective market that has had the ICC salivating most was not one of the new members who joined in the noughties but a country that had been a member for almost 50 years. A country that stands alone as the biggest market in global sport. The ICC had a recurring dream and it was American. For many, converting the USA's undoubted promise into reality was the key to justifying any claims to cricket being a global sport. Unfortunately, the story of American cricket over the last half century has been one of false dawn after false dawn: many of them as comical as they are depressing. US cricket has become a byword for maladministration.

America had been built on immigration long before the waves of post-war economic migration that has taken cricket to new outposts across the world. There are therefore plenty from cricket-playing backgrounds who play the game. This includes large populations of West Indians as well as those of Indian and Pakistani origin. Cricket communities can be found dotted across many of the key cities with centres in Florida, Texas and New York. Add this to a sporting culture, high potential for sponsorship and access to facilities and USA should have quickly developed to become a full member and a major cricket market.

So what has gone wrong? Well, where do we start? There has always been cricket in America but American cricket has never got going. This was partly due to the breathtaking ineptitude of its governing body the USA Cricket Association, that was forever imploding and characterised by infighting, self-interest and perplexing policies. It is not an organisation you'd want leading the development of cricket in the most important market in the world. Not quite the Monster Raving Loony Party getting a surprise mandate to rule Britain, but not far off. It has hoovered up money and spent it unwisely, and obsessed over power politics rather than leading a united cricket community towards a common goal.

Without strong and inclusive leadership America's dispersed and fragmented cricket communities were propelled by parochial self-interest. In many cases this meant expat clubs remaining insular and culturally distinct rather than reaching out to the mainstream population. Any far-sighted national body would have viewed success as transition to the sport being run and played by mainstream Americans rather than insular pockets of expats. It was only this, however long it took, that would ensure the USA reached its potential as a cricketing nation. But rather than adopt a systematic approach to achieving this long-term aim, the USACA has backed a succession of silken-tongued entrepreneurs promising the American dream in glitzy, get-rich-quick schemes. These have all fallen flat on their face and caused an equal share of amusement and bemusement. Playing high-profile matches in the USA was a wonderful idea; just look what it did for football after all. But tournaments underpinned by dodgy finances and unscrupulous egomaniacs with no thought of legacy or sustainable growth were never going to be the answer for American cricket. Stanford promised a lot but ultimately delivered nothing more than a riches to rags story that rubbed cricket's nose in the mud. There are many voices for sustainable growth in American cricket and many very laudable initiatives, including taking the game to young, white Americans. But they don't tend to grab the headlines and their voices don't tend to carry sway. More is the pity.

Chapter 18

The Woolf Review
and the Big Three

READING the ICC's annual reports from the noughties you are presented with a sport that is attracting unprecedented investment, growing rapidly and committed to development, tackling corruption and protecting the sport's integrity, and refining its governance. However, another version of the story was about to emerge that would cause something of a storm and reveal who really were the power brokers in cricket and how they wanted to mould the global game.

In 2011 the ICC embarked on its third strategic plan, titled 'A bigger, better, global game'. It reiterated existing commitments to expanding the game, introducing meritocratic pathways and maximising revenue generation for the good of all. The language was as glossy as the cover, carefully honed to give signals of a bold, inclusive strategy while not putting the cat amongst the full member pigeons and their privileged view of the world. In amongst the fine words was a commitment for an independent review of governance. This was the parting gesture of chief executive Haroon Lorgat, who had been ground down by the self-interest and politicking of the leading full members and wanted better for the sport.

The report was undertaken by leading British lawyer Lord Woolf and a small team from Price Waterhouse Coopers who reached out across members and stakeholders and ran a comprehensive consultation to hear and analyse views. Woolf was shocked by what he found purporting to be a global governing body in the 21st century and pulled no punches when the review was published:

'The ICC reacts as though it is primarily a members' club; its interest in enhancing global development of the game is secondary.'

Woolf concluded that cricket's archaic governance structure was designed to allow the game to be run by 'self-interested or parochial decision-making'. In a few short paragraphs, damning in their objectivity and simple truth, Woolf had made a mockery of the ICC's attempts to gloss over these fundamental governance shortcomings that had seen cricket shaped by the few for the benefit of the few.

The underlying issue was that ICC board members were not independent, being answerable to their member country's short-term financial objectives rather than accountable for the long-term health of the global game. In this context an Indian board member viewed success as increased revenue for the BCCI and no dilution whatsoever of India's ability to play who it wanted to when it wanted to on its own terms. It was impossible in this short-term 'members' club' mentality to take far-reaching, strategic decisions for the sport. The flawed governance model explains the Jekyll and Hyde nature of the ICC, in one breath supporting global development tournaments and in the next contracting World Cups. It explains why the Intercontinental Cup, such a laudable endeavour, was undermined by no clear pathway to Test cricket.

Woolf recommended that the old model be scrapped to be replaced by a board with no leadership or executive role within member boards, including five independent directors and an independent chairman and chief executive. Furthermore, Woolf attacked the culture of entitlement that came from the ICC being funded by its members through the subscription model. Instead he advocated that the ICC be independent and self-funding, with distribution of income based on need rather than historic rights and privileges.

Lorgat had let a viper loose in the ICC's nest.

Woolf recognised that the historic constitution of the ICC board not only promoted self-interest but also short-termism. No member wanted to deliver a message back to their board that a short-term reduction in income was needed for the long-term health of the game. To ensure a long-term, dispassionate view independent directors were recommended. Acknowledging a time-old shortcoming, he also recommended that all board resolutions should be binding.

Under the ethics section of the report the recommend-ations exposed skullduggery that everyone knew was commonplace but few had the confidence to call out. This included not seeking to 'place undue influence on other Members, nor allow themselves to be influenced inappropriately by other Members to support the interests of individual members'. This gave a firm nod to India's customary tactic of using the financial inducements of a bilateral series to gain endorsement for their voting positions.

On membership the report made some significant recommendations. It suggested a de-coupling of full member status from Test match status and called for transparent, measurable criteria for elevation to full member status. This echoed the frustrated efforts of Warren Deutrom and Ireland to know what they had to do so they could get on and do it. It called for the arcane, inherited rights of full membership to be replaced by, yes, you've guessed it, something clearly defined, measurable and enforced. The last point reflected a simple but quite shocking truth, that once you were a full member you were untouchable and unaccountable. You just took money and voted. There were less widely heralded but equally important recommendations too, for instance that the development committee come directly under the chief executive rather than risk recommendations being blocked by full members in the cricket committee. There was also the deliciously simple assertion that members of committees should have relevant skills.

The funding chapter was also an eye-opener for any cricket fan reading the report who wasn't aware of how the governing body operated. It included another strikingly simple recommendation: that funding should be allocated on the basis of need rather than historic privilege. This meant that richer boards would support the poorer ones for the good of the global game. It proposed a more equitable funding model for associates and proper funding for development of the game. For years the financial returns of associate and affiliate members had been pored over by regional development chiefs. Woolf recommended financial assessment and probity for full members too.

For associate members and supporters of global development the report echoed what many had been championing for years. The idea of a private members' club under siege and being forced into a fair, just, 21st-century reality was a romantic and compelling one and article after article appeared relishing the recommendations and keen to add another boot into the winded body of the ICC. An almost Leninist zeal to do away with status altogether was promoted. Anyone should be able to play anyone else in any format. Man the barricades! There was a feeling that unless all recommendations were accepted in full immediately that it was a conspiracy and stitch-up and the ICC should be strung up in a public square. Emotions ran very high indeed.

Here was an authoritative, independent voice telling the world and his slip cordon that cricket wasn't run as a modern, global sport. It was an anachronism, an imperial throwback, an oligarchy. It all began with a club in the form of the MCC and a club it remained.

The ICC must have wondered how it could have been so masochistic. Some believe Lorgat was put under pressure to suppress the report. Either way he left soon afterwards. The report was intended to be a key pillar of the ICC's new strategic plan. Instead it was a problem they wished would go away. While others called for action the ICC prevaricated. They would consider the recommendations in due course.

As Gideon Haigh pointed out in his brilliant essays on the review and its aftermath in *Uncertain Corridors*, the response of the full members was guided by the age-old truth that no one gives up power. While the ICC desperately attempted to buy some time India brazenly entered the fray, dismissing the notion that an English lawyer should be listened to. It was an echo of the bitter, post-imperial testiness seen in the infamous 1993 meeting Lord Cowdrey struggled in vain to chair. Their official position was stark and abrupt. The BCCI chief Srinivasan simply considered the recommendations 'unacceptable'. His role as BCCI chair and ICC director was, for the record, unacceptable to Woolf. The statement didn't even state which recommendations were unacceptable, or indeed whether any had any merit. It was the arrogant and dismissive behaviour of a board that knew it was untouchable.

In this book I have posed the question whether cricket had turned from an English game to an Indian one. India's response to the Woolf report provides an unequivocal answer. Unprompted and without consultation, they responded unilaterally on behalf of the game. India had pulled the strings for years and now under Srinivasan they didn't even want a veneer of discretion. The message was clear: this is our game and we won't be told how it should be run.

The ICC and other member boards had been blindsided and left powerless. Even if they agreed with all or none of what Woolf proposed what could they do now

India had made its stance clear? The report gave the ICC the moral authority to challenge India and claim control of a sport it purported to run. But how could it do that while locked into the governance limitations Woolf had so savagely exposed?

It wasn't just champions of the global game that were appalled by India's flat rejection of the report. Former Aussie Test spinner and Federation of International Cricketers' Associations chief executive Tim May called on the ICC to adopt the recommendations in full, pleading with board members to remember why they were there.

In this context the job of doughty former Test wicketkeeper turned ICC chief executive Dave Richardson was virtually impossible. His organisation had in effect been exposed as a sham of a governing body just as they were seeking to compete with football and other sports for broadcast rights deals. Expectation for reform was high but following India's early rejection of the report the chances of delivering reform were minimal. How could they be seen to implement the recommendations of a report they themselves commissioned when influential full members would block it? Richardson was at the tiller of a ship whose course was pre-determined by a computer in Mumbai.

In England the situation was made all the more depressing by the fact that due to the short-sightedness of ICC decision-making cricket was conspicuous by its absence in a memorable, nation-boosting Olympic Games.

As the months went by the silence from the ICC was deafening. Srinivasan, with a foul wind in his sails, used the threat of withdrawing India from the Future Tours Programme, in effect depriving all members of book balancing capital, if any of Woolf's recommendations were even proposed. The fate of the ICC was, it seemed, consigned to muddle through as before with its dirty laundry on full show to the watching world. But it was about to get worse. Not content with merely blocking Woolf's reforms, Srinivasan almost spitefully sought to break even more principles of good governance in a brazen coup in collusion with England and Australia. In a series of meetings in 2013 Srinivasan, his braying lieutenant Giles Clarke and Australian Wally Edwards set about recasting the world game to serve their own ends, for which read India's ends with the junior partners being thrown a few choice morsels from the table. Cricket was an Indian sport. India generated the lion's share of its wealth. India should therefore reap what it sowed.

The result of this colluding was the so-called 'Big Three' reforms. ICC decision-making would be concentrated in a new executive committee featuring the Big Three plus one other full member board. In addition, the Big Three would have a rotating chair of key ICC committees and the lucrative commercial affairs committee that agreed the broadcasting rights that funded the game. It hardly needed saying that all events would be hosted by one of the Big Three. The proposed distribution model would recognise the financial contribution provided by each member. This meant, of course, that India got most of it with England and Australia getting an uplift too. It was the opposite of the distribution on the basis of need model Woolf had recommended. The cabal needed the support of eight of the full members and used the old lure of the promise of bilateral tours as bait. But when the Big Three's reforms were presented to the ICC board in January 2014 they were met with shocked bewilderment. Ehsan Mani, former ICC president, was the first to take a stand, accusing Srinivasan and his stooges of undermining the global game and the integrity of the ICC. Others fell in behind him and once the document was leaked the media took aim too. The rich would get richer and the poor poorer. Was that really the way to globalise the game?

The opposition drew some concessions from the Big Three but ultimately the remaining full members were powerless to resist. The threat of India withdrawing from fixtures was simply too great a risk. The new redistribution model saw India claim a third of a bumper new €1.5 billion deal for the 2015–23 rights cycle. In contrast the budget for the associate and affiliate members was cut back dramatically and the regional development offices and High Performance Programme dismantled. The tide had most certainly receded from the high-water mark of development a few years before. A staff of 130 shrank to under 70, less than other major sports with significantly smaller budgets. This left the future uncertain for the tens of new members so recently welcomed into the fold. It also raised questions over the return on investment for the HPP with the risk that any ground made in closing the gap between full members and leading associates would be lost. Despite the performances of Kenya and Ireland at recent tournaments the World Cup was restricted to ten teams and the World Cricket League contracted back from eight teams to five.

The attempt to bring context to global cricket was also abandoned with the Test Championship removed and the cash cow of the Champions Trophy resurrected in its place. Only three years previously the ICC had promised 'A bigger, better global game.' Was this it?

Eventually his many enemies caught up with cement magnate Srinivasan and his replacement as ICC chairman, Shashank Manohar, set about reversing the retrograde 2014 reforms. Giles Clarke was invited to join a working group tasked with reversing the policies he had been influential in imposing. Under this new culture Richardson was finally able to deliver some of Woolf's recommendations, reducing to just two membership categories (all affiliates became associates), providing targeted assistance to weaker full members and leading associates and promoting Ireland and Afghanistan to full members. But without the governance reforms Woolf called for, full members could still thwart reforms that would see them lose out. Two divisions of tests with promotion and relegation was vetoed. Why would you risk relegation if you could protect your historic right for results and performances to be irrelevant and consequence-free?

As ever the two faces of the ICC worked against each other. The staff in the development wing worked up proposals for a 32-team World Cup. The board limited it to ten. The development team pushed for more games between associates and full members. The board were reluctant to commit to an FTP, let alone guarantee further fixtures for associate members. This institutional schizophrenia would continue as long as the flawed governance remained in place.

While the rollercoaster of the rogues' gallery, politicking and BCCI factional feuds played out cricket was revolutionising in a different way. Traditionally international cricket had always had primacy and at club level cricket didn't even begin to have the public draw, brand or financial might of football. But the invention of T20 was changing all that. While the BCCI had initially been very sceptical about the format they soon changed their tune and the Indian Premier League became, with its multi-million-pound franchises, a commercial behemoth. In the process it posed a major risk to international cricket. Leading players could command eye-watering salaries for a six-week stint and understandably were reluctant to commit to any international duties that could compromise this. When you add Australia's Big Bash, the Pakistan Super League, the Caribbean Premier League and the English Blast there was pressure to create multiple windows in the international calendar or risk second XIs playing internationals while the stars turned out for their franchises.

The last ten years have seen the rise of the franchise cricketer, the globe-trotting six-hitters for rent. No one embodies this modern variant of the cricketer better than the self-styled universe boss Chris Gayle. A talented and effective Test player in his youth, Gayle has turned out for franchises across the globe, having his passport stamped in multiple locations including Canada and Nepal. This saw his premature retirement from Tests and limited him to sporadic and occasional run-outs for his country. Pakistan's 'Boom Boom' Afridi has taken the same path and England's Kevin Pietersen fell out with the ECB over their lack of flexibility in accommodating his six-figure contracts. For servants like Alec Stewart the notion of picking and choosing when to represent your country was anathema. International cricket had always been the pinnacle. Was it any longer if you could become a millionaire in a month and a half for the Sunrisers or Super Kings?

The ICC saw the risk to weakening its brand and its revenue-generating ability. With high-profile franchise cricket popping up across the globe it was not only a crowded calendar but a crowded marketplace for broadcasters and sponsors. The ICC wrestled with fighting it or accommodating it. The latter was favoured by Srinivasan as he was himself a franchise owner!

The doom mongers of course had their say, prophesying the demise of Tests and international cricket. But somehow franchise cricket has been absorbed into the 21st-century game and while tensions inevitably exist and compromises have to be made it all appears to run along well enough. It is Packer on steroids. A bludgeoned six is simply incomparable to a caressed cover drive, the purists say. But in modern cricket you can watch both if you want to. Has cricket reached saturation point? Probably. But if you consider that many times over in the last four decades cricket has been labelled a dead man walking, reaching saturation point is in a way a significant success. Some would of course argue that cricket of all sports should focus on quality over quantity but it would take a blinkered view not to accept that the IPL has helped the modern generation develop an incredible level of skill that can make for breathtaking viewing.

In the last five years cricket has been wrestling with its conscience. The Woolf Report serves as a very public reminder of what the sport should be aspiring to: a modern and equitable governance enabling delivery of a long-term, development-focused strategy. But as turkeys wouldn't vote for Christmas so the most powerful full members will cling to power and block the most far-reaching reforms.

Slowly but surely the ICC have managed to introduce some of the recommendations. Although full members still can't be relegated and there has been no demotion in membership category they nevertheless don't enjoy the full suite of historic privileges they once did. Lower-ranked teams now have to pre-qualify for global events, for instance. These reforms have been piecemeal and deep inequity still exists. Looking on from the sidelines Woolf has been exasperated at the lack of commitment to the wholesale reform he thought was needed. Not just advisable, but essential.

The issue of ensuring all cricket has meaningful context has at least been addressed. There is a Test Championship again, albeit not including all the full members, and an ODI league structure with promotion and relegation that is linked to World Cup qualification. The Super League comprises 13 teams, with the Netherlands qualifying to join the big boys and secure regular, guaranteed fixtures with the leading teams. Something they had struggled to secure even when they had ODI status. Amsterdam is a good place to be as a cricket fan these days. Beneath this is a League Two featuring the next strongest associates, such as Scotland, Nepal and Papua New Guinea. All games at this level have ODI status, an improvement over the old

World Cricket League Championship where some games were ODIs and others weren't, a ridiculously contrived construct that undermined the profile and coverage of the league. Below League Two is a 12-team challenge league split across two groups, invested with List A status, itself fed by regional qualifiers in advance of each World Cup cycle. It is a good, progressive structure that provides teams with a pathway not just to World Cup qualification but also to regular fixtures against full members. But there is a sting in the tail. Of course there is. The World Cup continues to be restricted to ten teams so however good the structure is the World Cup dream remains strictly theoretical for the vast majority of members.

In the shortest format the ICC decided to get over its obsession with restricting status by enfranchising all of its members. All international teams can now play official T20 internationals. This puts the games on the statistical record, increases profile for sponsors and fans and opens up the prospect of Greece versus South Africa and Chile versus Australia. These games won't happen in practice of course but at least there is a veneer of a truly global game. All the fears and arguments against a more inclusive approach to status have proved unfounded. India versus Australia is not suddenly played in empty stadiums or dropped by broadcasters because Ghana versus Sierra Leone is afforded the same status.

Unfortunately, the progress made in opening up the T20 format has been balanced out by the removal of first class cricket from leading associate nations. This has gone largely under the radar, another example of what is omitted from ICC press releases often being more important than what is included. Without any exposure to the longest format it is difficult to imagine how any further associates can make a successful bid for full member status. After begrudgingly welcoming Ireland and Afghanistan into the fold, albeit without the full range of privileges of founding members, that might well be it. Countries like Scotland still harbour ambitions of course. But there certainly isn't a sense that the ICC are championing their cause and helping them get over the line. In truth, Ireland and Afghanistan have found it isn't quite the land of milk and honey they were expecting. There is no compulsion for teams to play Tests against them as they are outside the Test Championship. Tests are expensive to stage too and without a major broadcast deal they leave a huge hole in the finances. Ireland cancelled a planned Test in 2020 for this reason, declaring they would focus on white-ball cricket instead. A dream 20 years in the making, an emotional rollercoaster for players like Ed Joyce and Kevin O'Brien reduced to an exercise in book balancing. Very sad. Despite this though it has brought professional cricket to Ireland and Afghanistan. In the case of Afghanistan they boast the two highest-ranked bowlers, Rashid Khan and Mujeeb Ur Rahman, and the highest-ranked all-rounder, Mohammad Nabi, in T20 internationals. In the shortest format at least they are not just making up the numbers. Would the ICC's stance on elevation be different if the USA were the leading associate?

Test cricket lives on despite countless eulogies written. A popular film entitled *Death of a Gentleman* was released charting its fall. But defying all medical logic, the gentleman lives on with no sign of passing in his sleep. The Ashes in the summer of 2019 and that innings by Ben Stokes served as a reminder of the heights of emotion and entertainment Test cricket can reach. Everyone says it is the pinnacle of the game and everyone repeatedly commits to protecting it. Is it really as vulnerable as it is made out? Or do cricket fans perversely enjoy the existential crisis of obsessing over its demise whether true or not? It reminds them why they love the game, why cricket and its acolytes are on a higher plane than their brutish football compatriots. Crowds are down almost everywhere in the world and some series are alas uncompetitive and instantly forgettable. But if India and the IPL are meant to administer the final, mortal blow then why is Virat Kohli, the superstar Indian captain, one of Test cricket's staunchest advocates? Reality is not, at least not yet, conforming to the script written for Test cricket's demise.

Meanwhile, T20 leagues continue to pop up all across the world. In the Test nations of course, though some far more glamorous, glitzy and star-studded than others, but also beyond the historic cricket centres. Hong Kong, Canada, Afghanistan and Nepal have all launched tournaments on an IPL-lite model that have attracted professionals from Test nations. There is a pecking order, naturally, so if you don't get picked up in the IPL you may opt for the PSL or BPL. If you aren't on the radar for any of these then a much smaller salary but still handy bonus may be available in Nepal or Canada.

As well as giving full member journeymen like Luke Wright and Rilee Rossouw a plethora of options and their agents a busy schedule of phone calls, these leagues have also allowed the top associate players a route to become professionals. Scot Calum MacLeod, an unorthodox but on his day brutal batsman, is often picked up, raising the profile of Scottish cricket and giving him a handy bonus to his national contract. USA bowler Ali Khan has made a name for himself on the franchise circuit. But the breakthrough associate star has been Nepalese leg spin sensation Sandeep Lamichhane. Spotted as a teenager during regional trials, he was propelled to fame when taken under the wing of former Australia captain Michael Clarke. He is now one of the most sought-after bowlers in the world with franchises lining up to sign him. His example proves talent can prosper in modern cricket wherever it originates. Cricket can be a viable career path even if cricket is not professionalised in your country. But for every Lamichhane there are dozens of talented associates who don't get a lucky break and stay firmly under the franchise radar.

In addition to the larger-scale commercial T20 leagues, a raft of smaller, more localised tournaments have been founded, generally taking their inspiration from the IPL with amusingly absurd franchise names and colourful kits. They serve not to professionalise the game per se but certainly to energise and galvanise cricketing communities where the sport is small scale and low profile. A good example is the Mediterranean Cricket League played in Croatia and offering teams from across Eastern Europe a chance to gather and play competitive cricket. Another model that has emerged in recent years is the European Premier League, that mirrors the format of football's Champions League with leading clubs from each country competing to be kings of the continent. This provides a popular season highlight for the region that complements their domestic leagues. Social media has been an incredibly powerful tool for smaller cricket nations, giving them a platform to reach out to local players and raise the profile of cricket in their country but also create a supportive global community well below the radar of the ICC and most cricket fans. They can share best practice, arrange tournaments and secure sponsorship all through a Facebook page or Twitter account. Sierra Leone managed to get sponsorship for youth programmes to help overcome the social dislocation through Facebook and then use the same channel to help tackle Ebola.

The three formats have jostled for position in the new, crowded cricket calendar but none have been squeezed out. The 50-over game had looked under threat at times due to what was perceived to be pedestrian middle overs. T20 cut these out so why not just play that, so the argument went. But then England started scoring 400 plus regularly and the format got a new lease of life.

But has a relatively successful mix of three formats achieved the goal of making cricket attractive to the 21st-century fan? Are a new generation being attracted to the game or is cricket's demographic doomed to become more and more aged as younger generations eschew the game for other pleasures and diversions? Well, the ECB were certainly concerned that it was failing to capture the imagination of young fans and commissioned a very comprehensive behavioural study. This concluded that games were too long and the sport too inaccessible. They wanted a product that would fit in a two-and-a-half-hour broadcast window that enabled games to be shown on terrestrial TV. As with the creation of T20 fifteen years before the answer, they felt, was creating a new format. And so The Hundred was born. A game consisting of a hundred balls counted down on a big electronic screen with city-based franchises, jazzy clothing and top international stars. It came together to form a recipe to save cricket from being increasingly geriatric and irrelevant in the decades to come.

The trouble is that cricket fans hated it. The ECB's Twitter feed was hijacked by a torrent of abuse and mockery. No one seemed to have a good word to say about it. Not only did they hate it but they resented the huge gamble the ECB were taking in reducing the importance and profile of established formats to give pride of place to its new 'Down with the kids' format. The ECB simply rebuffed any criticism, claiming that existing cricket fans were not their market. This stirred up sentiment even more. The franchise names caused widespread mirth and mockery when they were announced and then the players were paraded in an absurd array of kits with children's snack brands emblazoned on the front. It was a scene from an Iannucci comedy. But the PR car crash made no difference. The Hundred was happening. No one took T20 seriously and that had saved the game (or ruined it depending on your perspective) so maybe, just maybe The Hundred would see youth take up cricket. Time will tell. Many boards across the world will be watching the inaugural season with interest. After all, they share the same struggles that led the ECB to take a gamble on a new format. Maybe by 2025 there will be Hundred leagues across the world, perhaps even a Hundred World Cup?

Maybe Chris Gayle, in his mid-forties, will hit the first Hundred double century? Can cricket accommodate four formats? And that isn't even to mention T10, which emerged in the UAE and attracted some top players only to become heavily associated with match fixing.

Chapter 19

The game in 2020

WHERE does the development dream stand in 2020? The commitment to a ten-team World Cup reveals that full members at least don't want a truly global sport. With the Intercontinental Cup gone and no hint of appetite to create future full members, true globalisation looks unlikely. Targeted efforts in the USA and Nepal, where the ICC stepped in directly to run cricket due to maladministration by the boards, appear to be reaping benefits and they may yet become major new markets. But China, Russia, Malaysia and Brazil aren't delivering on promise. No new members join these days, though some countries like Iceland are trying. Some have been thrown out. Existence is extremely precarious for the old affiliates who find themselves below the new World Cup qualifying tournament structure, desperately short of funds and jettisoned by regional offices stripped back to the bone. It would be no surprise if membership contracts down from a height of 108 to 75 or so. The meritocratic pathway still exists and there is a promising outlook for the top 40 countries. But those below that feel disenfranchised and let down. Many may not survive. That doesn't mean cricket won't be played. Economic migration from Asia and elsewhere has introduced cricketers to almost every country and they are likely to want to play cricket in one form or another. Whether they do so within a structure put in place by a formal board is less clear. Many who haven't liked the regulations of the board have just taken over the board themselves to get what they want. The reasons for such coups are just as likely to be a reduction in match fees and demanding less congested grounds than it is a five-year development plan.

Despite many predicting that cricket wouldn't survive as a 21st-century sport, it has held its own in the ultra-competitive sport/business world. It can't compete with football but neither has it been squeezed to the brink of extinction by it. Although it hasn't managed to claim any meaningful market share in the USA, China, Malaysia or South America, commercially cricket is buoyant with each new rights cycle bringing a significant increase in profits. This is of course largely down to the ever growing value of Asian markets where cricket remains the leading sport. As cricket has sought to break America so football has sought to break India. Many assumed it would have by now, but cricket still reigns supreme.

At recreational level in the full members the game faces challenges too. In England more and more clubs struggle to field an XI. People are less and less willing to commit the time to traditional league cricket and over time it has increasingly been perceived as a middle-class sport, not helped by the lack of cricket in state schools. When the sponsor for the national team is Waitrose it is difficult to argue cricket hasn't narrowed in its social appeal. One of the aims of The Hundred is to reconnect cricket to the working man. The flow of players is linked to exposure to cricket at school. Despite the efforts of organisations like Chance to Shine and others, many in the state school system simply do not get exposure. And without cricket on terrestrial TV, where exactly are people meant to get the opportunity to fall in love with the game? It is a similar story in some other Test nations. Although the reality in Southern Asia is markedly different. English tourists visiting India often remark on the impromptu games of cricket they see in the street. The game has a level of cultural penetration on the subcontinent that it simply doesn't have elsewhere. Add to that the revenue-generating ability of Asia and it is hard not to conclude that it is more an Indian game than an English one. Is it a global game? That is difficult to argue too. If you rephrased it as a game played throughout the world then that would be easier to make a case for.

Who are 21st-century cricketers? Let's meet a few. There are some like England's Rory Burns and India's Cheteshwar Pujara who have taken a traditional route through first class cricket to play in Tests, with the security of lucrative central contracts. But these are the exceptions not the rule in the 21st century. More common are those who have taken the lead from West Indian Kieron Pollard who as a young man turned his back on international service and central contracts to become a T20 mercenary across the globe. He's a lot richer than contemporaries who made Test cricket their goal but then a Test century may be a richer accomplishment than 50 T20 half centuries. In 2020 he made his 500th appearance in a T20 having represented more franchises than a Dubai shopping mall. Below professional level there is the city lawyer who played at school and shovels it to leg occasionally for his village side while taking in a Lord's Test with clients. There is the hearing-impaired boy who finds friends and confidence through cricket. There is the teenage Afghan immigrant who travels four hours up the autobahn to bowl ten overs in a Dusseldorf leisure centre. He is tipped to make the German team once he fulfils residency criteria. There is the leg-spinner from Papua New Guinea who becomes the eighth member of his family to play international cricket. There are the boys in Rawalpindi playing tape ball cricket in the concrete echo of a storm drain. There is the girl in Tokyo who discovers an intriguing game at university and tries to explain the rules to her bewildered father. There is the batsman in Sierra Leone looking to cricket to repair his community after the ravages of civil war and the threat of Ebola. It is a rich and varied cast list for an ever-unfolding drama.

The 2019 World Cup was watched by 1.6 billion people in over 200 countries across the world and yet how many in those countries have even heard of the sport? That is the enigma of cricket in 2020. In one sense it is a huge global enterprise with ambitious plans. In another it is a small, passionate community prone to fretting about what the future may hold.

Chapter 20

A brave new future

WHAT will cricket look like in 2050? Strangely it is a question hardly ever asked in the sport. Of all the thousands of articles and blogs only a handful look to the future. The nearest you will see are articles predicting Ashes squads in five or ten years' time. It is a very odd characteristic indeed that a sport that frets so much about the future doesn't really engage with it.

The halcyon past is far safer and regularly traversed territory. Setting goals for the future of the game very much depends on your perspective of what that future should look like. Many just want the highest quality cricket possible between just the top nations, with an almost maniacal desire to ensure that Test cricket doesn't die. Others just want to ensure that they can continue to put their whites on every Saturday without the worry of the ground being sold off or the club dying through lack of numbers. I'm more ambitious that that. I'd like to see cricket grow as a global sport and put down sustainable, local roots in countries across the world. Why, you may ask? Well, simple really, I believe cricket is the best sport ever invented and I'd like as many people to enjoy its excitement and beauty as possible. Selfishly, I'd also revel in the endless variety provided by fixtures like the USA versus China or Germany versus Iran, bringing infinitely more depth to the game.

The key to making this dream a reality is surprisingly simple. Cricket needs to look beyond short-term profit. It has been the greed and short-termism of the full members, particularly India, that has prevented cricket from making a genuine commitment to development. Woolf recognised this and called for dramatic, fundamental reform only to see India and its allies close ranks to retain a status quo that suits them very well. In the last few years the ICC have chipped away at his recommendations as best they can but have been blocked from delivering the most significant. By far the biggest opportunity missed has been ensuring that cricket features in the Olympics.

This would have a transformational effect on global cricket, not just through increased exposure, though this would be welcome, but because it would unlock government funding and support where cricket most desperately needs it. It is ironic that the ICC have been so desperate to reduce the reliance of its associate members on ICC grants while steadfastly ignoring a funding stream that would put global cricket on a sustainable footing. Quite mad really. Cricket is not in the Olympics because the full members desperately want to retain control of all profit from the game, ignoring the fact that in a few decades' time a genuinely global game would bring more profits to everyone.

In almost every interview with chairmen or development officers in emerging cricket nations there is a plea for cricket to be included in the Olympics. It would transform perception of the game from a minority sport associated with certain ethnic groups to a genuinely global sport that could see not just a step change in investment but attract a far broader base of players and fans in society. It could see cricket take off in China, Japan and Europe. It could also enable cricket to break out of its mould as an immigrant sport in the USA. Olympic inclusion would bring state investment, the development of facilities and the inclusion of cricket in school curriculums. It would enable the ICC to save a lot of money in direct grants that could then be targeted at specific development initiatives at regional and sub-regional level. This funding should be focused at broadening the ethnic base of cricket in its hinterlands so that it has the best chance of penetrating the national sporting consciousness. This is an ambitious goal and may not be possible in all countries. But there needs to be a sustained, concerted effort.

In support of Olympic inclusion the ICC should start viewing the status of matches as an opportunity for growth rather than protecting a product. Sadly, emerging cricket countries across the world have fought an uphill battle trying to promote games and build profile when matches aren't given status and statistics are rendered invisible. The extension of T20 international status for all was like the millennium bug. There was a lot of fear about it but in the end it had no negative impact whatsoever.

It was ludicrous to think that just because Belgium could play Tanzania in a T20I that India versus England would suddenly be unmarketable if they had the same status. Now countries can market their games as proper internationals, the fixtures get much more visibility on websites and the press and this in turn attracts fans and sponsors. ODI status should be extended in the same way to give countries flexibility in what formats they want to play. Full members worry about devaluing a product but do they honestly think broadcasters aren't able to recognise gradations in marketability?

There has been a very defensive attitude to status that has held the global game back. It isn't the answer in itself but a more open, inclusive approach would help the game become truly global. It is a lack of understanding, and perhaps even compassion too, of the pressures emerging cricket countries face that fails to identify these simple reforms that could make such a big difference. Unfortunately, it comes back to the fact that while many in the game may subscribe to vague rhetoric around developing a global game, in truth they'd rather it was just played between a few countries were the quality can be assured. Football doesn't seem to have the same hang-ups. Gibraltar can play Suriname at football and everyone seems happy enough. It is part of a rich tapestry of international competition. There will be higher quality in Brazil versus Argentina of course, but it doesn't render other fixtures meaningless.

There has to be a dream to inspire development. The World Cricket League provided this and the rise of Afghanistan into a major cricketing power has been one of the most uplifting stories in the game in the modern era. They started with nothing but the opportunity was there and it drove them on. Cricket has always been very keen on erecting glass ceilings. It is near impossible for the vast majority of teams to qualify for a World Cup. It is near impossible for teams to become full members. If you want cricket to be a truly global sport then why put so many obstacles in the way? Of course we need to be realistic. It is unlikely that the Czech Republic will become a cricket superpower. Perhaps they only have potential to build to a modest but sustainable player base with financial stability. That would be a great success in itself. Is it really necessary to stamp out inspiration and hope at their inception for emerging cricket nations? Surely they should feel that with a fair wind and concerted effort anything is possible for them in the sport. Cricket needs to fully enfranchise all its countries. It doesn't really deserve to be global sport if it doesn't.

Woolf advocated a funding model based on need only to see Srinivasan switch to a model where those that need it the least get the most. It is unlikely, sadly, that cricket's governance will reform to such an extent that full members will give up their historic pay packages for the greater good of the game. Supposing they did though, or did at least to some extent, how could a funding by need model work in practice? It could be an extension of two existing mechanisms, scorecard funding and the targeted assistance programme.

Traditionally funding has been targeted at either international fixture programmes or outreach programmes to attract more participants in the game (you'll remember that participants is a far more comfortable term for the ICC than players). There is a need though in many countries for more practical support. Many countries are overly reliant on a single ground. Investment for additional grounds and related facilities like nets would be a simple form of grant that would make a significant impact. It would allow more fixtures to be played by more players and build resilience of cricket in its outposts by guarding against pitch deterioration, flooding or financial pressures requiring land to be sold off or used for other purposes. Ideally the regional development office would help broker local development partnerships with town councils to match funding to provide greater value for money and for the local community to feel they had a vested interest in local cricket. At regional level the ICC should identify targeted interventions like this that can represent excellent value and really alter the trajectory of emerging cricket nations.

One of the constraints in development has been a lack of genuine commitment by full members to support associates in their region. Sending out the odd coach and providing coaching tools has largely been the limit of ambition as boards have been almost exclusively focused on their domestic game. This is understandable, of course, but if the game is going to grow sustainably full members need to be braver and bolder. This could take the form of integrating neighbours into domestic leagues, providing financial assistance and establishing twinning arrangements between clubs. Such partnerships and exchange programmes can provide a real spur to development.

A limitation in many emerging nations is difficulty in reaching a critical mass of players, clubs and media interest to break through from a peripheral game to a sport that engages broad sections of local communities. This isolation makes existence fragile and development very difficult. In Norway I helped developed a hub model for Oslo, Bergen and Tromso where clubs, local societies and businesses, municipal governments and a media group were to be formed to relaunch cricket as a community sport. Having investors and the media along for the journey from the outset guarantees coverage, profile and the necessary investment. It is such models that can gain the necessary critical mass and cultural penetration needed to put cricket on a sustainable footing. In so many countries cricket hangs by a thread as it lacks these community agents with a vested interest in its development. A further benefit of such integrated models is that cricket can be promoted as a game for everyone, helping break down stereotypes that it is only played by certain ethnic groups.

With such models delivering on the ground a long-term strategy developed by a more forward-looking and equitable governing body, cricket has a chance to be a truly global game. The innate virtues of cricket are such that once introduced to its charm many will want to take it up but it is critical that everyone feels it can be their game. The association of cricket as a foreign game in many parts of the world has constrained its ambitions even though levels of economic migration mean there are a lot more players internationally than ever before.

Expanded, inclusive global events, the profile of being an Olympic sport and an approach to status that is progressive and positive rather than reductive and repressive will also be critical ingredients for a bright future for the game. Full members must of course be innovative and financially astute to ensure cricket remains a popular game in its heartlands too, as there is no point in cricket having a late flowering in its outposts only to be balanced out by a depressing decline in its heartlands. Cricket can achieve all this and everyone in the sport needs to channel confidence, will and determination to make it happen. Obsessing over decline, as so many cricket fans do, will likely see what we all fear most become a reality. Test cricket may become more of a niche variant of the sport. Let's do all we can to make sure it doesn't, but equally let's not let fear of a decline in Test cricket inadvertently lead to a decline in the sport.

Is modern cricket an Indian sport with an English soul, or an English sport with an Indian heart? In truth it belongs to all of us who love the game and we all hold its future in our hands.

Epilogue

IT is the cusp of April 2020. Spring has come early and the smell of mown grass delights the nostrils. Ordinarily double centuries would be in progress at Fenners and clubs would be desperately trying to pin players down to ensure they can fulfil their fixtures. But it is all a bit different this year. Coronavirus has stopped everything, including cricket. The Pakistan Super League carried on briefly before various players succumbed to symptoms. The ECB are looking at whether games could be played later in the season behind closed doors with extremely stringent testing in place. To be denied that stirring feeling of the cricket season commencing, compounded of course by the broader anxiety about the short-term victims and long-term consequences of the virus, is dispiriting indeed.

Starved of a season to preview and matches to cover, cricket journalists have turned either to dewy eyed nostalgic pieces or reflection on how the game could be improved when it finally returns. We all take cricket for granted; indeed many fear that we have such an incessant diet of it these days that it has reached saturation point.

If absence makes the heart grow fonder then we expect a passionate, emotional outpouring when bats are picked up once more. But along with relief will we all also have a greater sense of perspective, a new-found clarity on where the game should go? Perhaps we will conclude that the game was hurtling almost unknowingly down a certain road it should never have turned down. Many thought that about The Hundred of course. Maybe after due reflection we will think the game has been a bit stubborn in guarding status, unduly pessimistic about the decline of Tests and oddly complacent about growing the global game. Can this moment be a catalyst to take a fresh approach or will it merely reinforce old power politics and further calcify the status quo?

The confluence of writing a history of cricket at the very time play is stopped has the effect of heightening feelings of love and loss. Coping with a hiatus in the game provides a desperately stark glimpse of what it would be like if it stopped. The world would be incalculably the poorer. So, if you turn that sentiment around it would be incalculably richer if it was truly global: with an English spirit, an Indian passion and the endeavour of all.